AF365853

Certification Manual

# LEAN SERVICES

*Collection:* Gestiona
*Publishing director:* David Soler

Lean Service. Certification Manual
1st Edition, 2019

© 2019, Luis Vicente Socconini Pérez Gómez
© of this Edition: ICG Marge, SL

*Publisher:* Marge Books
València, 558 – 08026 Barcelona
Tel. 931 429 486 – marge@margebooks.com
www.margebooks.com

*Managing editor:* Adrià Gibernau
*Make-up editor:* Mercedes Lara
*Printed by:* Prodigitalk, SL (Martorell, Barcelona)

Paper Edition ISBN: 978-84-17903-28-2
Digital Edition ISBN: 978-84-17903-29-9
Legal Deposit: B 26441-2019

 The paper used in this books has not been bleached with elemental chlorine ($CI_2$).

# The autor

**Luis Socconini**

Luis Socconini is an Industrial Engineer from the ITESM Campus in Guadalajara. He has a Master's Degree in Quality and Productivity and is a Master Black Belt.

He is certified in Strategic Management by Stanford University, in Leading Product Innovation by Harvard University and in Industry 4.0 by M.I.T.

He has worked for the business school of Wharton, Pennsylvania, as a business consultant; at the Grolsch Brewery, in the Netherlands, as a process engineer, and at IBM as a manufacturing engineer.

As director of Lean Six Sigma Institute, he develops high impact projects in companies such as Abbott Laboratories, Kraft Heinz, Coca Cola, BMW, Bimbo, Fender, among others. Luis has a broad base of experience and is continually developing productivity applications in diverse industries such as construction, mining, agriculture, government, energy, services, etc.

He has been a distinguished professor at several prestigious universities in Mexico.

Luis is the author of the book **Lean Company, Lean Manufacturing, The Process of the 5's in action,** as well as co-author of the book **Lean Six Sigma Management System** and **Lean Energy.**

www.socconini.com

# Index

# Foreword

The practical use and implementation of the Lean Manufacturing Six Sigma philosophy in the manufacturing industry has proven with results to be the best way to design waste-free processes and products. Consequently, it has drawn the interest of managers to diversify its implementation beyond manufacturing processes. This is a reason why professionals focusing on continuous improvement have tried to convert the tools and best practices they learned in our courses and certifications into practical implementations for their services and support processes.

*Lean Service* simplifies the work of experts in continuous improvement by delivering services in a simple and clear manner through the use of Lean tools, thus presenting readers with practical implementations focused on improving customer satisfaction.

The goal of *Lean Service* is to help readers achieve high-value experiences, especially given the opportunities found in a daily exposure to all kinds of services, including but not limited to: public transportation, coffee shops, restaurants, hotels, self-service shops, airports, hospitals, consulting, telephone services, private or public security, news, casinos, internet service, cable, etc.

We must also consider our own internal processes as services. These may include overseeing a company's medical service, administering payroll, etc.

For some years, we have focused our research, teaching material, and consulting practices to services due to the *speed* and *quality* required when delivering results to our clients and performing services ourselves. That is why this book has been written – so that students, professionals, and experts in the Lean Six Sigma philosophy have a compendium of tools, resources, and examples that allows them to rapidly create designs and implement changes that their processes require and to remove waste that affects customers and ultimately threatens to put organizations at risk if time and resources are not devoted to this important task.

So far, we have seen that lives can be saved in healthcare services, for instance, when simple and highly effective processes are developed and implemented. We also see how hospitality services such as hotels, restaurants, casinos, and cafes – to name a few – benefit from a significant reduction in unnecessary costs and activities that do not add value.

We want this book to open up new opportunities for the services you provide. We are sure that your customers will soon return and recommend your services to others, and your staff will become ambassadors who astonish your customers every day by developing life experiences that create an impact and are remembered.

# Introduction
# to Lean Service

1

## Objectives

1. Develop *agile* and *high quality* services for customers.
2. Implement the Lean Six Sigma philosophy to *design* and *manage* highly effective services.
3. Prepare the *organizational* and *strategic structure* to develop world-class service companies.

## Content

I. Background
II. Productivity and its limitations
III. Business development model
IV. What is Lean Six Sigma?
V. Benefits
VI. Implementation process
VII. Change management
VIII. Roles and structure
IX. Six Sigma methodology and tools

## I. Background

What is a service?

- **It is a job done for the benefit or pleasure of someone else and may be:**
  - A gardening company
  - A firm of accountants
  - A bank
  - An entertainment company
  - An airline
- **Even manufacturing companies integrate services:**
  - Customer service
  - Repair
  - Installation
  - Internal Services Departments

## Services...

- Currently, 3 out of 4 workers (75%) are dedicated to services.

- Services grow at an annual rate of 13% while manufacturing does so at only 3% on average.

- In fact, practically all of us offer a service, either a direct service to a customer or in some function within a company.

- So far, Lean Six Sigma has been applied in 5% of manufacturing companies worldwide but only 1 to 2% of service companies are beginning to apply it.

## Classification of service companies

| Category | Examples |
| --- | --- |
| Professional and personal services | Doctors, lawyers, builders, consultants, financial analysts, insurance agents, customs agencies, accountants, beauty salons, travel agencies. |
| Entertainment | Casinos, theatres, cinemas, comedians, actors. |
| Government services | Procedures for licenses, passports, permits, customs. |
| Hospitality and food | Hotels, restaurants, bars, discos. |
| Support and representability | Departments, Call centres, Chambers, Associations. |
| Maintenance and repair | Car agencies, maintenance of houses or appliances. |
| Medical services | Hospitals, clinics, diagnostic centres, surgeries. |
| Transport | Airlines, airports, trains, boats, buses. |
| Retail services | Department stores, pharmacies, online sales. |
| Training and education | Universities, schools, technological institutes. |
| Essential services | Water, electricity, telephone, gas. |
| Financial services | Banks, brokerage firms, insurers, exchange houses. |
| Use of equipment or facilities | Car rental, rental of function rooms, golf courses, gyms. |

## Many companies continue to encounter

- Slow delivery of products or services
- Constant customer complaints
- High inventory levels and struggles to deliver their products and services
- Inconsistent quality
- Poor customer service
- High costs and prices
- Poor internal communication
- Steady or declining sales and decreasing margins

**THESE COMPANIES ARE DESTINED TO VANISH!**

*"It's not the big who eat the small...*
*It's the fast who eat the slow."*
*Jason Jennings*

## Lean Six Sigma

**Eliminate overload, variation, and waste**

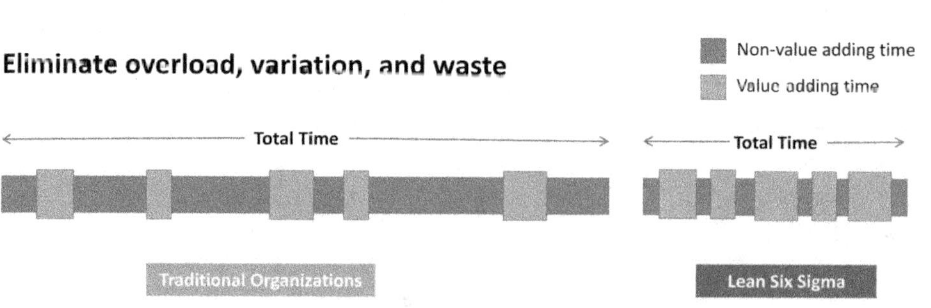


**Reduce:** Time, Costs, Defects, Inventory, Space, Waste.

**Increase:** Productivity, Customer Satisfaction, Quality, Cash Flow.

# Which model represents your business?

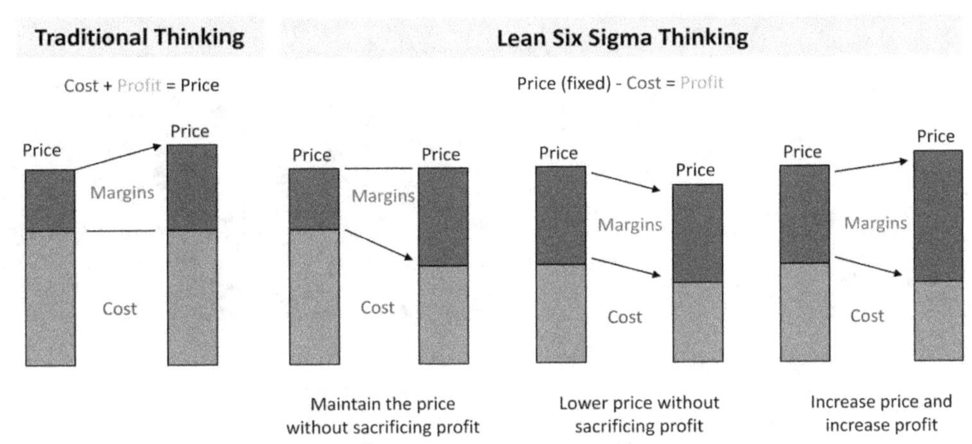


**The key to increasing profits:** *reduced costs & increased revenues*

# Evolution of Productivity and Quality

# Industry evolution

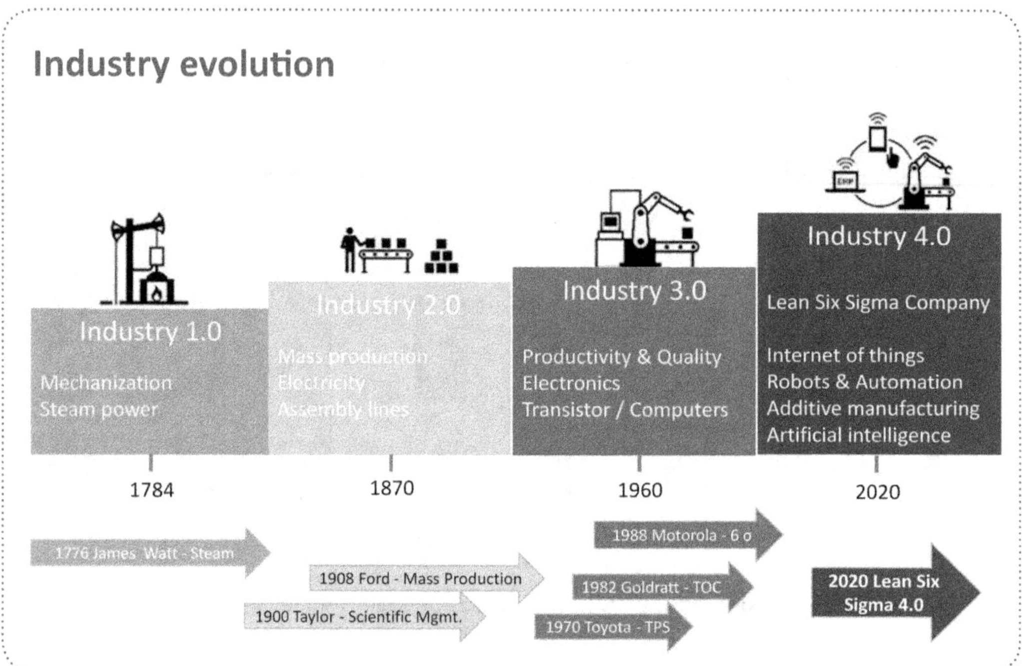



# What is Industry 4.0?



Platforms that connect people, objects and systems.

## II. Productivity and its limitations

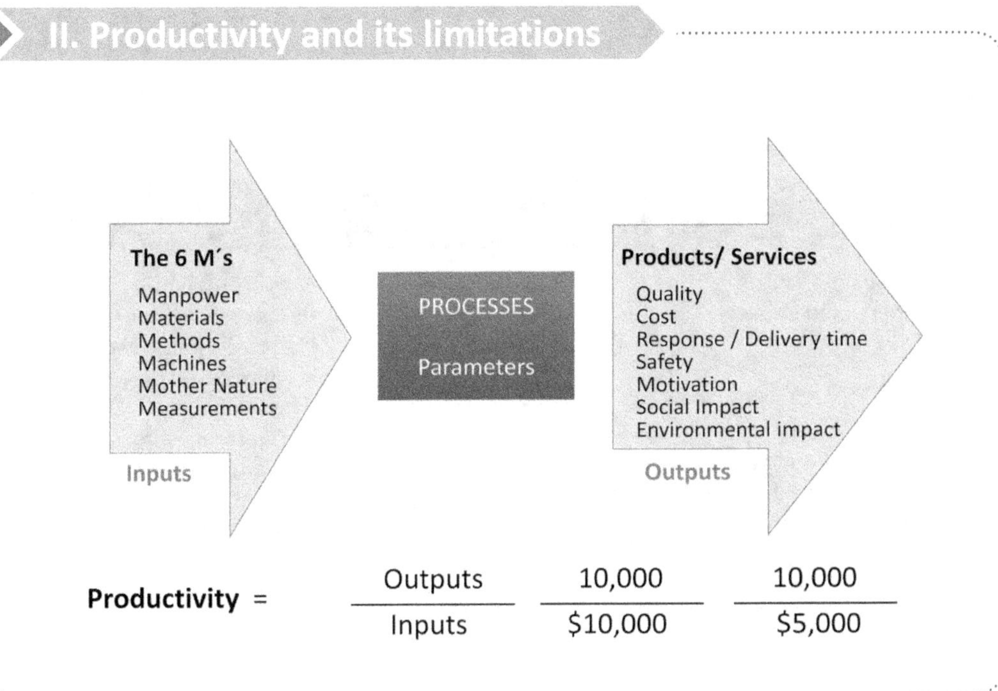


$$\text{Productivity} = \frac{\text{Outputs}}{\text{Inputs}} \quad \frac{10,000}{\$10,000} \quad \frac{10,000}{\$5,000}$$

# Methods to increase productivity

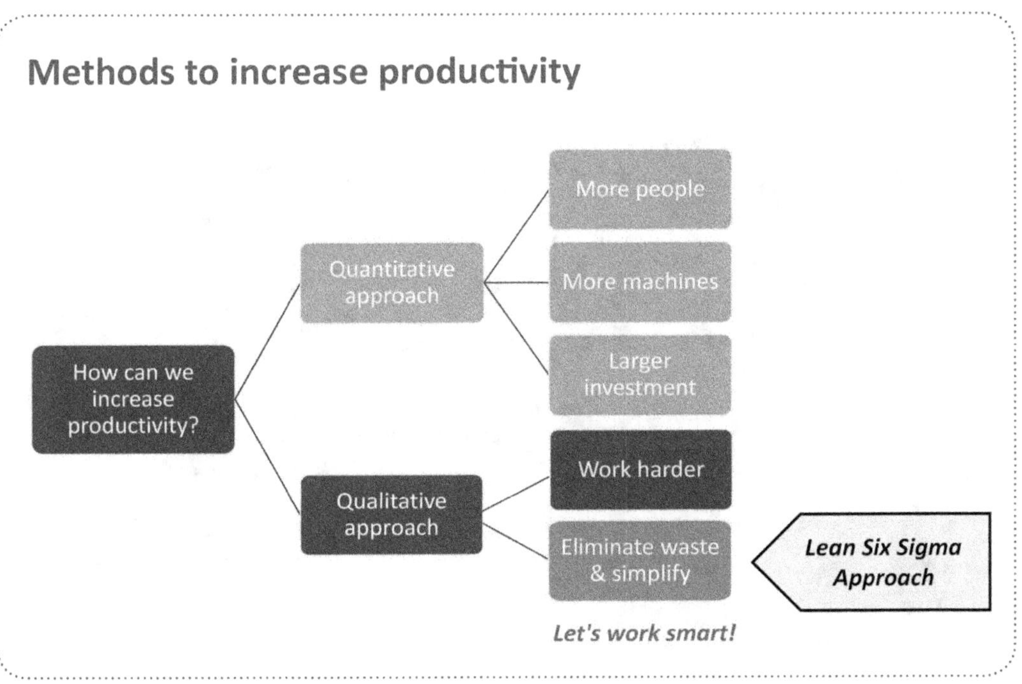

# Limitations to Productivity

| Muri<br>Overburden | Mura<br>Variability | Muda<br>Waste |
|---|---|---|

**Muri / Overburden**
- Overbearing Tasks
- Work related stress
- High-Risk Tasks

**Mura / Variability**

**Total Variability**
- The variation that results from all process inputs

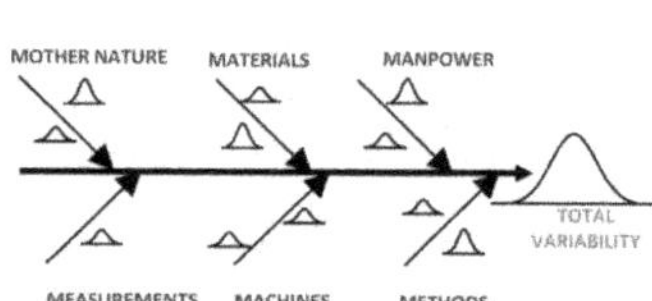


**Muda / Waste**
- Overproduction
- Excess inventory
- Defects and Rework
- Unnecessary movements
- Overprocessing
- Waiting and Searching
- Transport
- Waste of energy
- Talent without action
- Contamination / Pollution

## III. Business development model

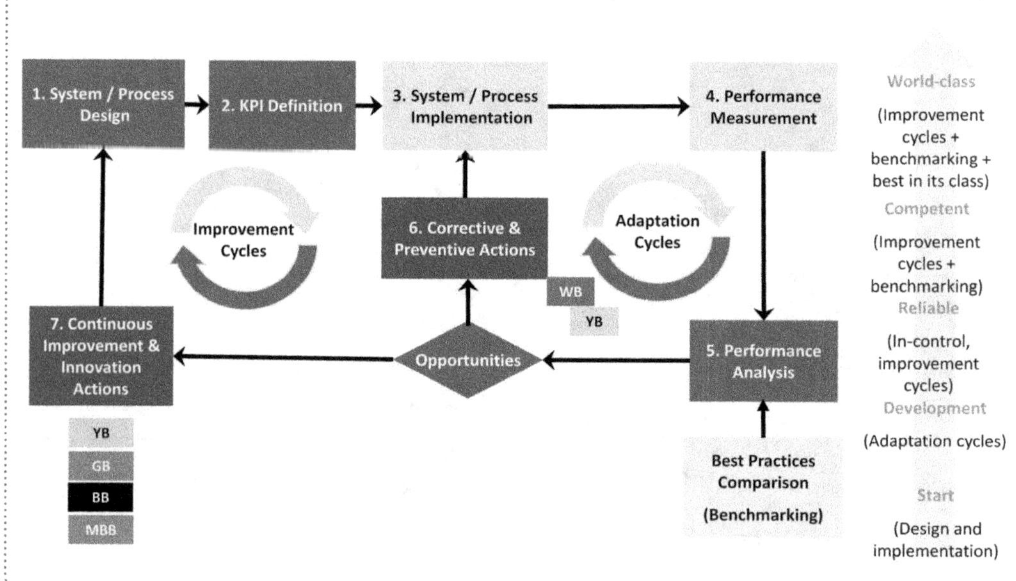

## IV. What is Lean Six Sigma?

- **Lean = Speed**

  Improves flow by eliminating waste

Motorola

- **Six Sigma = Quality**

  Improves the process by reducing variation

1. Work **philosophy**
2. Work **methodology**
3. Strategic and tactical **toolset**

*The path to improvement
does not have an end.*

## Lean Six Sigma Model

Source: Lean Company, Luis Socconini

## Lean Principles  "The 4 P's"

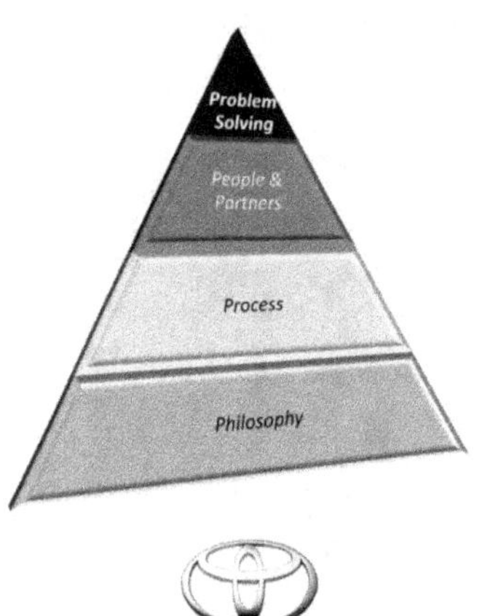


***Philosophy***
1. Base management decisions on a Long-term philosophy

***Process***
2. Create process flow
3. Use "Pull" systems
4. Level out workload
5. Stop when needed to avoid defects
6. Standardize processes
7. Visual control
8. Only use reliable technology

***Developing our people and suppliers***
9. Develop leaders
10. Develop and challenge your people
11. Respect your suppliers by challenging them

***Solving problems generates learning***
12. See for yourself
13. Make decisions
14. Learn through Kaizen

## Lean Six Sigma in services

- In services, unlike manufacturing, the challenge is even greater.
- In services, we create **life experiences** which will be remembered forever by our satisfied customers.

**But bad experiences will also be remembered!!!**

LSSI
LEAN SIX SIGMA INSTITUTE

## Why Lean Six Sigma in services?

- Service organizations face enormous challenges, like never before.
- The modern consumer is better educated and informed and expects services to be:
    - More accurate
    - Quick
    - Friendly
    - Less expensive
- Implementing Lean Six Sigma in services will increase the perceived value of the customer experience and therefore make enduring organizations.

## It is no longer acceptable

- Having to give the same information more than three times when once should be enough.
- Waiting for hours to receive a service when the wait should only be seconds or minutes.
- Registering at an unwelcoming and error-prone reception desk.
- Receiving services without added value, without quality and having to pay a high price for them.

## Critical processes in services

- Manage an appointment.
- Receive customers.
- Fill out an application.
- Provide a quote.
- Place an order.
- Provide consultation or specific service work.
- Generate an invoice.
- Make a payment.
- Follow up on customer satisfaction.

## V. Benefits

**Hard Savings**

**Soft Savings**

- Reduce costs
- Increase capacity
- Increase demand
- Improve margin
- Reduce capital structure:
  - Inventory
  - Accounts receivable
  - Building, equipment, etc.
- On Time delivery
- Improve quality

- Improve communication
- Improve customer satisfaction
- Improve employee satisfaction
- Reduce employee turnover
- Improve safety and environment
- Continuous improvement culture
- Better decision making



**LSSI**
LEAN SIX SIGMA INSTITUTE

## Benefits of Lean Six Sigma vs. other methodologies

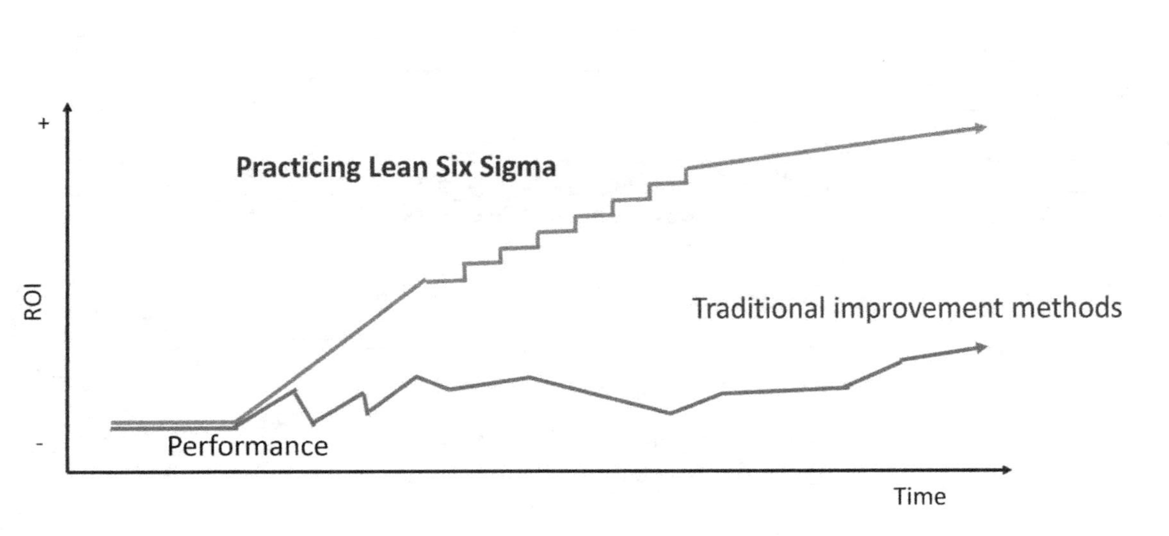


**Lean Six Sigma =** Breakthrough Results

# Lean Six Sigma is applied throughout the company

| LEAN SIX SIGMA COMPANY | | | | | | | | | | | |
| --- | --- | --- | --- | --- | --- | --- | --- | --- | --- | --- | --- |
| Upper Management | Human Resources | Research & Development | Sales & Marketing | Accounting & Finance | Procurement | Service | Manufacturing | Maintenance | Logistics | Quality | IT |

**STRATEGIC TOOLS**
- Hoshin Kanri
- Value Stream Structure
- Value Stream Map
- Talent Development
- Agile Project Management
- Standard Work for Leaders
- Kata
- Gemba Walks

## Strategic Tools

All areas use management tools to define, execute and follow up on strategies.

**BASIC TOOLS**
- 5S Housekeeping
- Visual Management (Andon)
- Standardize Work
- Personal (Self) Management

## Tactical Tools

All areas use basic tools to support identification, development and sustainment of improvements.

| | LEAN | SIX SIGMA | Upper Management | Human Resources | Research & Development | Sales & Marketing | Accounting & Finance | Procurement | Service | Manufacturing | Maintenance | Logistics | Quality | IT |
| --- | --- | --- | --- | --- | --- | --- | --- | --- | --- | --- | --- | --- | --- | --- |
| DMAIC | | | | | | | | | | | | | | |
| Tool Set | | | Planning | Talent Attraction | Product Development | Mktg. Campaigns | Budget Cost Acct. | Supplier Development | Lean Service | Lean Manufacturing | Autonomous | Incoming Warehouse | Quality Deployment | Hardware |
| | | | Strategic Mgmt. | Talent Development | Lean Startup | Surveys | Inventory / Payroll | Purchasing | | | Preventive | Routing / Loading | Quality System | Software |
| | | | Decision Making | | Design for Six Sigma | Pricing | Invoicing / Credit | Warehouse | | | Predictive | Transportation | Calibration | Communication |
| | | | | | | Lean Retail | Acct. Payable / Financial Statements | | | | Energy | | | Help Desk |

## Industries

- Food & Beverage
- Electronics
- Services
- Automotive
- Government
- Agriculture
- Mining
- Packaging
- Airports
- Military

- Pharmaceutical
- Banking
- Insurance
- Hotels
- Restaurants
- Construction

- Healthcare
- Plastics
- Lubricants
- Logistics & Customs
- Education
- Cosmetics
- Footwear
- Textile
- Printing
- Foundry

LEAN MANAGEMENT | WHITE BELT | YELLOW BELT | GREEN BELT | BLACK BELT | MASTER BLACK BELT

## Traditional vs. Lean Six Sigma

### Traditional

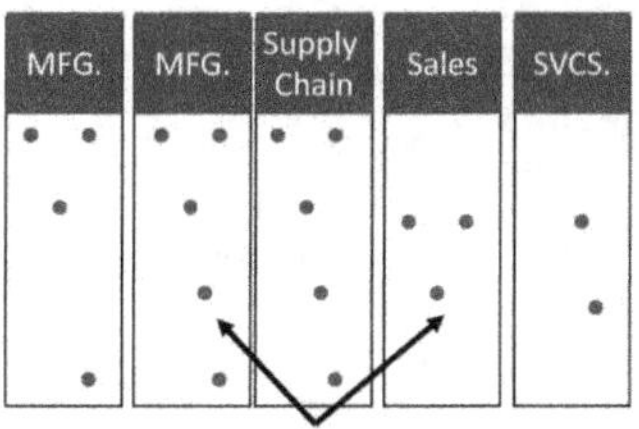


Isolated Projects by departments

### Lean Six Sigma

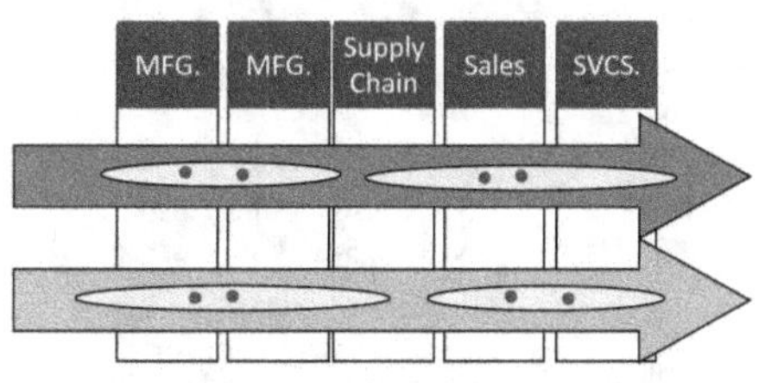


A few high-impact projects in the value stream or service family

*"If I could change the way we implemented it,
I would have started with Lean and then Six Sigma."*

Jack Welch, Ex-CEO GE

## LEAN SIX SIGMA COMPANY
### Transformation Model

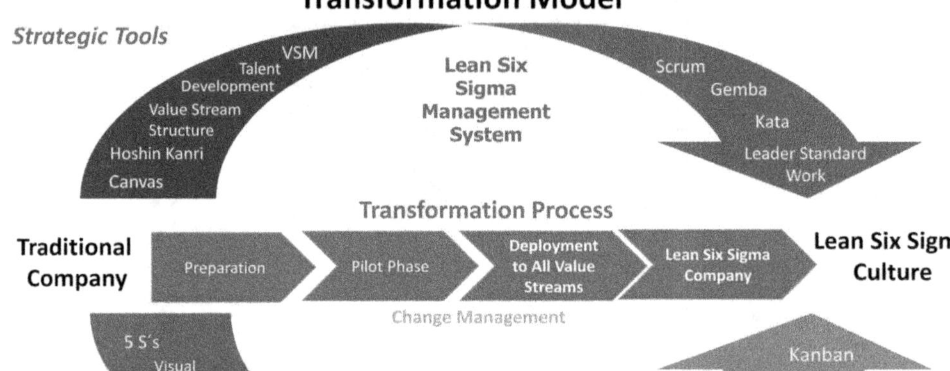


## VI. Implementation process

|  | 1 -3 months | 4 - 6 months | 1 – 2 years | 1 – 2 years and onward |

|  | **Preparation** | **Pilot** | **Deployment to All Value Streams** | **Lean Six Sigma Company** |

**Preparation**
- Initial training (LM, WB)
- Initial assessment
- Develop Hoshin Kanri
- Define leader team
- Select pilot projects
- Value Stream / Service Family Map
- Design initial plan
- Communicate plan
- Kick off

**Pilot**
- Certify White & Yellow Belts
- Certify Processes

Basic Tools
- 5 S Housekeeping, Visual Mgmt., Standard Work, etc.

Adaptation Cycles
- DMAIC Kaizen blitz for:
  - Problem solving
  - Failure Mode and Effects Analysis

Improvement Cycles
- DMAIC Kaizen for:
  - Continuous Flow, TPM, Quick Setups, Kanban
- DFSS Kaikaku for:
  - Product Design, etc.

**Deployment to All Value Streams**
- Certify GB, BB & MBB
- Certify Value Streams
- Design Value Stream
- Implement Value Stream Office
- Select team members

Continue
- Basic tools
- Adaptation Cycles
- Improvement Cycles

Develop
- Supply chain Kaizen
- Supplier Kaizen
- Customer Kaizen

**Lean Six Sigma Company**

Certify entire company

Implement Lean Six Sigma
- Accounting
- Human Recourses
- Sales & Marketing
- Logistics
- Service / Manufacturing
- IT
- Quality
- Maintenance

## VII. Change management

**1. Create a sense of urgency**
- Analyze the market
- Analyze the competition
- Identify possible risks and opportunities

**2. Build a guiding team**
- Form a group of influential and responsible individuals
- Teamwork

**3. Develop a vision & strategy**
- Develop the vision
- Develop strategies to carry out the vision

**4. Communicate the change vision**
- Communicate and share the vision and strategy
- Determine the leader team

**5. Empower action**
- Avoid obstacles
- Improve and modify the structure
- Increase risk taking

**6. Secure short term gains**
- Plan performance improvements
- Achieve & announce victories
- Reward the responsible parties

**7. Consolidate improvements & produce more change**
- Expand growth to other areas
- Constantly evaluate results
- Support successful processes

**8. Make it last**
- Continue to support the change
- Focus on values and the customer
- Improve management effectiveness

Preparation → Pilot Phase → Deployment to All Value Streams → Lean Six Sigma Company

# Resistance to change

It has been proven that, faced with important and transcendental changes:

**20 % +**
20% of people will be positive in their implementation and their contributions will be very valuable.

**60 % Neutral**
60% of people tend to be neutral.

**20 % −**
20% tend to have a negative attitude towards change.

With **good leadership**, many negative people and neutral people will become positive. Otherwise, it will be just another forgotten project.

# Why some companies can and others don't?

| Vision | + | Skills | + | Incentives | + | Resources | + | Planning | = | Change |
| X | + | Skills | + | Incentives | + | Resources | + | Planning | = | Confusion |
| Vision | + | X | + | Incentives | + | Resources | + | Planning | = | Anxiety |
| Vision | + | Skills | + | X | + | Resources | + | Planning | = | Slow change |
| Vision | + | Skills | + | Incentives | + | X | + | Planning | = | Frustration |
| Vision | + | Skills | + | Incentives | + | Resources | + | X | = | False start |

# Lean Six Sigma certifications

## There are four certification categories:

| 1. People Certification | 2. Process Certification | 3. Value Stream Certification | 4. Company Certification |
|---|---|---|---|
| Training and certification as:<br><br>• White Belts<br>• Yellow Belts<br>• Green Belts<br>• Black Belts<br>• Master Black Belts | • Evaluate if the processes meet the requirements.<br>• Make sure that the methods are supported and the tools work. | All value stream processes have achieved a certain level of progress and people are exercising the correct habits. | The company has a Lean / agile management culture and a leadership team that makes decisions based on facts and data. |
| 2 Projects per year | 2 Evaluations per year | 2-4 Evaluations per year | 2 Evaluations per year |

# Certification levels

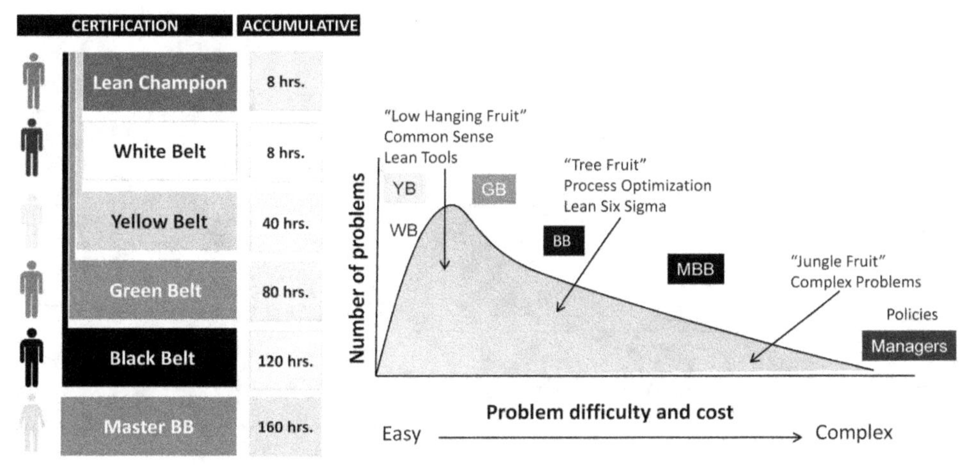



## VIII. Roles and structure

| CHAMPION LSS Management | WHITE BELT | YELLOW BELT | GREEN BELT | BLACK BELT | MASTER BLACK BELT |
|---|---|---|---|---|---|
| Responsible for budget and resources | Project Team Member | Lean Practitioner | Small Project Leader | Project Leader & Coach | Experienced Implementation Expert and BB coach |
| Lean Six Sigma Project Sponsor | Practices the basic tools every day as part of his/her work | Ensures philosophy is sustained on a daily basis | Provides specific support | Ensures correct implementation for the value stream or Service Family | Expert in practicing Lean Six Sigma throughout the company and supply chain |
| | | | Ensures sustainability in his / her area of responsibility | | |
| Leaders | 100% | 20 - 50% | 10 - 20% | 1 - 3% | 1 % |

## Lean Six Sigma Structure

| | | Executive Staff | | Staff | Experts | Selected People |
|---|---|---|---|---|---|---|
| **Corporate Office Region Country** | |  | |  |  |  |
| | | | | Corporate Champion | Master BB | Improvement Teams |
| **Family of Products / Services** | Value Stream Teams  | | Support Teams  |  Value stream / Service Family Champion | Black Belt | Improvement Teams |
| **Productive Teams** |   Products / Services | | 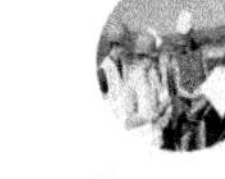 Transactions |  Project Champion |  Green Yellow Belt Belt |  Improvement Teams |

## IX. Six Sigma methodology and tools

**Define**  >  **Measure**  >  **Analyze**  >  **Improve**  >  **Control**

**DEFINE**

- Secure management commitment and active participation.
- Be familiar with the strategy and how the projects relate to the company's plan.
- Secure the resources that will be allocated to projects: people, time, tasks.
- Define the project.
- Define the team and clarify the roles.
- Identify the main cause-effect relationships

**MEASURE AND MAP**

- Understand customer requirements.
- Know the process in detail.
- Define and evaluate measurement systems.

**ANALYZE**

- Develop a clear understanding of productivity constraints to successfully reach the full potential of the service.
- Analyze the process to understand where the improvements will be made.

**IMPROVE**

- Establish new conditions in the service process.
- The benefits associated with the proposed solution are estimated by the team and approved by the Director.
- The improvements are implemented and verified.

**CONTROL**

- Control and follow up the service process.
- Standardize new methods.
- Document the lessons learned.
- Continuously improve.

# Lean Six Sigma Tools

| | | | |
|---|---|---|---|
| **1** | **Introduction** | | |

| Introduction | Problem Solving Methodology |
|---|---|

| | |
|---|---|
| **2** | **Define** |

| | | | |
|---|---|---|---|
| | Define the Strategy | | |
| | Define the Team | | |
| | Define the Project | | |

| Hoshin Kanri | Value Stream Structures | Talent Development |
|---|---|---|
| Teamwork | | |
| A3 | | |

**3 Measure**

Measure the Voice of the Customer
Measure the Service
Map the Service

| NPS | Kano | Needs Map |
|---|---|---|
| Box Score | 4 Q's | |
| Cross - functional | Data Collection | VSM |

**4 Analyze**

Analyze the Bottleneck
Limitants to Productivity
Failure Mode and Effect Analysis

| Spaghetti | Balance | |
|---|---|---|
| Overburden | Variability | Waste |
| FMEA | | |

**5 Improve**

Basics Tools
Reliability
Continuous Flow
Future Value Stream Map

| 5 S's | Andon | |
|---|---|---|
| TPM | | |
| Cells or Pods | SMED | Kanban |
| VSM Future | Kaizen Plan | |

**6 Control**

Control the Service

| Standardized Work | Poka Yoke | Kata |
|---|---|---|

# Conclusion

"No organization, large or small, local or global, is immune to change."

"To address new technological, competitive, and demographic forces, leaders from all sectors are trying to fundamentally alter the way their organizations do business."

John P. Kotter

# Problem solving

**How to transform problems into solutions**

## Objectives

1. Apply a practical and simple method for *defining* problems.
2. Use a *structured* approach to understand the *root cause* of a problem.
3. *Solve* problems using a practical and simple methodology.

## Content

I. Background
II. What is problem solving?
III. Benefits
IV. When do we use it?
V. Methodology
VI. Exercise

## I. Background

- Everyone faces different types of problems at work and personally.

- When trying to solve problems, most of the time we attack symptoms and NOT causes.

- How many of us know and apply a problem solving methodology?

## How do we normally solve problems?

**The general tendency is:**

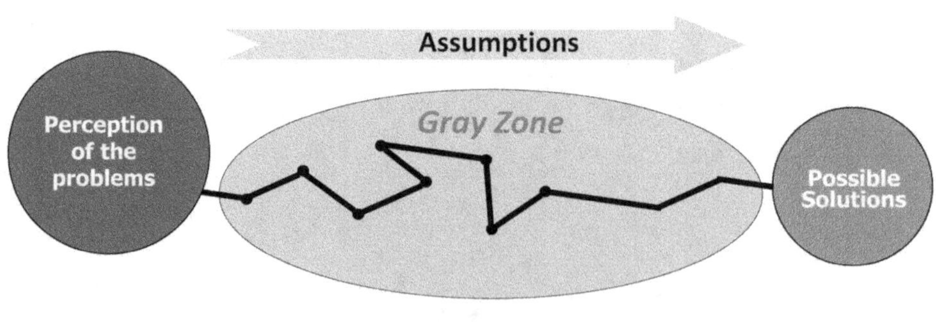

# How are we going to solve the problems now?

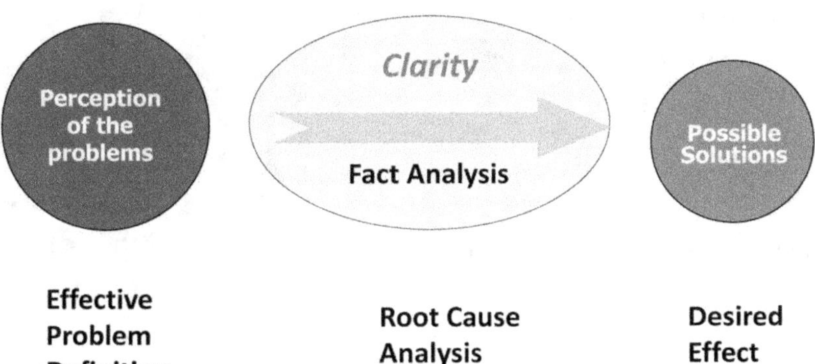


**Effective Problem Definition**

**Root Cause Analysis**

**Desired Effect**

## II. What is problem solving?

A methodology to solve problems based on the root cause.

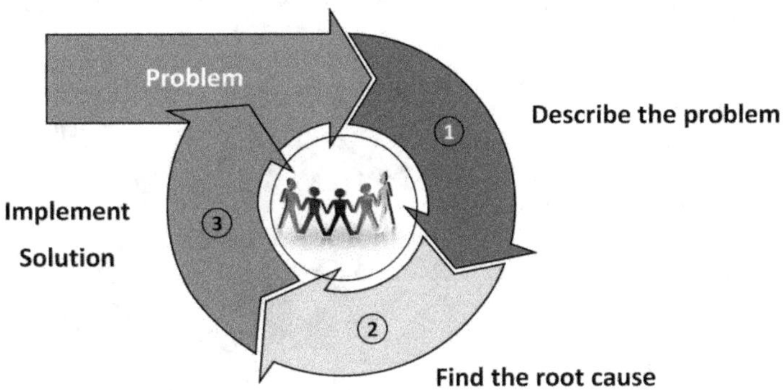

# Problem solving



- It provides the team with an approach to define causes of the problem
- Prevents recurrence
- Create better standards
- Motivate teamwork
- It helps solve the problems permanently

**"Working as a team ensures success."**

Henry Ford

## IV. When do we use it?

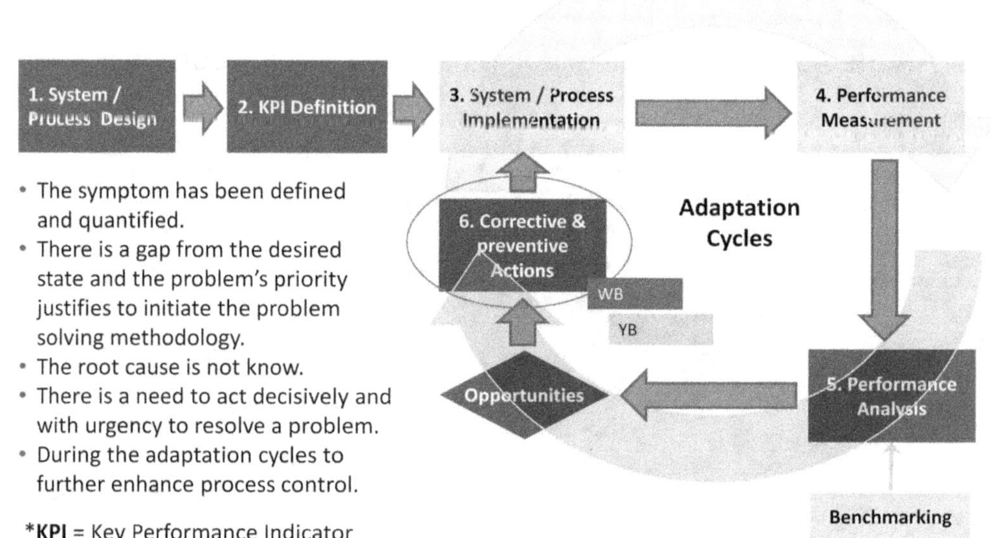


- The symptom has been defined and quantified.
- There is a gap from the desired state and the problem's priority justifies to initiate the problem solving methodology.
- The root cause is not know.
- There is a need to act decisively and with urgency to resolve a problem.
- During the adaptation cycles to further enhance process control.

**KPI* = Key Performance Indicator

## V. Methodology

# How does it work?

| | |
|---|---|
| **Problem** | **STEP 1. DESCRIBE THE PROBLEM** |
| Cause | **STEP 2. FIND THE CAUSE** |
| Solution | **STEP 3. IMPLEMENT SOLUTION** |
| | **PDCA - Share learning** |

# Problem

- Define the problem as accurately as possible
- The problem is defined in the present tense

It should be written as a simple and concise statement that identifies the problem's subject using a present tense verb , along with the respective defect / situation.

**Define the Problem**

Find the Cause

Solution

Confirm

Subject + present tense verb + (defect/situation)

**Defect / situation** is an undesirable characteristic, present in a product or process.
**Subject** is the name given to a specific product or process containing the defect.

**e.g.** The pizza is **delivered late.**
The company produces **defective screws.**

# Define the problem

To make a scientific description of any event,
the following information needs to be provided.

- What is the problem and <u>what it's not</u>
- Where is the problem and <u>where it's not</u>
- When does a problem happen and <u>when it doesn't</u>
- How big is the problem and <u>how big it's not</u>

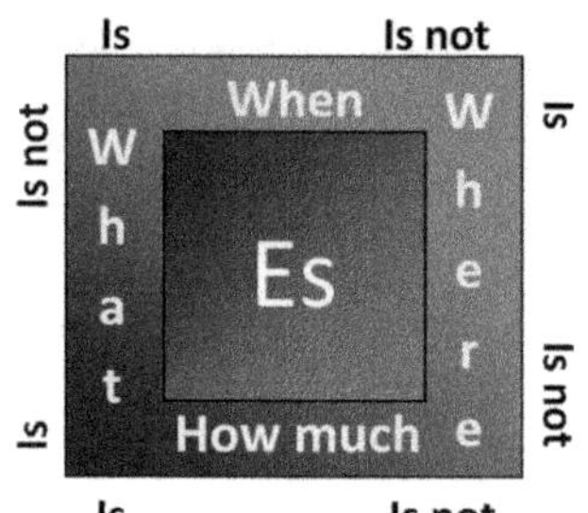


| The problem in its right dimension |
| --- |

## Guide for Problem Analysis

| | IS | IS NOT |
| --- | --- | --- |
| **WHAT** <br> (Identity) | What SERVICE has an ERROR / PROBLEM / DEFECT <br> What ERROR does it have? | Another SERVICE could have this ERROR but does not have it <br> It could have another ERROR, but does not have it. |
| **WHERE** <br> (Location) | Where are the SERVICES with this ERROR (place) <br> Where is the ERROR found in the SERVICE | Where could there be SERVICES with ERROR, but they are not <br> Where could be the ERROR in the SERVICE but it is not |
| **WHEN** <br> (Time) | When did the SERVICES with ERRORS appear (date, hour, minute) <br><br> When did the ERROR appear in the "life" of the SERVICE (Time, Phase, Event, First time) <br><br> Frequency that the PROBLEM is observed (Continuous, sporadic or periodic) | When could the SERVICES with ERROR have appeared but they did not <br><br> When could have the ERROR have appeared, but did not <br><br> Frequency that the PROBLEM is NOT observed |
| **HOW MUCH** <br> (Magnitude) | How many SERVICES have the ERROR <br> What is the magnitude of the ERROR <br> The PROBLEM increases or decreases <br> Write any other quantitative data | How many SERVICES could have ERROR, but they don't <br> What could be the magnitude of the defect, but it isn't |
| **MOST PROBABLE CAUSES**: What changes could cause the problem? How does this change cause the problem? | | |
| **TEST**: If this would be the cause, how is it explain that the IS happens and the IS NOT doesn't? | | |
| **VERIFICATION**: The easiest, cheapest, fastest. In the place of the scene - where the problem happens | | |

# The problem statement should comply with the following

1. **Be specific:** problems are usually stated vaguely:
   "The water is too hot."

2. **Describe the problem, not its symptoms:**
   "The morale of the department is low."

3. **Avoid causes and solutions:**
   "The response time for providing the service is the cause of the customer's dissatisfaction, which indicates a potential problem."

# Use the brainstorming process to define the problem

**Objective:** to express without bias all the opinions of the group.

To achieve this goal, all participants should be asked to write on a small paper (post-its) all the ideas generated from the question:

**What do you think is the problem?**

The facilitator gathers and classifies all the ideas and presents them in an un-biased way.

## SOS Example / Brainstorming

## What is the problem?

### 1 Problem

**Define the problem / SOS Example**

Orders are delivered late to customers.

## 2 Cause

Define the problem

Find the Cause

Solution

Confirm

- Observe and answer **"Why does this happen?"**

- If you cannot answer the previous question: Use some of the basic tools for problem solving (fish diagram, 5 whys, current reality tree, etc.)

- Prioritize if there is more than one cause (use FACTS)

---

## What is the cause?

**Basic Tools**

| Fishbone Diagram (Ishikawa) | 5 Whys | Current Reality Tree |
| --- | --- | --- |

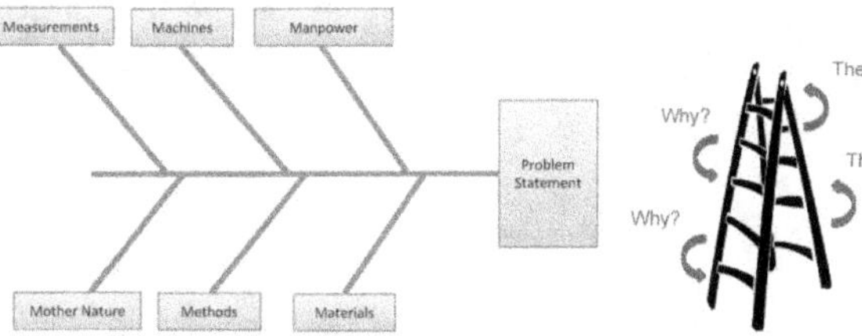

# Fishbone Diagram / Ishikawa

Is a graphical tool that results from a brainstorming session in which all potential causes for a particular effect are listed and organized into categories. This makes it easier to separate problems and possible improvements.

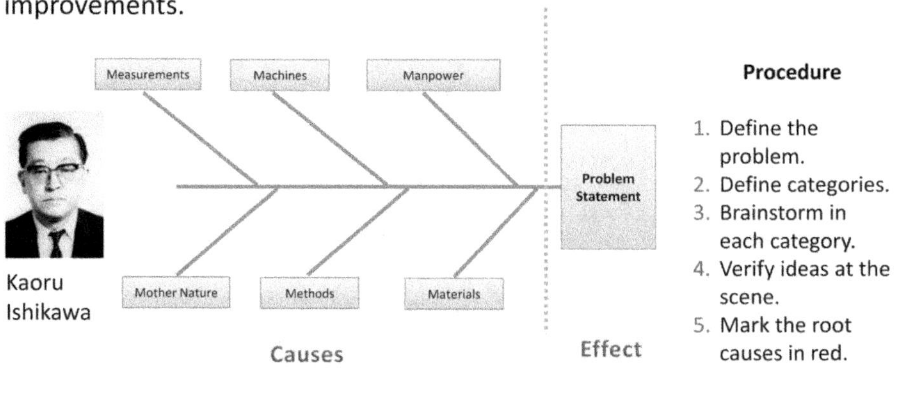


### Procedure

1. Define the problem.
2. Define categories.
3. Brainstorm in each category.
4. Verify ideas at the scene.
5. Mark the root causes in red.

# Example SOS

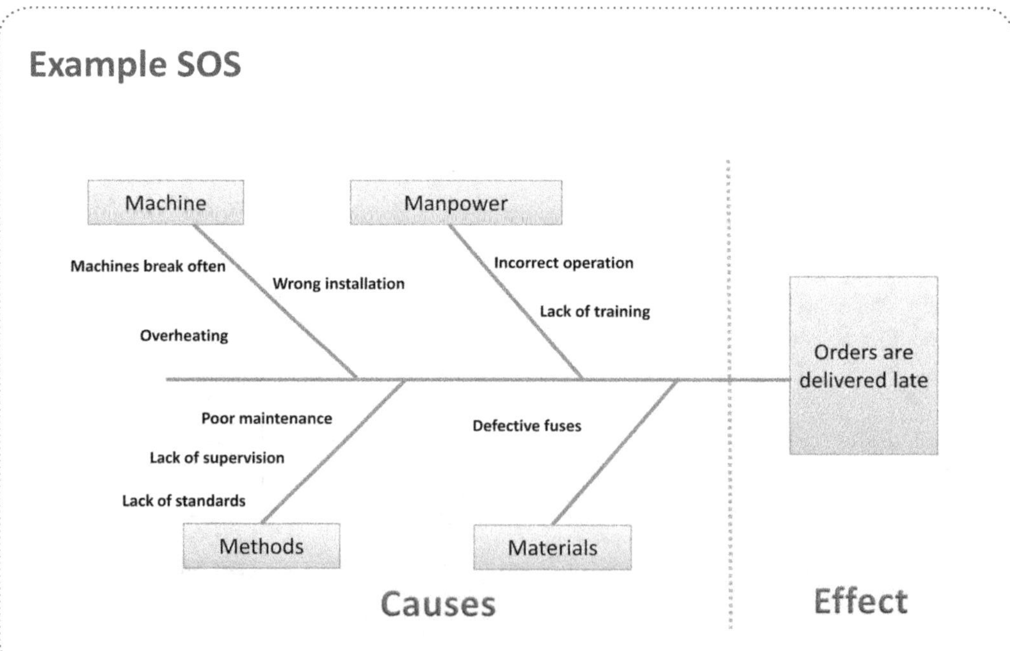

# 5 Whys

Define the problem: Orders are delivered late to customers

1. **Why?**
   Because the machines are broken down

2. **Why?**
   Because the fuses are melted

3. **Why?**
   Because the machines are overheating

4. **Why?**
   Because the oil changes are not made in time

5. **Why?**
   Because there is no formal maintenance program

# Current Reality Tree

A diagram that shows the cause and effect relationships, while taking into consideration all variables that influence a problem or a given situation. It includes circumstances, causes, effects, that pertain to the problem.

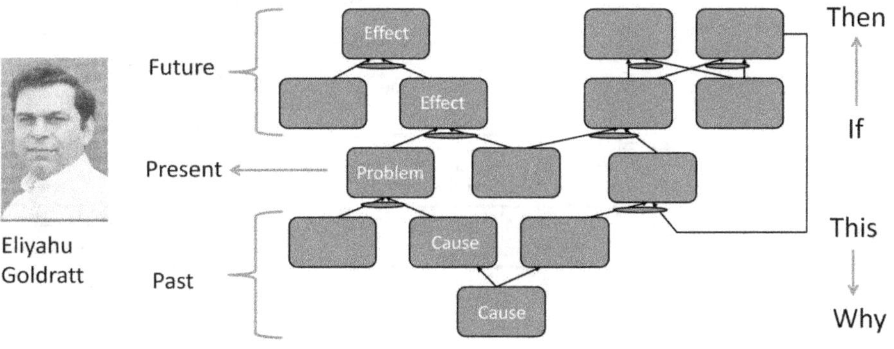

**2** Cause

## Find the Cause / SOS Example

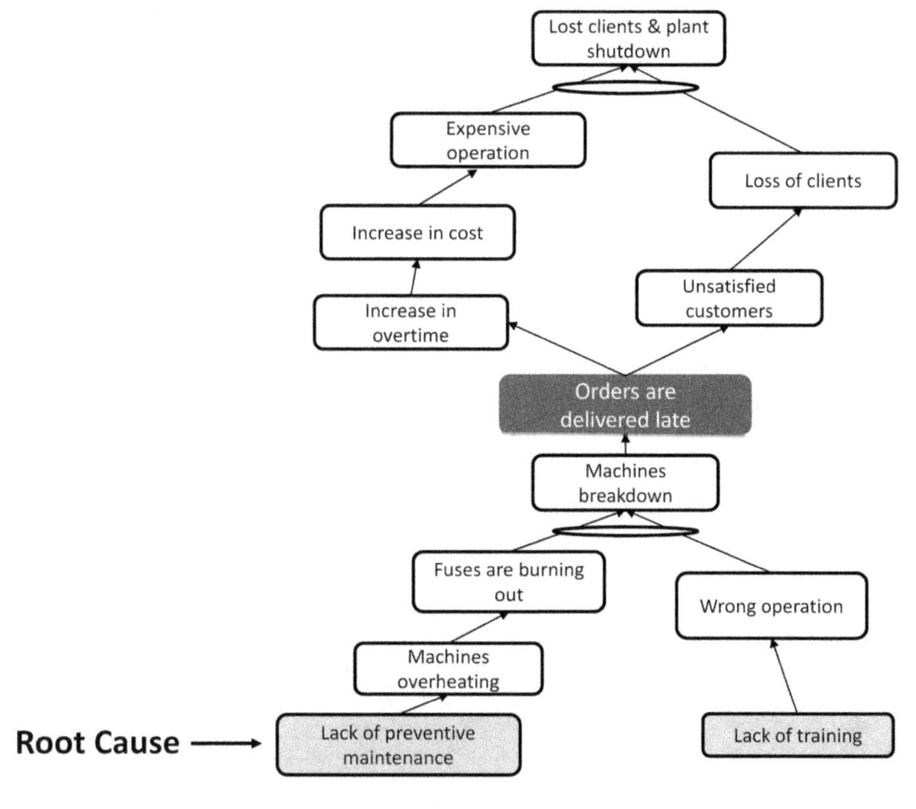

# 3 Solution

- Select the best permanent correct action to eliminate the root cause.
- Verify that actions are successful when implemented.
- Document the case.

## What is the solution?

### Tools

**Future Reality Tree** — To establish the best solution sustained in actions and effects.

**Decision Matrix** — When you have to decide between two or more options to solve a problem.

**A3** — To document the problem solving process.

# 3 Solution

## Solution / SOS Example - Future Reality Tree

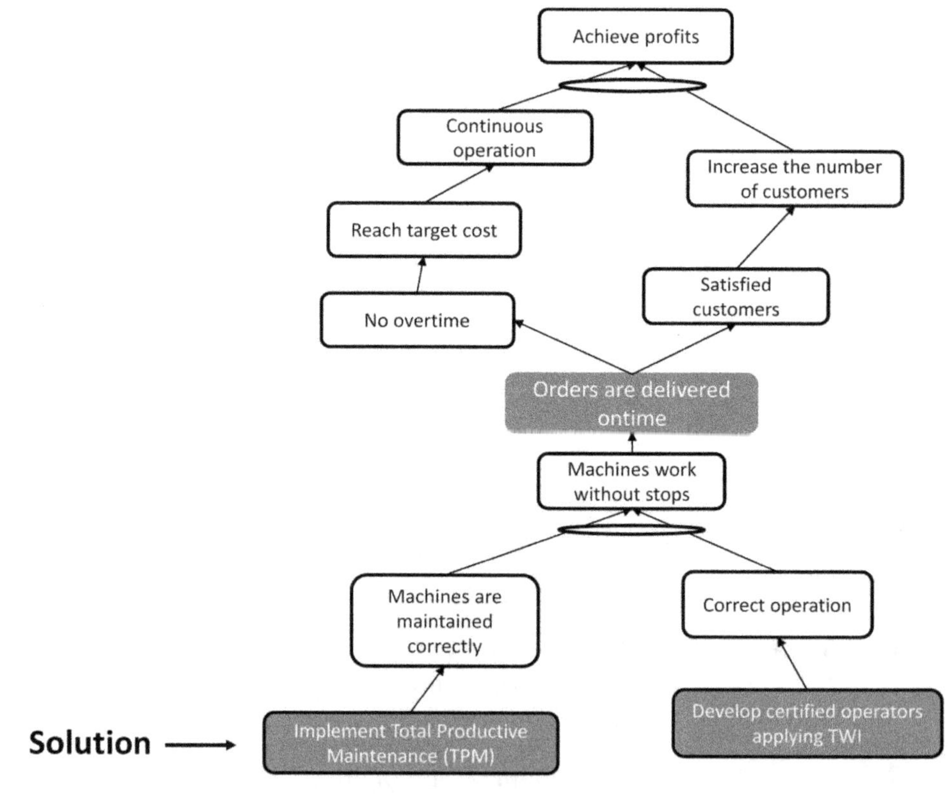


**Solution** ⟶

# Example: A3

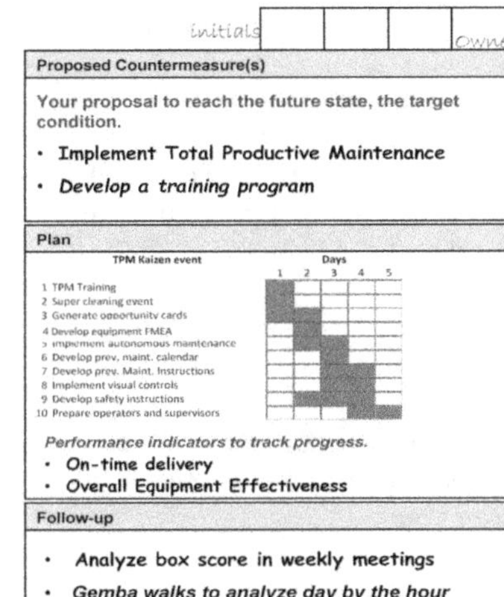


We will see the **A3 with more detail** in the project definition topic.

# What we accomplish?

Apply the problem solving process to:

- Define the problem properly.
- Identify the root cause and effects.
- Define actions that eliminate the problem.
- Efficiently document the problem solving process.

Now it is very important to consider:

- Use the simple problem solving method.
- Teach our classmates, students and family how to solve problems in an easy way.
- Constantly improve our problem solving process.

## VI. Exercise

Bayside is one of our best customers. Lately, we haven't been able to deliver a single order to them on time. Our facility is a mess. Nothing is ever produced as planned.

The production supervisor blames maintenance personnel for being too slow when fixing maintenance issues. The maintenance staff blames the operators for not taking care of the machines and letting them breakdown constantly. The bottom line is that we are not delivering products on time to our customers, and they are assessing the possibility of going with other more reliable suppliers.

Every day, we try our best to meet our production schedule. However, issues keep coming up, and as the production manager, I spend much of my time resolving them.

In the last few days, we have had to pay for excessive maintenance costs and overtime to ensure that our orders are complete. However, we still can't meet our expected delivery dates and requirements.

I really don't know what is going on with the company. I am beginning to feel desperate and am not sure what the solution is. I have morning meetings every day with my production personnel and we review the production schedule. The meetings are chaotic since everyone is placing blame on each other and no one can agree on the best problem solving method.

In the maintenance report, I have noted high reliability/performance fuses are being changed frequently. Lately, I have had to approve urgent purchase orders for fuses to avoid stopping the production machines.

I think we need to establish a preventive maintenance plan, but with all the problems we are facing, I don't see how we can put one together since there is not enough time to focus on both production and maintenance.

The operators are constantly reporting that the machines are overheating, but I think they are just using the machines as an excuse to evade their responsibility for not meeting production and delivery requirements. I have been wanting to launch a training program to teach the operators how to operate the machines correctly, but we haven't had time since we are almost always behind schedule.

At this point, I don't know what the solutions are to address our problems and I am totally overwhelmed. I need to solve our issues quickly or we might have to completely shut the plant down due to low productivity.

# Lean Strategy:
# Hoshin Kanri



## Objectives

1. Understand the *key elements* of Strategic Planning.
2. Understand the Hoshin Kanri *implementation* process.
3. *Start* the Hoshin Kanri planning process in a company.

## Content

I. Background
II. What is Hoshin Kanri?
III. Benefits
IV. When is it used and how long does it take?
V. Procedure

## I. Background

- Only between 10% and 20% of companies in the world make a strategic plan

- Only between 10% and 20% execute successfully

- 91% of executives qualify as "exceptional decision-makers"

Source: Harvard Business School

## What is strategy?

**STRATEGY**

***Strato*** = A group of people
Ex: Army

***Agein*** = Guide
Ex: Direct

*"Art of conducting military operations"*

## Strategy deployment

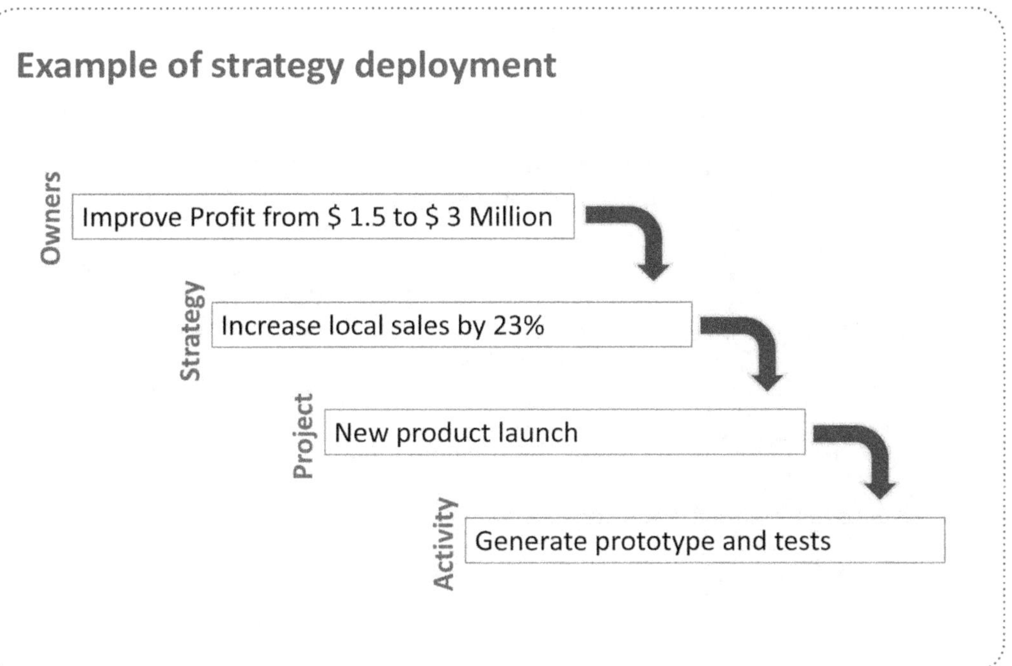


## Example of strategy deployment

## Symptoms of companies in need of Hoshin Kanri planning

- No connection between strategy and continuous improvement

- Too many projects in process

- The plans from one year to the next never seem to connect

### II. What is Hoshin Kanri?

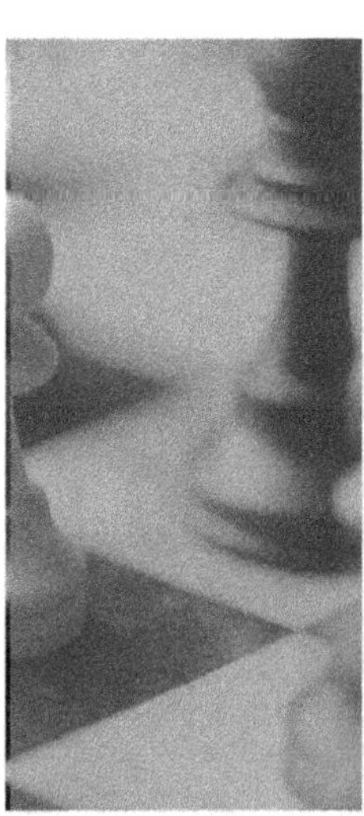

Hoshin is a management tool to address 4 fundamental questions:

- **What is it about?** - vision and key results areas

- **How will we measure our performance?** - key metrics and objectives

- **What are we going to do?** - strategies, action plans

- **How will we behave?** - core values

## What is Hoshin Kanri?

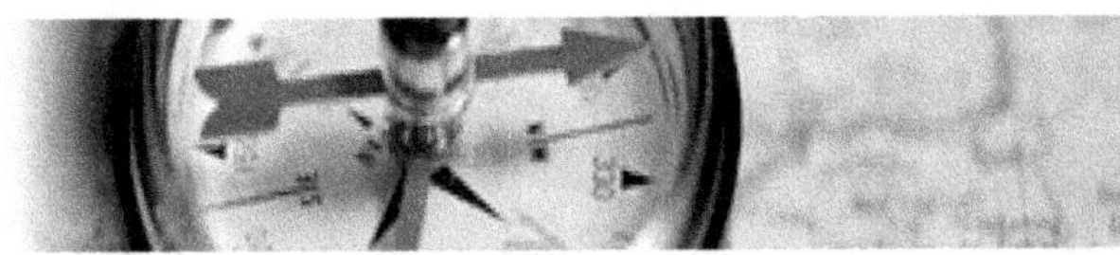

- *ho* = direction
- Shin = needle
- Hoshin = direction of needle or compass

- Kan = control
- ri = reason or logic
- *kanri* = administration control

方針　　　　　　　管理

Hoshin Kanri means management and control
of an organization's direction or focus.

## Other terms used for Hoshin Kanri

- Hoshin Planning (Hewlett-Packard)
- Policy Deployment (AT&T, Infineon Technologies)
- Policy Management (Texas Instruments)
- Management by Results (Xerox)
- Priority Management
- Goals Deployment
- "Catch-ball" Process

## III. Benefits

- **Focuses** the whole company on a few **vital goals**, instead of the many trivial ones
- Creates alignment towards objectives through the **participation** of the entire management team in the planning process
- **Leadership** at **all** levels
- **Communicates** key goals to all managers and staff
- **Integrates and encourages** inter-functional cooperation to achieve significant progress. A review process that holds participants accountable for achieving their part of the plan

## IV. When is it used and how long does it take?

- **Start of operations:** fundamental plan (Hoshin Kanri and box score).
  - Realization time: 1 week
- **Annually:** update of the fundamental plan (Hoshin Kanri).
  - Realization time: 2-4 days
- **Monthly:** evaluation of global progress (balance scorecard).
  - Realization time: 1 hour
- **Weekly:** evaluation of value streams (box score).
  - Realization time: 30 minutes
- **Daily:** evaluation of progress per hour (process board).
  - Realization time: 5 minutes

## V. Procedure

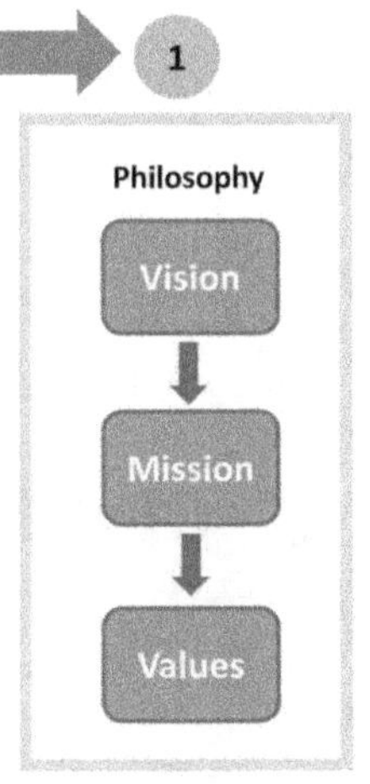

## 1. Establish the philosophy of the company

**VISION**
**What do we want to be?**

**MISSION**
**What is our business?**
**Why do we exist?**

**VALUES**
**What do we believe in and
how do we behave?**

## Examples of vision / mission

**Disney:** "We create happiness by providing the finest entertainment for people of all ages, anywhere."

**Google:** "Organize world information so that it is universally accessible and useful."

**eBay:** "Providing a global electronic market in which virtually anyone can trade with almost any product, thus creating economic opportunities throughout the world."

**Apple:** "Produce high quality and easy-to-use products that incorporate high technology for the individual. We are demonstrating that high technology does not have to be intimidating for non-computer experts."

**Nike:** "Bring inspiration and innovation to every athlete in the world. If you have a body, you are an athlete."

## Example

**A strategic plan on a single sheet**

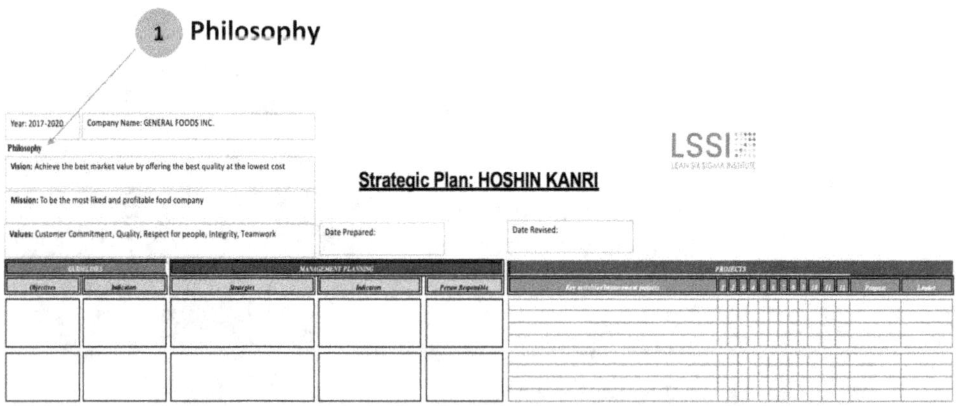

**1  Philosophy**

## 2. Establish objectives (what's)

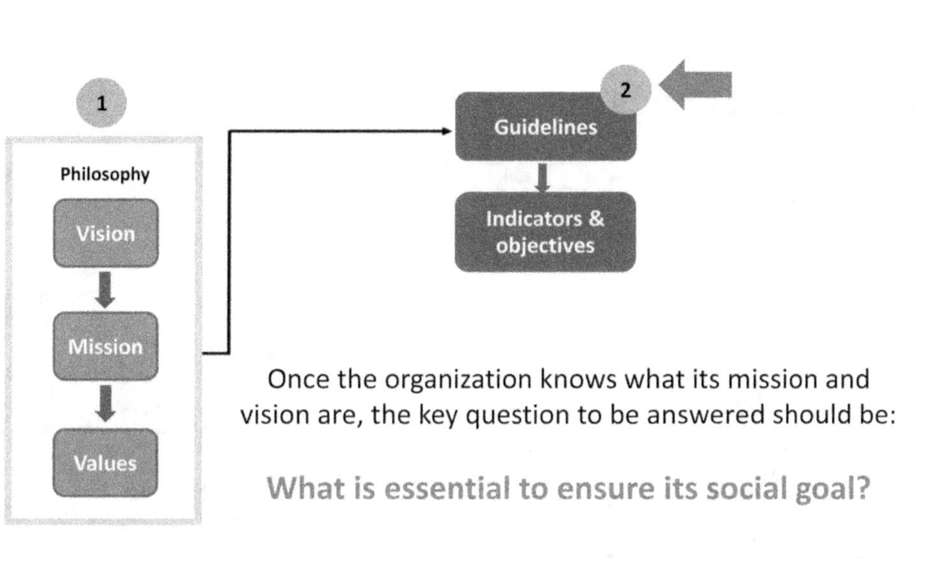



Once the organization knows what its mission and vision are, the key question to be answered should be:

**What is essential to ensure its social goal?**

## Example

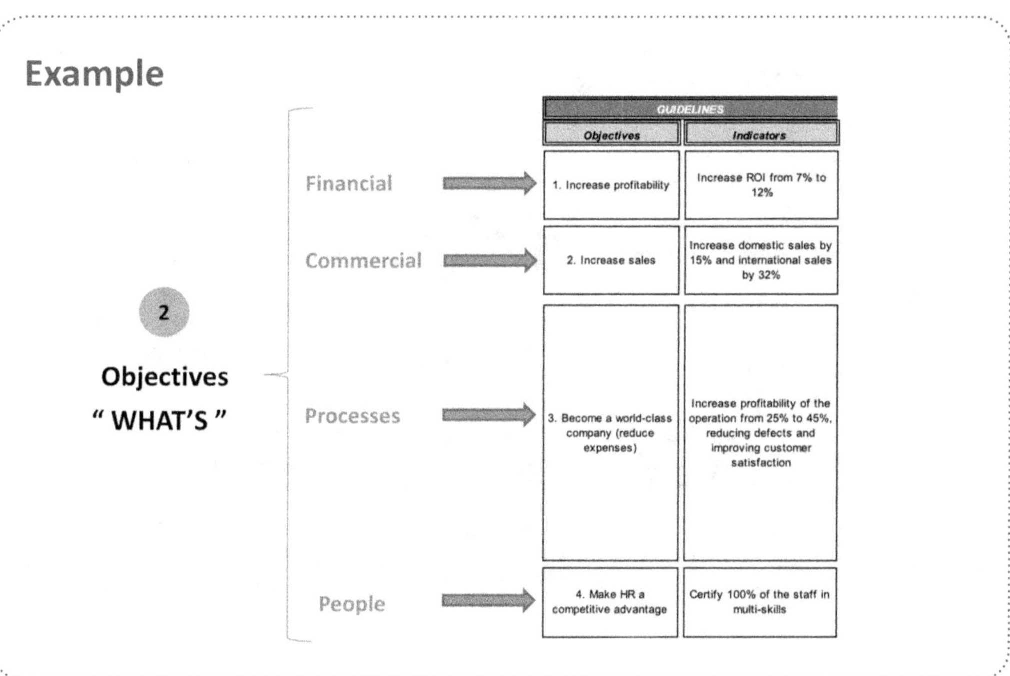



| GUIDELINES | |
|---|---|
| Objectives | Indicators |
| 1. Increase profitability | Increase ROI from 7% to 12% |
| 2. Increase sales | Increase domestic sales by 15% and international sales by 32% |
| 3. Become a world-class company (reduce expenses) | Increase profitability of the operation from 25% to 45%, reducing defects and improving customer satisfaction |
| 4. Make HR a competitive advantage | Certify 100% of the staff in multi-skills |

## Indicators and objectives of the guidelines

**BALANCE SCORECARD**  **Monthly Executive Indicator**

| Guidelines | Objectives | Goal | (YTD) | January | February | March | April | May |
|---|---|---|---|---|---|---|---|---|
| Financial | Economic Value Added | 4% | | | | | | |
| | ROI | 12% | | | | | | |
| | RONA | 18% | | | | | | |
| | $ Backlog | $100,000 | | | | | | |
| | Throughput | $4,010,000 | | | | | | |
| | Cash Flow | $800,000 | | | | | | |
| Commercial | Profit / Loss | $2,060,000 | | | | | | |
| | Revenue | $5,000,000 | | | | | | |
| | Net Promoter Score | 78% | | | | | | |
| | Market Share | 22% | | | | | | |
| Processes | Conversion Costs | $1,250,000 | | | | | | |
| | Direct Cost | $990,000 | | | | | | |
| | Inventory Value | $650,000 | | | | | | |
| | Total Investment | $27,364,000 | | | | | | |
| People | Internal NPS | 90% | | | | | | |
| | Employee engagement | 90% | | | | | | |
| | Turnover | 1% | | | | | | |
| | Talent Development | 85% | | | | | | |

## 3. Development of strategies

Strategies represent actions that must be completed to achieve medium and long-term company objectives. The strategy defines a conceptual structure or frame of reference to guide these actions.

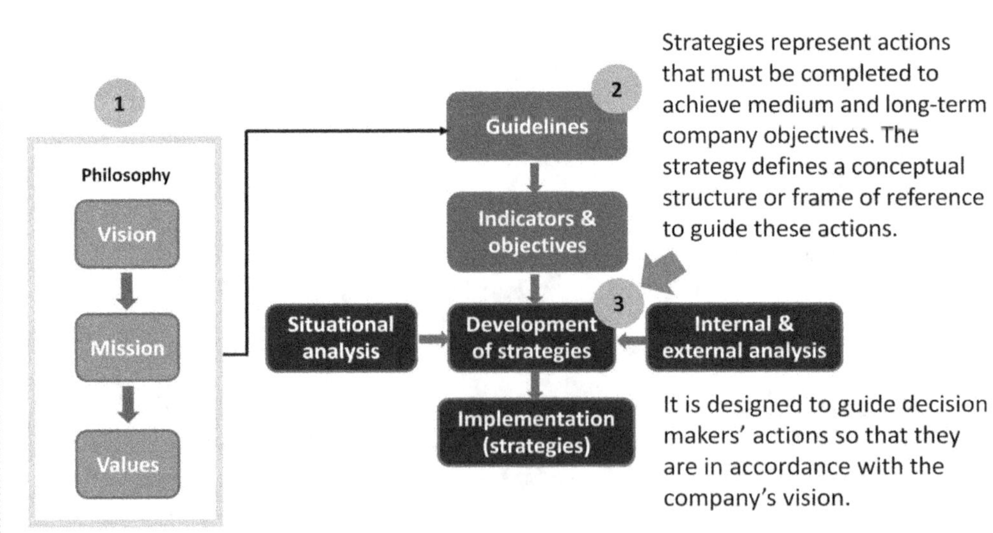


It is designed to guide decision makers' actions so that they are in accordance with the company's vision.

# Example

| GUIDELINES | | MANAGEMENT PLANNING | | |
|---|---|---|---|---|
| **Objectives** | **Indicators** | **Strategies** | **Indicators** | **Person Responsible** |
| 1. Increase profitability | Increase ROI from 7% to 12% | 1.1 Increase profit / sales to 18% <br> 1.2 Increase sales to 24% | Profits / sales <br> Sales / investments | VT, MK, DG <br> VT, MK, DG <br> VT, MK, IN |
| 2. Increase sales | Increase domestic sales by 15% and international sales by 32% | 2.1 Sell services that add value to our customers <br> 2.2 Increase sales with current customers <br> 2.3 Launch products in record time <br> 2.4 Enter new niche markets | Sales in $ <br> NPS <br> Days to launch <br> Targeted segments | VT, MK, DG <br> VT, MK, DG <br> VT, MK, IN |
| 3. Become a world-class company (reduce expenses) | Increase profitability of the operation from 25% to 45%, reducing defects and improving customer satisfaction | 3.1 Implement Lean Company | Facility sigma level <br> Level of customer satisfaction <br> OEE <br> Delivery days <br> Inventory turns <br> Operation expenses <br> % scrap | IN, CA, DG, RH <br> IN, CA, DG, RH <br> IN, CA, DG, RH <br> IN, CA, DG, RH <br> IN, CA, DG, RH <br> IN, CA, DG, RH <br> IN, CA, DG, RH |
| | | 3.2 Maintain ISO 9000:2000 certification | Number of nonconformities | CA <br> All |
| | | 3.3 Implement lean logistics | On-time deliveries (punctuality) | CA, SE, DG <br> All <br> IN, CAL |
| 4. Make HR a competitive advantage | Certify 100% of the staff in multi-skills | 4.1 Establish talent development program | % progress of the program <br> % of certified personnel | HR |

**3**

**Strategies**

**"HOW'S"**

# SWOT Matrix

| Method: <br> SWOT Matrix | Strengths <br> 1. <br> 2. <br> 3. | Weaknesses <br> 1. <br> 2. <br> 3. |
|---|---|---|
| Opportunities <br> 1. <br> 2. <br> 3. | Use the strengths to take advantage of the opportunities | Overcome weaknesses while taking advantage of opportunities |
| Threats <br> 1. <br> 2. <br> 3. | Use the strengths to avoid threats | Minimize weaknesses and avoid threats |

## 4. Indicators

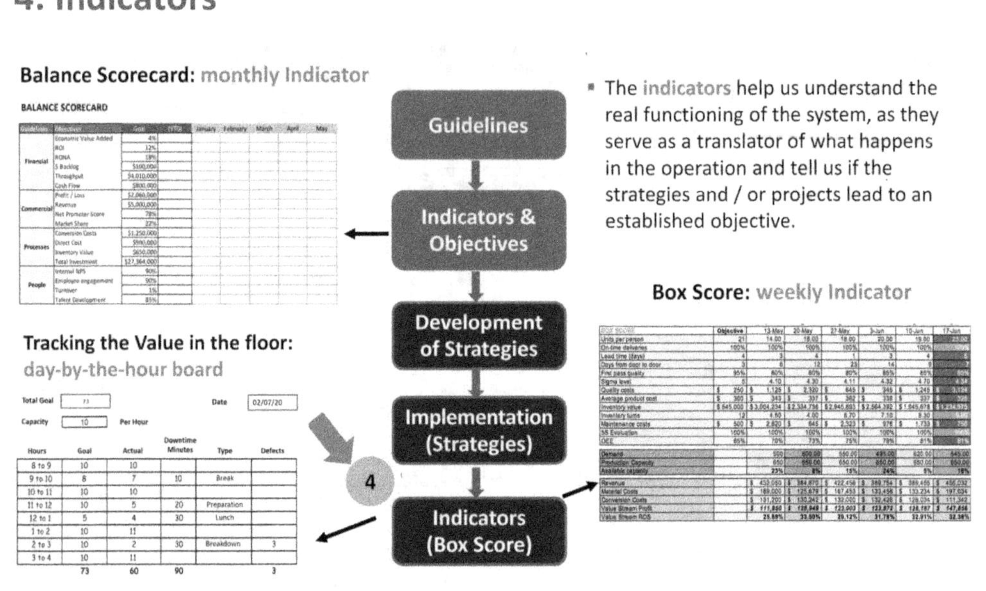


* The indicators help us understand the real functioning of the system, as they serve as a translator of what happens in the operation and tell us if the strategies and / or projects lead to an established objective.

# Integration of indicators

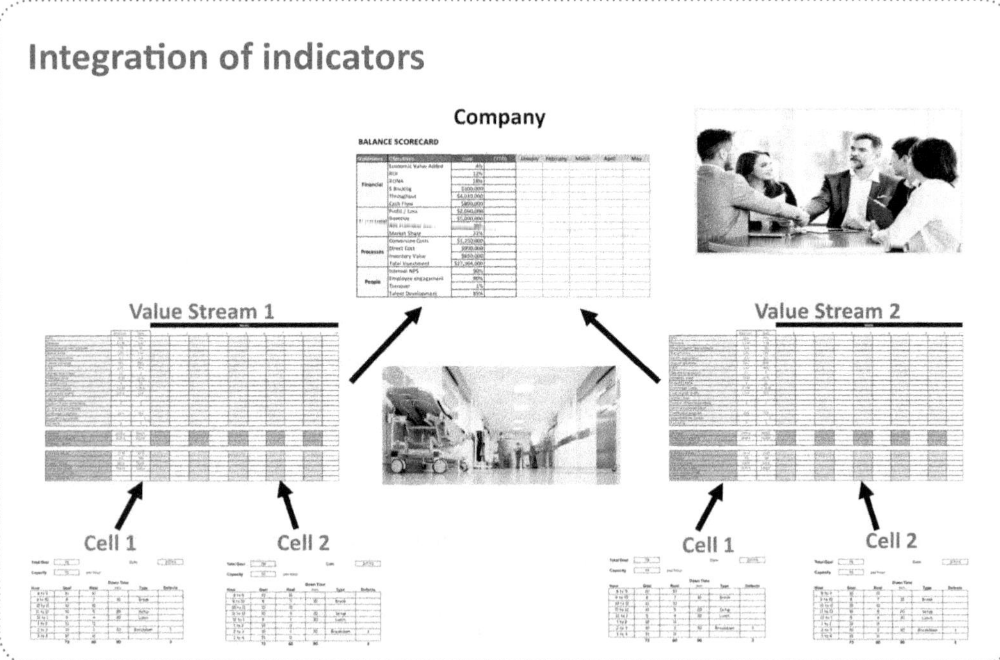

# Box Score - weekly indicators

| BOX SCORE | Objective | 1 13-May | 2 20-May | 3 27-May | 4 3-Jun | 5 10-Jun | 6 17-Jun |
|---|---|---|---|---|---|---|---|
| Units per person | 21 | 14.00 | 16.00 | 18.00 | 20.00 | 19.00 | 23.00 |
| On-time deliveries | 100% | 100% | 100% | 100% | 100% | 100% | 100% |
| Lead time (days) | 4 | 3 | 4 | 1 | 3 | 4 | 5 |
| Days from door to door | 3 | 6 | 12 | 23 | 14 | 9 | 7 |
| First pass quality | 95% | 80% | 80% | 80% | 85% | 85% | 85% |
| Sigma level | 5 | 4.10 | 4.30 | 4.11 | 4.32 | 4.70 | 4.34 |
| Quality costs | $ 250 | $ 1,125 | $ 2,320 | $ 645 | $ 345 | $ 1,245 | $ 3,124 |
| Average product cost | $ 300 | $ 343 | $ 337 | $ 362 | $ 338 | $ 337 | $ 325 |
| Inventory value | $ 545,000 | $ 3,004,234 | $ 2,334,756 | $ 2,945,893 | $ 2,564,392 | $ 1,945,678 | $ 1,234,975 |
| Inventory turns | 12 | 4.50 | 4.00 | 6.70 | 7.10 | 8.30 | 9.00 |
| Maintenance costs | $ 500 | $ 2,820 | $ 645 | $ 2,323 | $ 976 | $ 1,733 | $ 756 |
| 5S Evaluation | 100% | 100% | 100% | 100% | 100% | 100% | 100% |
| OEE | 85% | 70% | 73% | 75% | 79% | 81% | 81% |
| Demand | | 500 | 600.00 | 550.00 | 495.00 | 620.00 | 545.00 |
| Production Capacity | | 650 | 650.00 | 650.00 | 650.00 | 650.00 | 650.00 |
| Available capacity | | 23% | 8% | 15% | 24% | 5% | 16% |
| Revenue | | $ 432,050 | $ 384,870 | $ 422,456 | $ 389,754 | $ 389,455 | $ 456,032 |
| Material Costs | | $ 189,000 | $ 125,679 | $ 167,453 | $ 133,456 | $ 133,234 | $ 197,034 |
| Conversion Costs | | $ 131,200 | $ 130,242 | $ 132,000 | $ 132,426 | $ 128,034 | $ 111,342 |
| Value Stream Profit | | $ 111,850 | $ 128,949 | $ 123,003 | $ 123,872 | $ 128,187 | $ 147,656 |
| Value Stream ROS | | 25.89% | 33.50% | 29.12% | 31.78% | 32.91% | 32.38% |

**Color codes**

Prompt attention

Good

Alert

- The results of quality, delivery and costs are analyzed weekly to ensure that they are studied and  decisions can be made weekly.
- Now there are 52 opportunities to make good decisions, contrary to only 12 when it is done monthly.

# 5. Development of tactics

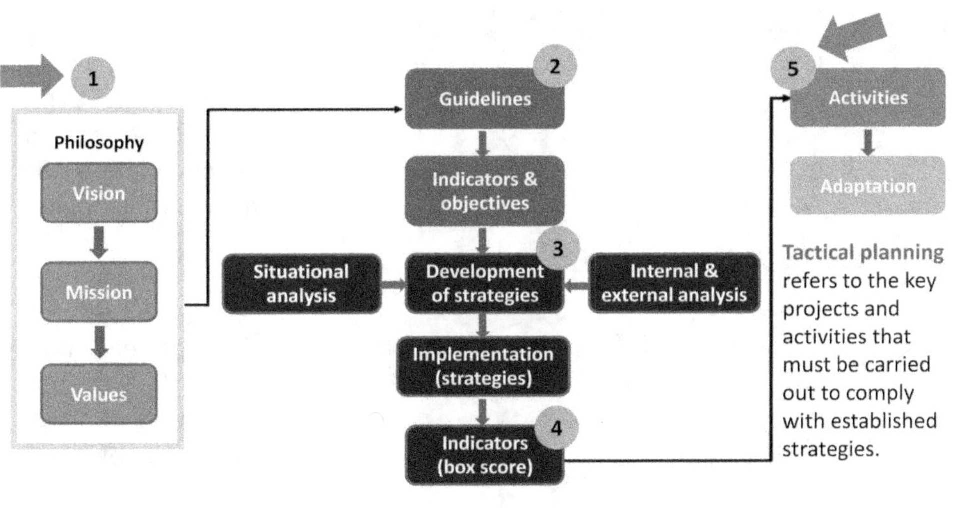


Tactical planning refers to the key projects and activities that must be carried out to comply with established strategies.

## Development of tactics

| GUIDELINES | | MANAGEMENT PLANNING | | | PROJECTS | | |
|---|---|---|---|---|---|---|---|
| **Objectives** | **Indicators** | **Strategies** | **Indicators** | **Person Responsible** | **Key activities/Improvement projects** | **Progress** | **Leader** |
| 1. Increase profitability | Increase ROE from 7% to 12% | 1.1 Increase profit / sales to 18%<br>1.2 Increase sales to 24% | Profits / sales<br>Sales / investments | VT, MK, DG<br>VT, MK, DG<br>VT, MK, IN | 1.1 Reduce inventories<br>1.2 Improve the use of our investments<br>1.3 Reduce costs without sacrificing quality<br>1.4 Achieve an agile costing to detect variations | | |
| 2. Increase sales | Increase domestic sales by 15% and international sales by 32% | 2.1 Sell services that add value to our customers<br>2.2 Increase sales with current customers<br>2.3 Launch products in record time<br>2.4 Enter new niche markets | Sales in $<br>NPS<br>Days to launch<br>Targeted segments | VT, MK, DG<br>VT, MK, DG<br>VT, MK, IN | 2.1 Design customer service packages<br>2.2 Analyze purchase frequency and identify trends<br>2.3 Implement SCRUM for product development<br>2.4 Introduce concurrent engineering and DFSS | | |
| 3. Become a world-class company (reduce expenses) | Increase profitability of the operation from 25% to 45%, reducing defects and improving customer satisfaction | 3.1 Implement Lean Company | Facility sigma level<br>Level of customer satisfaction<br>OEE<br>Delivery days<br>Inventory turns<br>Operation expenses<br>% scrap | IN, CA, DG, RH<br>IN, CA, DG, RH<br>IN, CA, DG, RH<br>IN, CA, DG, RH<br>IN, CA, DG, RH<br>IN, CA, DG, RH<br>IN, CA, DG, RH | 3.1.1 Train personnel on Six Sigma<br>3.1.2 YB, GB, BB certification<br>3.1.3 Executive training<br>3.1.4 Pilot implementation in area A<br>3.1.5 Certify personnel as multiskilled operators<br>3.1.6 Implement 5S in facility 1<br>3.1.7 Implement TPM in the pilot area<br>3.1.8 Implement continuous flow in the pilot<br>3.1.9 Implement SMED in the pilot area | | |
| | | 3.2 Maintain ISO 9000:2000 certification | Number of nonconformities | CA<br>All | 3.2.1 Conduct internal audits<br>3.2.2 Perform all corrective actions | | |
| | | 3.3 Implement lean logistics | On-time deliveries (punctuality) | CA, SE, DG<br>All<br>IN, CAL | 3.3.1 Implement kanban<br>3.3.2 Implement heijunka<br>3.3.3 Implement software | | |
| 4. Make HR a competitive advantage | Certify 100% of the staff in multi-skills | 4.1 Establish talent development program | % progress of the program<br>% of certified personnel | HR | 4.1.1 Conduct a diagnosis of the organizational climate<br>4.1.2 Train Coaches<br>4.1.3 Develop training materials<br>4.1.4 Perform pilot implementation | | |

**Tactics: Projects** (5)

## Development of tactics

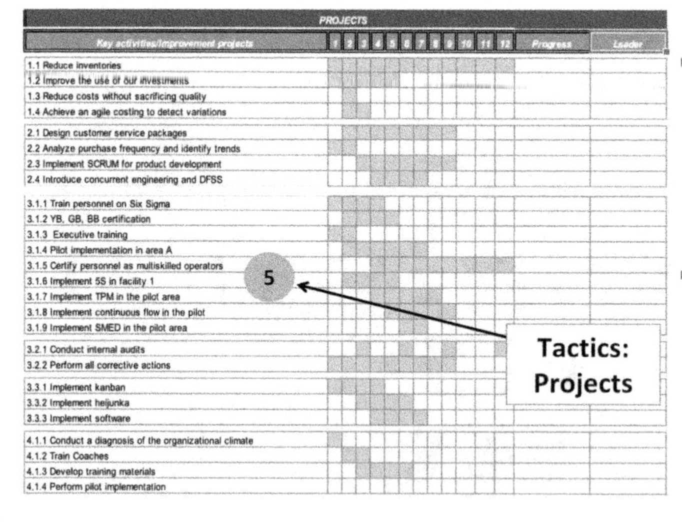



- Once the tactical planning has been defined, work on the development of the projects can begin.

- To ensure that the strategy is executed, these projects must be successfully carried out through an agile management system called **SCRUM**.

# Value Stream Structure

**Teamwork is possible if the structure is right**

## Objectives

1. Understand *how companies of the future* will be designed by *value streams.*
2. Show how *self-managed* teams can perform.
3. Understand the basic concepts of *Lean Accounting* in value streams.

## Content

I. Introduction
II. Background
III. What is value stream structure?
IV. Why implement value streams?
V. Who participates?
VI. Procedure

## I. Introduction

A company that has decided to be agile in response to the client's needs, and is sufficiently productive to stay in the market, should consider:

- Direct and effective communication.

- A flat and agile organization.

- Teamwork

## A good strategic plan is not enough

## II. Background

Companies are traditionally organized by departments and use structures similar to family trees.
Currently many companies are still organized in this way.

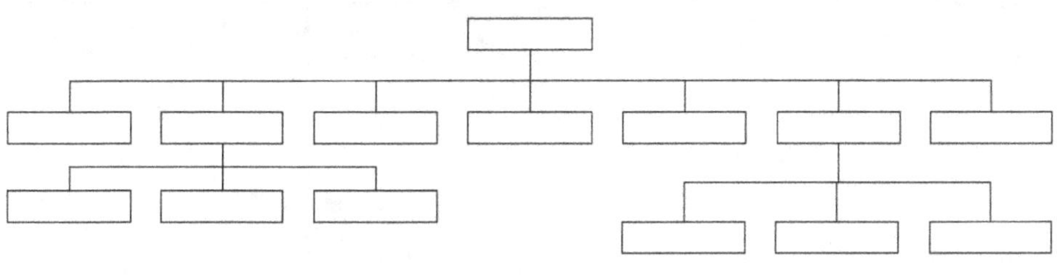

# Example of traditional structure

| Planning | Sales | Safety | Legal | Design | Costs |

| Engineering | Manufacturing | Packaging | Marketing | Service | Client need |

## Organizational structure types

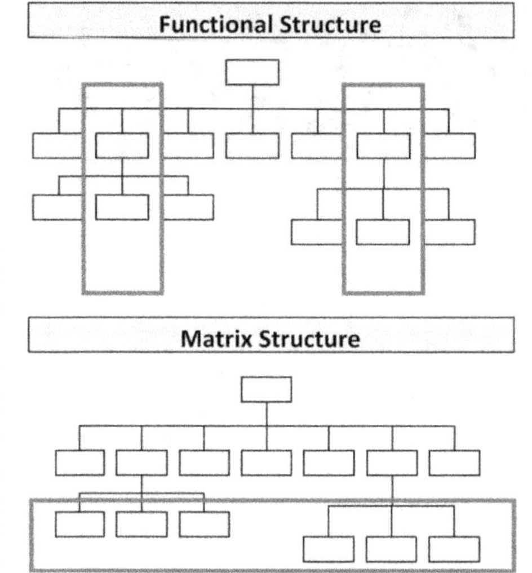


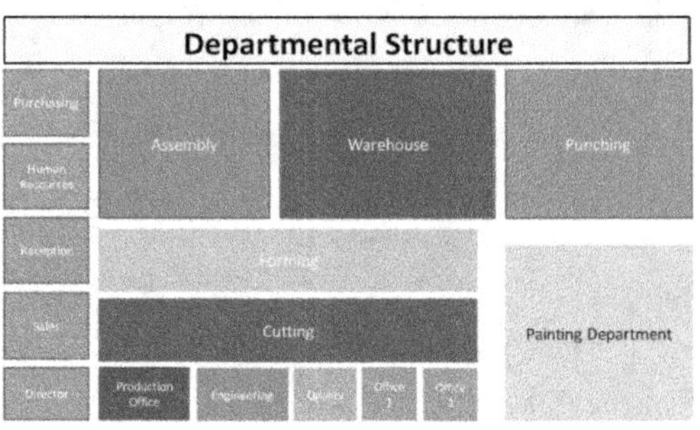


## Conclusions

- Managers delegated poorly or tried to solve problems at all levels.
- Lower-level staff simply received orders and didn't always understand why they were doing certain activities.
- It was rare that everyone involved in the processes could answer the following questions:
    - At what speed the customer is willing to buy? (Takt-time)
    - What is the companies' capacity?
    - Where is the main constraint?
    - Are we delivering our products or services on time?
    - Do you really know what the customer thinks about your products?
    - Are you reaching the costs goals and are you making money?
    - Does everybody knows the same?

## III. What is value stream structure?

- They are business units composed of all those directly responsible for the activities of a family of products or services.

- Decisions are made and results delivered from start to finish.

- They are developing cross functional teams taking responsibility for the entire process, analyzing information and making decisions.

- Each value stream will be analyzed through a map (VSM), where you will see the process flow of information, activities and materials.

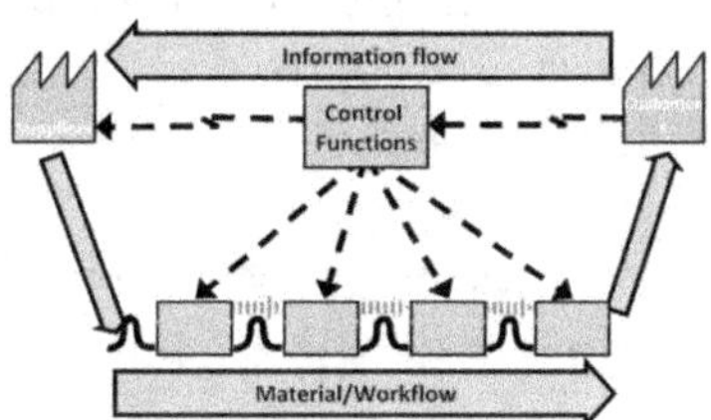


*"The way companies of the future are being designed"*

## Value stream structure

Management Team

Value Stream 1

Value Stream 2

Value Stream 3

| Business Development | Product Development | Human Resources | Admin. & Finance | Information Technology | Quality Control | Maintenance |

**Each Value Stream represents a product or service family**

### IV. Why implement value streams?

- To eliminate all the bureaucracy that prevents to develop successful businesses.

- It gives management time to plan, analyze the future of the business, and devote more energy to future development.

- It allows strategies such as Lean Six Sigma to be successful.

### V. Who participates?

**Level 3: Owners and Directors**

**Level 2: Value Stream Teams and Support**

**Level 1: Production or Service Teams**



**LSSI**
LEAN SIX SIGMA INSTITUTE

### VI. Procedure

1. Define **level 1** staff and train them on their roles (standardized work).
2. Define **level 2** staff and train them on their roles (leader standard work).
3. Design the value office and boards for the reviews of each level (andon, leader standard work, etc.)
4. Analyze the performance of the value stream:
   - Update the box score and floor boards
   - Value stream cost analysis
5. Design how the **level 3** (management team) will work, if the pilot was successful in the deployment phase.

## 1. Define level 1 staff and train them on their roles

Leaders, Operators, Material Handlers, and Technicians

### Responsibilities

- Conduct meetings at the beginning and end of a shift

- Daily planning and hourly analysis of progress

- Team-based decision making

- Analyze their own results

- Solve problems

## Update the day-by-the hour board

**Goal** 73 units                                      **Date:** 02/07/19
**Capacity** 10 units per hour

| Hours | Goal | Actual | Acumulated | Downtime (minutes) | Type | Defects |
|---|---|---|---|---|---|---|
| 8 to 9 | 10 | 10 | 10 | | | |
| 9 to 10 | 8 | 7 | 17 | 10 | Break | |
| 10 to 11 | 10 | 10 | 27 | | | |
| 11 to 12 | 10 | 5 | 32 | 20 | Setups | |
| 12 to 1 | 5 | 4 | 36 | 30 | Lunch | |
| 1 to 2 | 10 | 11 | 47 | | | |
| 2 to 3 | 10 | 2 | 49 | 30 | Breakdown | 3 |
| 3 to 4 | 10 | 11 | 60 | | | |
| Total | 73 | 60 | | 90 | | 3 |

## 2. Define level 2 staff and train them on their roles

Value stream manager, financial analyst, customer service representative, sales associate, scheduler, manufacturing engineer, quality analyst, etc.

### Responsibilities

- Work in the "value office"
- Weekly planning and review of box score
- Daily analysis of obligations, profitability, potential problems  and requirements
- Daily analysis of results
- Take action
- Solve level 2 problems
- Support level 1



**LSSI**
LEAN SIX SIGMA INSTITUTE

Support areas: HR, maintenance, IT, etc.

## Responsibilities:

- They work in their processes as internal service providers
- Weekly planning
- Daily analysis of box score results, responsibilities, profitability, and potential problems
- Take action
- Solve level 2 problems

# Value stream board

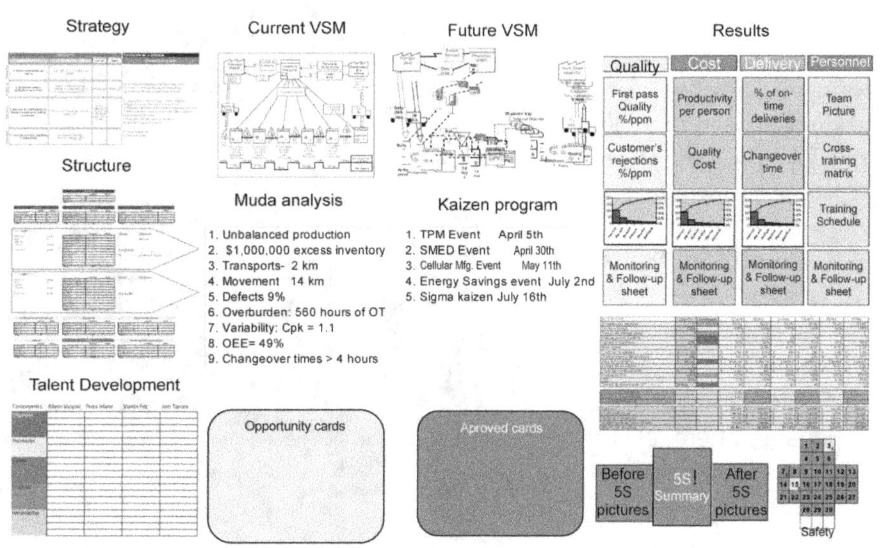

## 3. Value office design

You must select an area in which the value stream team members will work.

**The room must have:**

- Visibility to areas that generate value
- A strategic location
- Proper lighting
- Work stations for each member
- A meeting table at the center of the room
- A projector and screen
- Writing board

## Value office / Control tower

People responsible for the value stream work full-time in the value office. They have scheduled meetings to review and analyze results, and make decisions.

- Value stream Manager
- Sales
- Planner/Buyer
- Finance
- Process Engineer
- Quality Engineer
- Equipment Engineer



**LSSI**
LEAN SIX SIGMA INSTITUTE

# 4. Analyze the performance of the value stream

## A. Update the box score

| BOX SCORE | Objective | Progress | 7-Jan | 14-Jan | 21-Jan | 28-Jan | 4-Feb | 11-Feb |
|---|---|---|---|---|---|---|---|---|
| Units/person | 21 | | 14 | 16 | 18 | 20 | 19 | 23 |
| On-time deliveries | 100% | | 100% | 100% | 100% | 100% | 100% | 100% |
| Lead time (days) | 4 | | 3 | 4 | 1 | 3 | 4 | 5 |
| Days from door-to-door | 3 | | 6 | 12 | 23 | 14 | 9 | 7 |
| First pass yield | 95% | | 80% | 80% | 80% | 85% | 85% | 85% |
| Sigma level | 5 | | 4.10 | 4.30 | 4.11 | 4.32 | 4.70 | 4.34 |
| No quality cost | $ 250 | | $ 2,345.00 | $ 3,112.00 | $ 645.00 | $ 345.00 | $ 1,245.00 | $ 3,124.00 |
| Average product cost | $ 300 | | $ 343.00 | $ 337.00 | $ 362.00 | $ 338.00 | $ 337.00 | $ 325.00 |
| Inventory value | $ 545,000 | | $ 3,004.23 | $ 2,334.76 | $ 2,945.89 | $ 2,564.39 | $ 1,945.68 | $ 1,234.98 |
| Inventory turns | 12 | | 4.5 | 4 | 6.7 | 7.1 | 8.3 | 9 |
| Maintenance cost | $ 500 | | $ 2,820.00 | $ 645.00 | $ 2,323.00 | $ 976.00 | $ 1,733.00 | $ 756.00 |
| 5S evaluation | 100% | | 100% | 100% | 100% | 100% | 100% | 100% |
| OEE | 85% | | 70% | 73% | 75% | 79% | 81% | 81% |
| Launch time (days) | 25 | | 42 | 42 | 42 | 42 | 37 | 37 |
| Demand | | | 100 | | | | | |
| Production capacity | | | 200 | | | | | |
| Available capacity | | | 50% | | | | | |
| Revenue | | | $ 432,050 | $ 384,870 | $ 422,456 | $ 389,754 | $ 389,455 | $ 456,032 |
| Material cost | | | $ 189,000 | $ 125,679 | $ 167,453 | $ 133,456 | $ 133,234 | $ 197,034 |
| Conversion cost | | | $ 131,200 | $ 130,242 | $ 132,000 | $ 132,426 | $ 128,034 | $ 111,342 |
| Value Stream Net Profit | | | $ 111,850 | $ 128,949 | $ 123,003 | $ 123,872 | $ 128,187 | $ 147,650 |
| Return | | | 25.89% | 33.50% | 29.12% | 31.78% | 32.91% | 32.38% |

- Every week the box score is updated to identify opportunities and to know if the established goals have been reached.

- The box score meeting is held every week with all members of the value stream.

## B. Value stream cost analysis

**Traditional cost method**

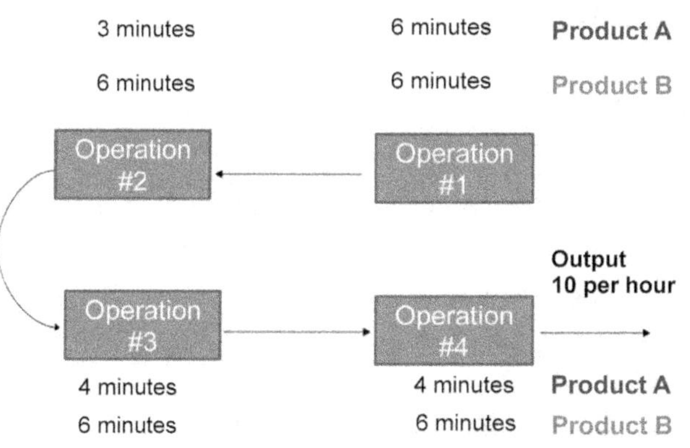


**Product / Service A**

**Labor = 17 minutes**
**Labor rate: $24.23**
**Overhead rate: 600%**

Labor = $6.87
Overhead = $41.19
Material = $42
**Total Cost = $90.06**

**Product / Service B**

**Labor = 24 minutes**
**Labor rate: $24.23**
**Overhead rate: 600%**
Labor = $9.69
Overhead = $58.15
Material = $42
**Total Cost = $109.84**

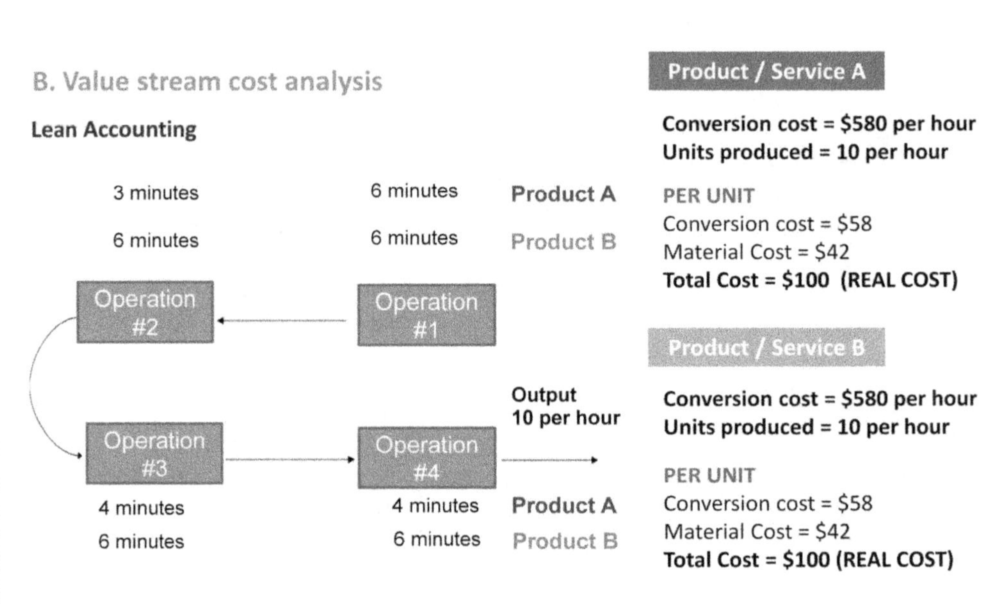


# Benefits

- Eliminate waste from administrative and accounting processes
- Internal understanding of the real costs of a company's products and/or services
- Better marketing and sales strategies
- Members of the value stream share a common objective
- Guides decision-making in relation to the value created for customers and the business
- Financial statements delivered every week
- Eliminate bureaucracy that prevents better communication and therefore better results
- Calculate and evaluate the benefits of a Lean implementation

## 5. Design how level 3 (management team) will work, if the pilot was successful in the deployment phase

Managers, directors, and chief executives

**<u>Responsibilities:</u>**

- Strategic planning and monitoring
- Monthly review of results and annual strategic planning
- If necessary, weekly meetings for decision making
- Look for new business opportunities
- Solve level 3 problems
- Support level 2
- Conduct "Gemba Walks" frequently

## Balance Scorecard

| Guidelines | Objectives | Goal | (YTD) | January | February | March | April | May |
|---|---|---|---|---|---|---|---|---|
| Financial | Economic Value Added | 4% | | | | | | |
| | ROI | 12% | | | | | | |
| | RONA | 18% | | | | | | |
| | $ Backlog | $100,000 | | | | | | |
| | Throughput | $4,010,000 | | | | | | |
| | Cash Flow | $800,000 | | | | | | |
| Commercial | Profit / Loss | $2,060,000 | | | | | | |
| | Revenue | $5,000,000 | | | | | | |
| | Net Promoter Score | 78% | | | | | | |
| | Market Share | 22% | | | | | | |
| Processes | Conversion Costs | $1,250,000 | | | | | | |
| | Direct Cost | $990,000 | | | | | | |
| | Inventory Value | $650,000 | | | | | | |
| | Total Investment | $27,364,000 | | | | | | |
| People | Internal NPS | 90% | | | | | | |
| | Employee engagement | 90% | | | | | | |
| | Turnover | 1% | | | | | | |
| | Talent Development | 85% | | | | | | |

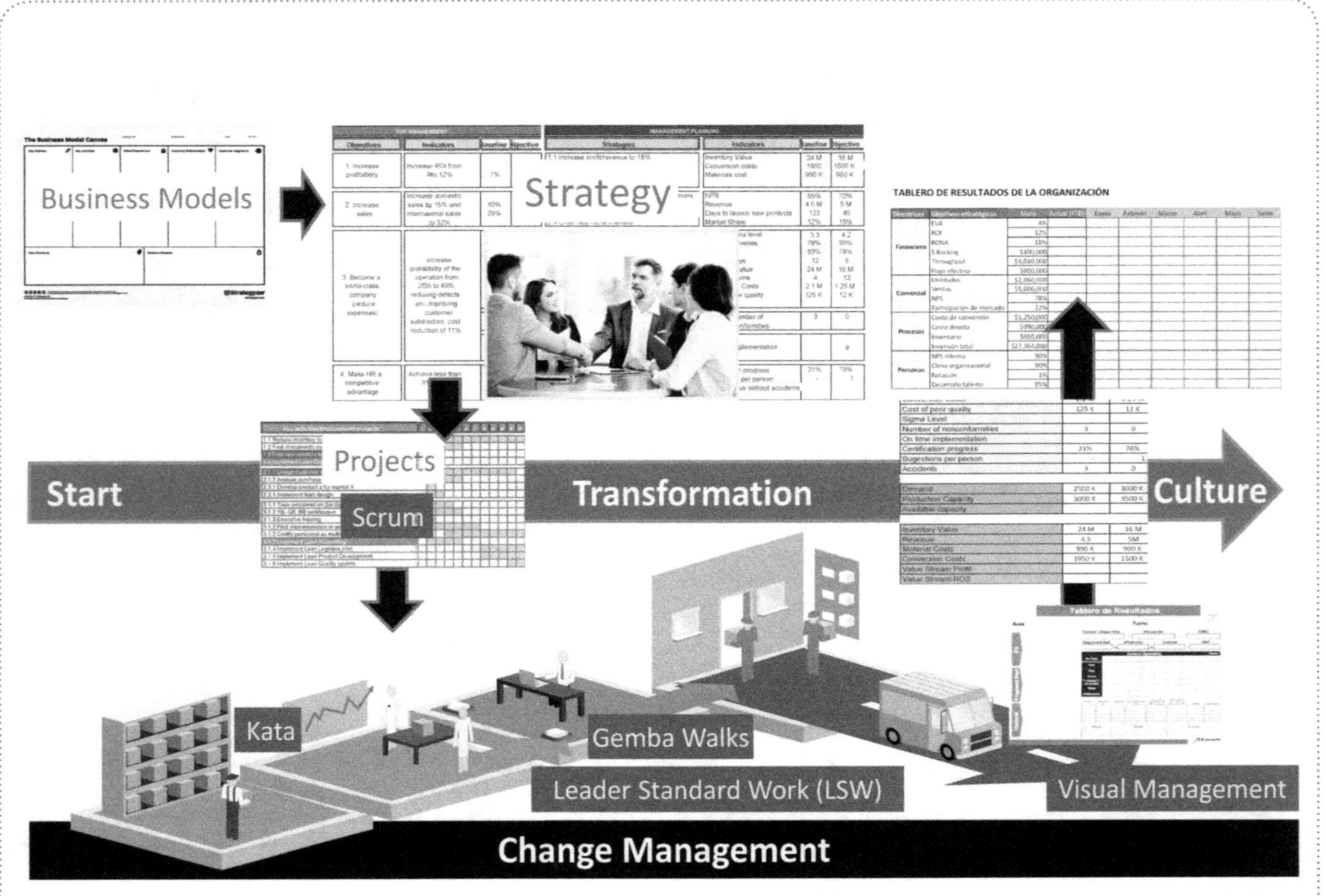

Business Models
Strategy
TABLERO DE RESULTADOS DE LA ORGANIZACIÓN
Start
Projects
Scrum
Transformation
Culture
Kata
Gemba Walks
Leader Standard Work (LSW)
Visual Management
Change Management
Tablero de Resultados
Cost of poor quality
Sigma Level
Number of nonconformities
On time implementation
Certification progress
Suggestions per person
Accidents
Demand
Production Capacity
Available capacity
Inventory Value
Revenue
Material Costs
Conversion Costs
Value Stream Profit
Value Stream ROS

# Talent Development

**The art of developing learning organizations**

## Objectives

1. Understand the *importance* of talent development in an organization.
2. Understand the *process to implement* talent development as a competitive advantage.
3. Apply a creative and effective *method* to *transfer knowledge.*

## Content

## I. Introduction

- Many quality, communication, and productivity issues are not due to a lack of technology or special resources.

- What is really needed is sufficient time dedicated to teaching, learning and practicing.

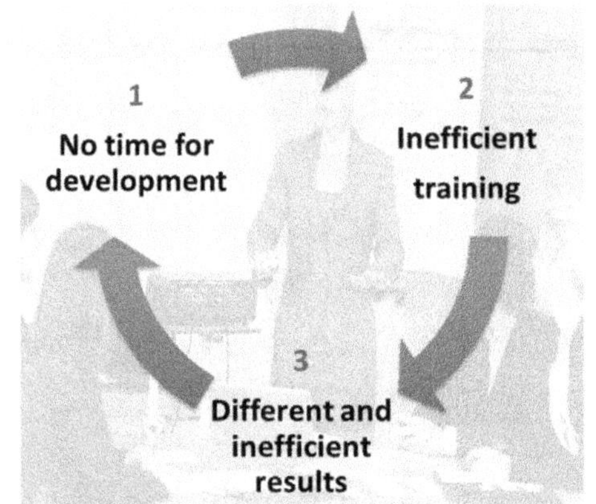


## People are the most important resource

- Only people can think about how to solve problems

- Only people can understand the customers

- Only people can provide support to the processes

*Knowledge creates understanding, but only practice creates confidence.*

- When the United States entered WWII, they began to deploy young working men to the war. However, the country still had to produce day-to-day products required by the country and its people.

- The new labor force was made up of older men and women, who were not necessarily prepared to take over those jobs.

The US government decided to develop the Training Within Industry (TWI) service to train the employees who would be replacing the workers going to war.

The program would prepare trainers in any industry who are capable of teaching employees key skills, in order to help these employees perform their jobs effectively (i.e., leadership  skills, teaching skills, improvement skills, etc.)

The program was aimed for: managers, supervisors and team leaders.

The training program included 3 courses:

- Job Instruction (JI)
- Job Methods (JM)
- Job Relations (JR)

The TWI program helped the United States win the war.

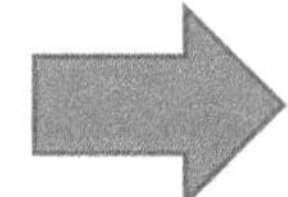

## TWI: A forgotten program

## Toyota brings it back

- At the end of World War II, the United States stopped the TWI program.

- The teaching system is not encouraged or promoted among U.S companies.

- Toyota reinvented the TWI program.

- Toyota produces cars and also talented people.

- Processes are designed to be analyzed and taught by leaders, who will then challenge the system continuously.

## III. What is Talent Development?

- Talent development is a methodology used to develop a learning culture by **attracting, training, and retaining employees**.

- It includes accompanying each person on their journey to help them reach their full potential.

## IV. Key elements

### TWI Components

| Charles Allen 4-step Learning Process | TWI | | | PDCA Cycle | Scientific Method |
| | Job Instructions | Job Methods | Job Relations | | |
| --- | --- | --- | --- | --- | --- |
| Preparation | Prepare the Worker | Breakdown the job | Get the facts | **Plan** - Observe data and reality; decide on a problem; define it | Observation & Description |
| Presentation | Present the Operation | Question every detail | Weigh & decide | **Do** - Analyze the problem; propose a countermeasure | Formulation of an hypothesis |
| Application | Try Out Performance | Develop new method | Take action | **Check** - Try the countermeasure; check the results | Use the hypothesis to make predictions |
| Testing | Follow Up | Apply new method | Check results | **Act** - If successful, standardize the change; if not, start the cycle over | Test the predictions through experiments |

## V. When to implement it?

- As soon as an organization is established

- Any time where lack of knowledge is generating problems. Example: quality, speed, cost, sales, etc.

## VI. Procedure

1. Prepare the organization to develop exceptional people.

2. Identify critical knowledge.

3. Transfer the knowledge to others.

4. Verify the learning process and success of the program.

# 1. Prepare the organization

### Assess the Needs

- Develop the strategy (Hoshin Kanri) to focus on critical knowledge

- According with box score results, define where training is required

- Results determine the areas of focus for Talent Development

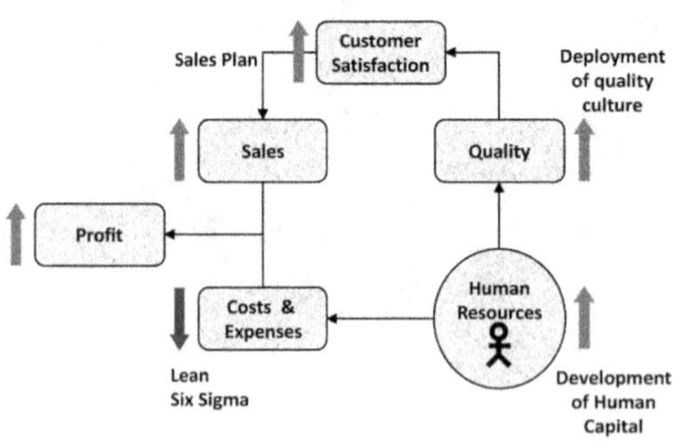


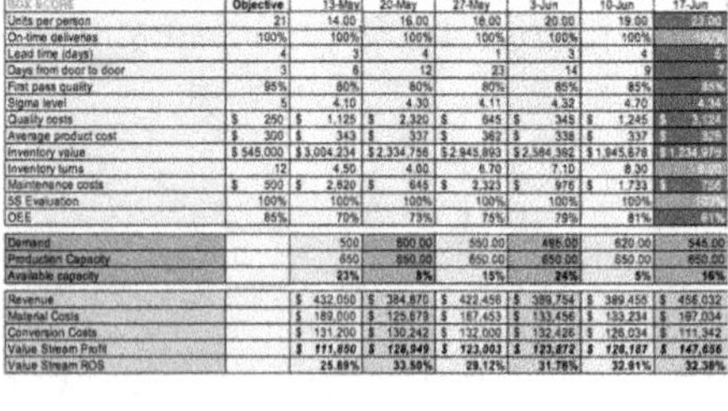

| BOX SCORE | Objective | 13-May | 20-May | 27-May | 3-Jun | 10-Jun | 17-Jun |
|---|---|---|---|---|---|---|---|
| Units per person | 21 | 14.00 | 16.00 | 16.00 | 20.00 | 19.00 | 23.00 |
| On-time deliveries | 100% | 100% | 100% | 100% | 100% | 100% | [illegible] |
| Lead time (days) | 4 | 3 | 4 | 1 | 3 | 4 | 5 |
| Days from door to door | 3 | 6 | 12 | 23 | 14 | 9 | 7 |
| First pass quality | 95% | 80% | 80% | 80% | 85% | 85% | 85% |
| Sigma level | 5 | 4.10 | 4.30 | 4.11 | 4.32 | 4.70 | 4.34 |
| Quality costs | $ 250 | $ 1,125 | $ 2,320 | $ 645 | $ 345 | $ 1,245 | $ 3,124 |
| Average product cost | $ 300 | $ 343 | $ 337 | $ 362 | $ 338 | $ 337 | $ 326 |
| Inventory value | $ 545,000 | $ 3,004,234 | $ 2,334,756 | $ 2,945,893 | $ 2,584,382 | $ 1,945,678 | $ 1,234,979 |
| Inventory turns | 12 | 4.50 | 4.00 | 6.70 | 7.10 | 8.30 | [illegible] |
| Maintenance costs | $ 500 | $ 2,820 | $ 645 | $ 2,323 | $ 975 | $ 1,733 | [illegible] |
| 5S Evaluation | 100% | 100% | 100% | 100% | 100% | 100% | [illegible] |
| OEE | 85% | 70% | 73% | 75% | 79% | 81% | 61% |
| Demand | | 500 | 800.00 | 550.00 | 495.00 | 620.00 | 545.00 |
| Production Capacity | | 650 | 650.00 | 650.00 | 650.00 | 650.00 | 650.00 |
| Available capacity | | 23% | 8% | 15% | 24% | 5% | 16% |
| Revenue | | $ 432,050 | $ 384,870 | $ 422,456 | $ 389,754 | $ 389,456 | $ 456,032 |
| Material Costs | | $ 189,000 | $ 125,679 | $ 187,453 | $ 133,456 | $ 133,234 | $ 197,034 |
| Conversion Costs | | $ 131,200 | $ 130,242 | $ 132,000 | $ 132,426 | $ 126,034 | $ 111,342 |
| Value Stream Profit | | $ 111,850 | $ 128,949 | $ 123,003 | $ 123,872 | $ 126,187 | $ 147,656 |
| Value Stream ROS | | 25.89% | 33.50% | 29.12% | 31.78% | 32.91% | 32.38% |

## 2. Identify critical knowledge

Break down the job into steps for teaching

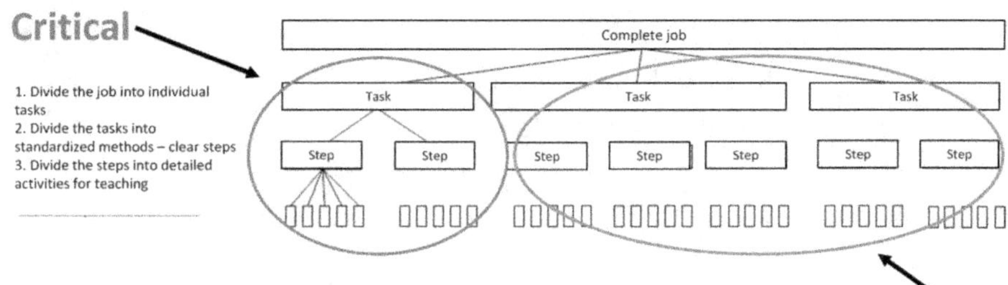


Job breakdown includes three main parts:

1. Identify key steps in the work task.
2. Identify important information within the steps (key points).
3. Why are the key points important?

## Identify critical knowledge

Critical knowledge must be documented in a work instruction format.

| WORK INSTRUCTION | | | | | | |
|---|---|---|---|---|---|---|
| Department: | | Area: | Operation: | Type of product: | Made by: | Pg. 1 of 1 |
| NO. | SEQUENCE OF OPERATIONS | | KEY POINTS | | ILLUSTRATIONS | |
| 1 | | | | | | |
| 2 | | | | | | |
| 3 | | | | | | |
| 4 | | | | | | |
| 5 | | | | | | |
| | CHANGES | | SAFETY CONSIDERATIONS | | SIGNATURES | |
| Date | Rev | Description of Change | Elim. | Approved | Date | Shift | Supervisor | Operator |

# 3. Transfer the knowledge

| Job Instruction | **Present the Operation** |
| --- | --- |
| Prepare the Worker | **Step 1:** Trainer performs the task (without speaking) |
| **Present the Operation** | **Step 2:** Trainer mentions the steps as he/she performs the task |
| Try Out Performance | **Step 3:** Trainer mentions the steps, as well as the key points, as he/she performs the task |
| Follow Up | **Step 4:** Trainer mentions the steps and key points and explains why the key points are important, as he/she performs the task |

# 4. Verify the learning process and success of the program

- Continuous monitoring and review of tasks

- Guide the student towards independence

- The team leader trains each member of the team

- Success is shown through results, not only actions

# Evaluate knowledge and performance

## Multi-skills Matrix

Each task has to be learned at the highest level of detail and must be evaluated according to the skills shown during practice.

| Name | Register | Get info. | Diagnose | Fix | Testing | Invoice | Check out | Total | Ranking |
|---|---|---|---|---|---|---|---|---|---|
| John Smith | 1 | 3 | 4 | 0 | 2 | 1 | 1 | 12 | C |
| Bob Hope | 5 | 5 | 5 | 5 | 5 | 5 | 5 | 35 | G |
| Robert Mills | 3 | 4 | 2 | 1 | 5 | 4 | 2 | 21 | E |
| Dave Jones | 1 | 0 | 4 | 4 | 2 | 2 | 1 | 14 | C |

| Description | Values |
|---|---|
| Beginner (No experience) | 1 |
| Learning (Has a notion about the process) | 2 |
| Good (works well, with good quality & speed) | 3 |
| Expert (mastered the operation) | 4 |
| Trainer (can train others) | 5 |

| Ranking | Point Range | Salary |
|---|---|---|
| A | 1 to 5 points | $ 750 |
| B | 6 to 10 points | $ 890 |
| C | 11 to 15 points | $ 990 |
| D | 16 ato20 points | $ 1,025 |
| E | 21 to 25 points | $ 1,290 |
| F | 26 to 30 points | $ 1,440 |
| G | 31 to 35 points | $ 2,000 |

## VII. Benefits

- A more stable workforce
- Reduces accidents
- Documented knowledge of critical processes
- People who are willing and motivated to learn
- People who are willing and motivated to teach
- Creates quality excellence
- Greater job satisfaction
- Minimal costs arising from poor quality
- High employee retention rates

**Companies that have implemented TWI have reported improvements of at least 25% in their productivity.**

# Define Team

**Nothing better than a crisis to get the best out of a Team**

## Objectives

1. Understand the *importance* of working as a team to implement Lean Six Sigma.
2. Get to know and re-examine the *roles* of team members.
3. Recognize the importance of *personal quality* in teamwork.

## Content

I.    Teamwork
II.   Roles and Responsibilities
III.  Personal Quality
IV.  Time Management

## Who will win the competition?

Team A

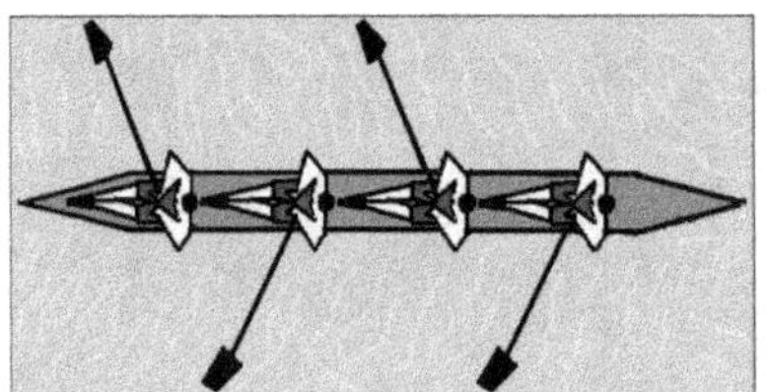

Team B

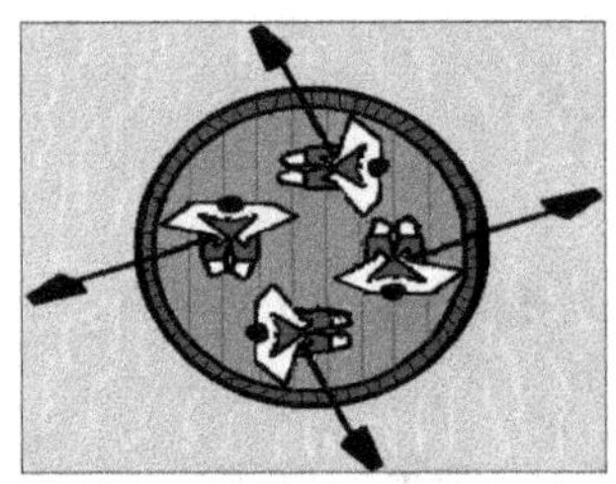

Is the problem the people or the system?

## Characteristics of Effective Teams

- **Common approach or method**
  - Each team member performs the same amount of real work.

- **Mutual responsibility**
  - Sincere promise to maintain trust and responsibility.

- **Conflicts**
  - They exist but they get resolved.

## Team Definition

A team is a group of people with complementary skills who are committed to a common purpose and who set performance goals and an approach that makes them interdependent.

Characteristics of Effective Teams

- Reasonable number of members (between 4 and 25).

- Right combination of skills:

  - Technical or functional experience.
  - Analytical and problem solving skills.
  - Interpersonal skills.

United Team

A winning team combines good teamwork
with individual skills.

Its power is based on the understanding
of these two factors.

## Requiring...

- Time.

- Active participation of all members.

- Communication skills: listen, present ideas clearly, resolve conflicts.

- Creative thinking and open-mindedness.

## Synergy

- It's a way of working where cooperation is encouraged between all those who make up a team.

- It's a work philosophy that upholds the priority of group interests.

- It's an all-inclusive pursuit of the whole via the best efforts of the individual parts.

- Teams often generate better results than any individual group member's.

"When a team matches or surpasses...

the best of its members."

$$1 + 1 = 3$$

All teams are groups, but,
not all groups are teams.

Teamwork consists of the coordinated work of
a group of people to reach a common goal.

## Groups vs. Teams

### DIFFERENCE BETWEEN

### Group

- Strong and clearly focused leader.
- Individual responsibility.
- The purpose of the group is the same as that established by the Mission.
- Individual results.
- Efficient meetings.
- It measures its effectiveness indirectly by its influence on others.
- Discuss, decide and delegate.

### Team

- Leadership is shared.
- Mutual responsibility.
- Specific purpose of the group.
- Collective work results.
- Discussions and active problem solving are encouraged.
- It measures performance when evaluating collective work results.
- Discuss, decide and do the work together.

## Stages of team development / Tuckman Model

| Forming | Storming | Norming | Performing |
|---|---|---|---|
| • Lack of integration or group maturity | • Team members start to voice their opinions | • Team members resolve their conflicts | • Synergy is created |
| • Effort to be pleasant among team members (complacent) | • The understanding of roles and responsibilities is questioned | • The team reaches an understanding through mutually accepted ideas | • Interdependence is evident and accepted |
| • Little progress in terms of work completed | • Conflict arises due to different ideas and conclusions | • Some work is completed (team progress) | • Team-based problem solving skills are developed |
| • Roles and responsibilities are clarified and understood | • Lack of agreement delays the team's work | • Team members start to work as a team | • Agreements are achieved |
| • "Honeymoon" phase | | • Trust is developed and more ideas are shared | • Significant and noticeable progress in terms of work completed |

Source: Adapted from Bruce W. Tuckman

# Team Rules

- ❖ _____ Open-mindedness to receive opinions and comments.
- ❖ _____ Build relationships of mutual support.
- ❖ _____ Positive attitude: Build instead of destroy. Help-vs-Block.
- ❖ _____ Get to the point, be specific.
- ❖ _____ Committed participation. Listen carefully, speak sincerely.
- ❖ _____ Informal atmosphere.
- ❖ _____ Creativity in solutions.
- ❖ _____ If I oppose, what do I propose?
- ❖ _____ Be flexible.
- ❖ _____ Confront, don't evade.
- ❖ _____ Do not "pass the buck."
- ❖ _____ Be sincere, honest and genuine.
- ❖ _____ See the what if instead of the why not.
- ❖ _____ Be willing to act differently from the past.
- ❖ _____ Confront the negative with a positive spirit.
- ❖ _____ Use our sense of humor positively.
- ❖ _____ Communicate and work as a team.
- ❖ _____ Follow up on commitments.

## II. Roles and Responsibilities

In Lean Six Sigma there are 2 types of teams:

- Service Teams.
- Project Teams.

- The service teams work continuously on their process and their function is to maintain the service within the established parameters of quality, promptness, cost, etc.

- Project teams work on specific activities and tasks for the duration of the project and their function is to improve or innovate the service.

- Normally people who have a specific function in the service participate in certain projects when they are invited.

## Roles and Responsibilities in Projects

| Member | Responsibility | Role |
|---|---|---|
| Champion | He is a manager who proposes and supports projects and has the responsibility of delivering results and ensuring that projects are carried out on time and within budget. | Define strategy, define projects, select teams, support project development. |
| Sponsor | He is the owner of the process to which the project applies, his responsibility is to provide resources to the project and remove obstacles. | Suggest members, free up member time, take action decisions, ensure compliance with dates. |
| Leader | He is generally a certified Black Belt, dedicated to improvement projects, knowledgeable of the Lean and Six Sigma methodology and tools. | Design the project, select members, conduct the methodology and meetings, guide the members. |
| Member | He has a specific job and is invited at certain times to participate in meetings or improvement events. It is desirable that they are certified as WB, YB, GB. | Propose ideas, perform certain tasks, attend project meetings. |

## Considerations

- Individual public recognition is important to increase respect among team members.

- Don't repress the discussions, let everyone state their opinions and solve the problem.

- Encourage "brainstorming" among team members to generate more innovative solutions to problems.

- Support and always be available to help team members when necessary.

- Develop team ideas through the contribution of ideas from team members.

- Set team goals as well as individual ones.

- Conduct team meetings properly in order to increase trust and respect among the members.

- Motivate and encourage all team members to take responsibility for the objectives and be perseverant in reaching the goals.

- Have team members share their individual goals in order to develop team goals.

- Motivate individuals to generate ideas and projects that are important for the team's goal.

## III. Personal Quality

- Teams are made up of people and that's why, to form a good team, we must first have quality people.

- Quality is not in the things that people do, but in the people who do things.

"Personal quality is the basis of all types of quality."

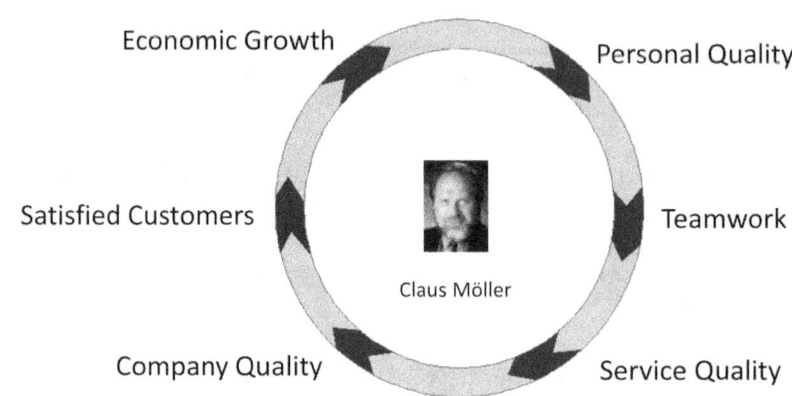


## Quality means being fully involved

Quality creates self-esteem.
Self-esteem is the basis of quality.

# Would you use a parachute folded by...

Would others use one folded by you?

# Personal Quality may determine a company's future

- Studies reveal that not all employees are motivated every day.

- Everyone is responsible for being motivated.

- It is important to realize that not only the organization benefits from the improvement in personal quality.

- Improving personal quality benefits the individual as well as his family and friends.

## Two Levels of Personal Quality

- **A Level** (Current Action Level):
  - This is the current satisfaction with the way we lead our own lives.

- **I Level** (Ideal Action Level):
  - These are the wishes, expectations and demands of a person with respect to their performance.

## What is your Development Potential range?

- It is the distance between what I am capable of doing and what I really do.

- The range of potential can vary from one situation to another.

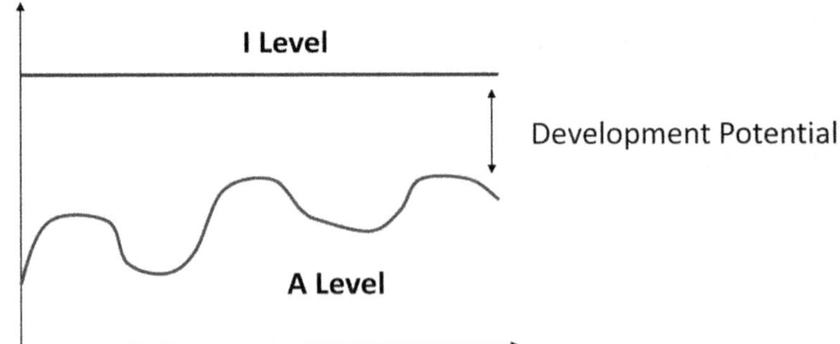

# A Level may change

- It is dynamic, it can change dramatically from one minute to the next.

- It is subject to influences that may increase or decrease A level:

  - Recognition / Rewards
  - Success / failure
  - Physical environment
  - Psychological environment
  - Experience and skills
  - Nature of the task
  - Time available
  - Others' A Level
  - Your I level

# I Level

- Ideal level of your own personal quality.

- It is closely linked to your personality.

- You will have reached your I Level when you feel that:

  - You can't do better.
  - You are proud of your performance.
  - You sign off your work with satisfaction.

## The Meaning of Ideal Level

- It is the way we would like our life to be: social, work, family, spiritual, physical.

- The ideal quality standard determines how one's own and others' quality is assessed.

- The ideal level may vary as the years go by.

- Examples:

  - Child: "I want to be a detective, travel the world and be a super-athlete"

  - Adult: «I want to study engineering, get married and have children»

## How to improve your Current Level

- Personal
  - Learn and apply new and interesting activities.
  - Get along with family and friends.
  - Eat well and get enough sleep.
  - Do sports 5 to 7 of the 168 hours in each week.
  - Do recreational activities.
  - Save and plan your family finances.
  - Do voluntary community service.

- Professional
  - Do what you really enjoy.
  - Always do your work right the first time.
  - Study to improve your ability.
  - Spend time teaching and helping others.

## The Power of Thoughts

- ❖ Cultivate a good **thought** and you will reap a good **deed**.

- ❖ Cultivate a good **deed** and you will reap a **habit**.

- ❖ Cultivate a **habit** and you will reap your **character**.

- ❖ Cultivate your **character** and you will reap your **destiny**.

- ❖ A wonderful destiny!

## IV. Time Management

- One of the most important causes of low team performance is a lack of time management skills

- Time is our **most valuable resource**

- By analyzing how we use our time, we will realize how we are wasting it and how we can find better ways to use it

## Parkinson's Law

- It was first articulated by Cyril Parkinson in 1957 as a result of his research in the British Civil Service.
- Examples:
    - Time: Work expands so as to fill the time available for its completion.
    - Income: Expenditures rise to meet income.
    - Space: Storage resources tend to increase (racks, drawers, etc.) to meet storage capacity.

For many people, the more time they have to complete a task, the more their minds will wander, which can create problems.

## Time management best practices

1. Plan your day
2. Use the Pomodoro Technique
3. Use your email effectively
4. Conduct effective meetings
5. Make effective phone calls
6. Take notes effectively using Bullet Journal

# 1. Plan your day

- Spend at least 15 minutes to plan your day.
- Schedule the activities in the medium to long-term.
- Plan daily life activities (exercise, food, transportation).
- Classify activities as A, B or C.

    - A: Important and urgent
    - B: Important and not urgent
    - C: Less important and not urgent

- When taking notes, define your tasks and schedule.
- Before you start your day,  picture what your day will look like.

## Daily planning example

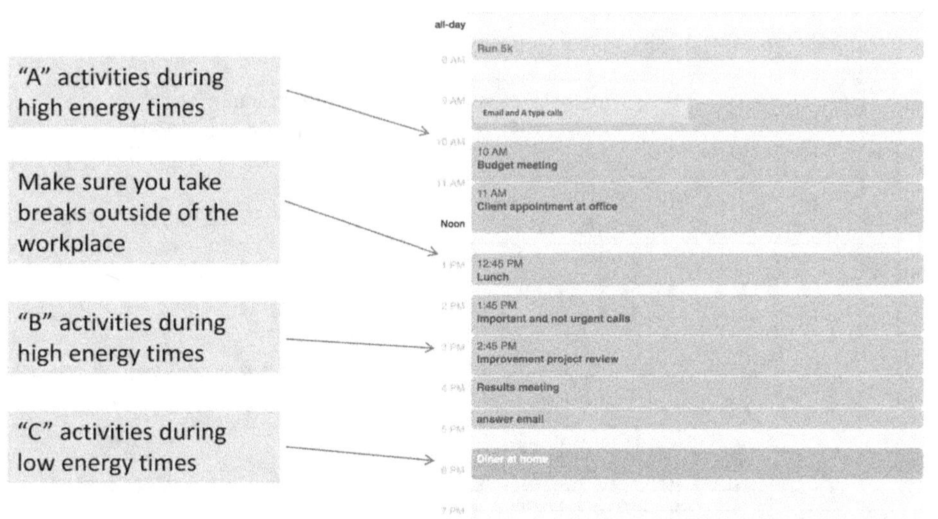


"A" activities during high energy times

Make sure you take breaks outside of the workplace

"B" activities during high energy times

"C" activities during low energy times

## 2. Use the Pomodoro technique

- The Pomodoro Technique is a time management method developed by Francesco Cirillo in the late 1980s.
- The technique uses a clock to divide the time spent on a job in 25 minute intervals called 'Pomodoro' that are separated by pauses.

> A key objective of the technique is to eliminate interruptions
> (internal and **external**) on focus and flow.
> When interrupted, the other activity must be recorded and postponed.

- Pick the task
- Set the Pomodoro (watch or clock) to 25 minutes
- Work on the task until the clock rings and record it with an X
- Take a short break (5 minutes)
- After 4 "Pomodoro", take a longer break (15-20 minutes)

## 3. Use your email effectively

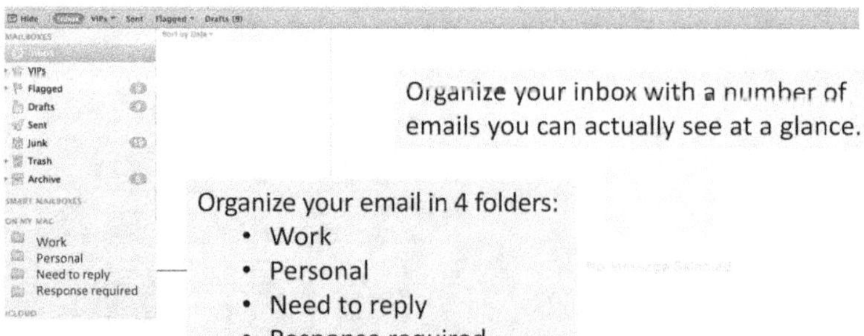

Organize your inbox with a number of emails you can actually see at a glance.

Organize your email in 4 folders:
- Work
- Personal
- Need to reply
- Response required

1. Answer only the emails you can complete in 2 minutes or less.
2. Eliminate the emails you don't need.
3. Archive the emails you need to keep.
4. Flag the emails you still need to reply to.

## 4. Conduct effective meetings

1. Plan the meeting
2. Send invitations
3. Confirm the logistics
4. Use an attendance sheet
5. Explain the objective of the meeting
6. Assign specific times during the meeting and follow them
7. Take notes
8. Write down the tasks to be completed and the person responsible
9. Summarize the meeting (confirm the objective)
10. Send a "meeting report" to all participants
11. Follow-up on the activities
12. Evaluate the meeting

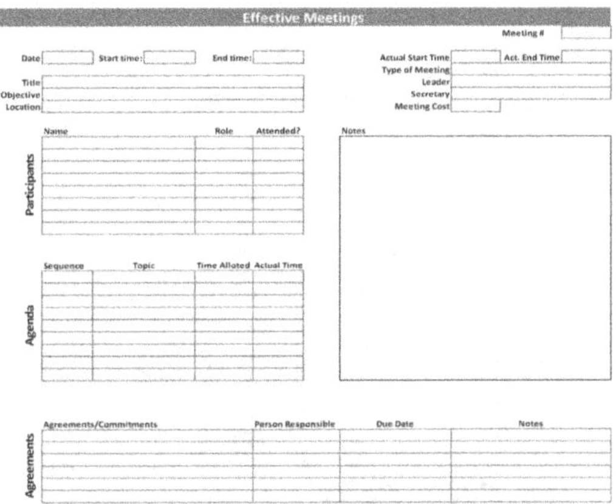

## 5. Make effective phone calls

1. Prepare for the conversation as if it was a meeting
2. Group phone calls together so that you can continue with other calls if one number is busy
3. Prioritize your calls
4. Use the speakerphone or headset so you can continue with other activities (only type C calls)
5. Schedule your phone calls

## 6. Take notes effectively / Bullet Journal

- The Bullet Journal is a customizable organization system.

- It can be your to-do list, sketchbook, notebook or diary, but most likely, it will be all of the above. It will teach you to do more with less.

*By Ryder Carroll*
*Product designer*

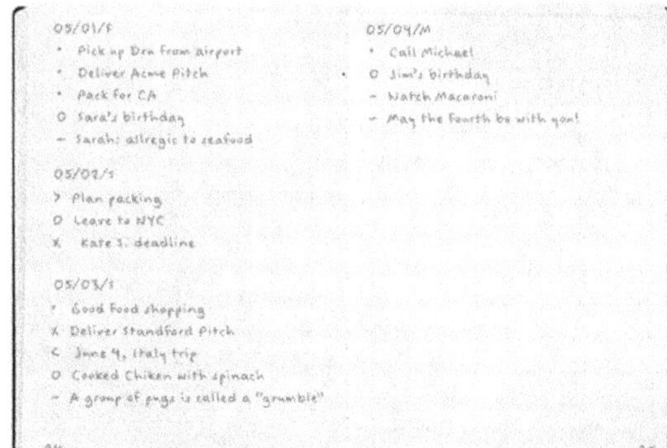

### Index

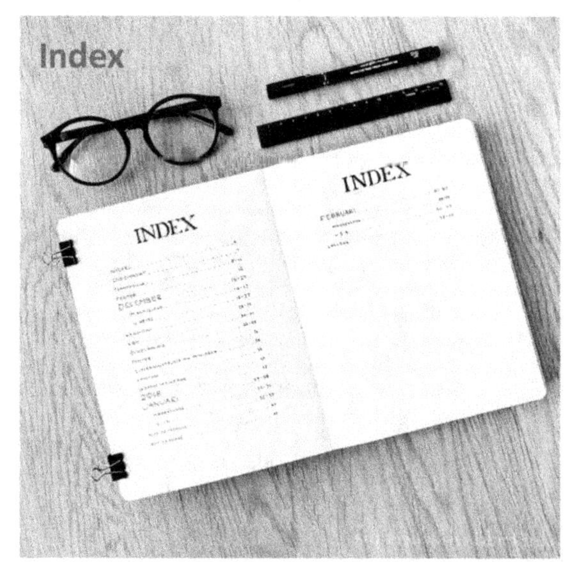


### Bullets

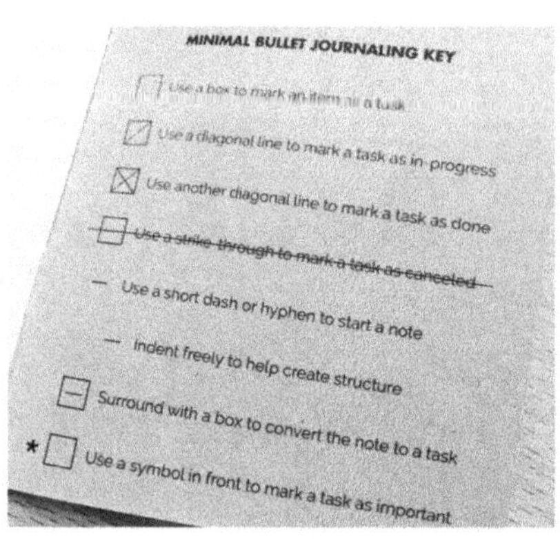

## Bullet Journal

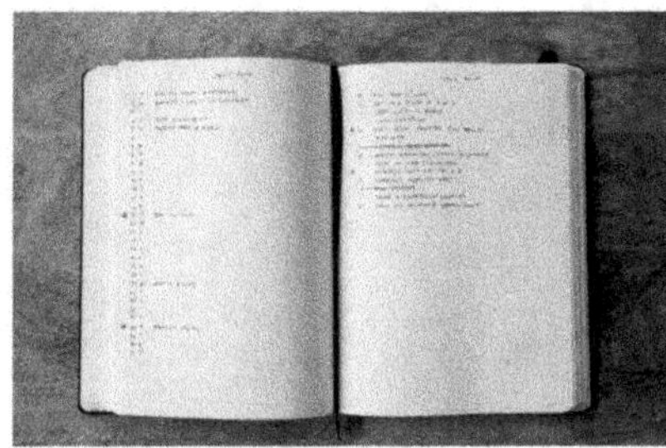

**Monthly Planner**

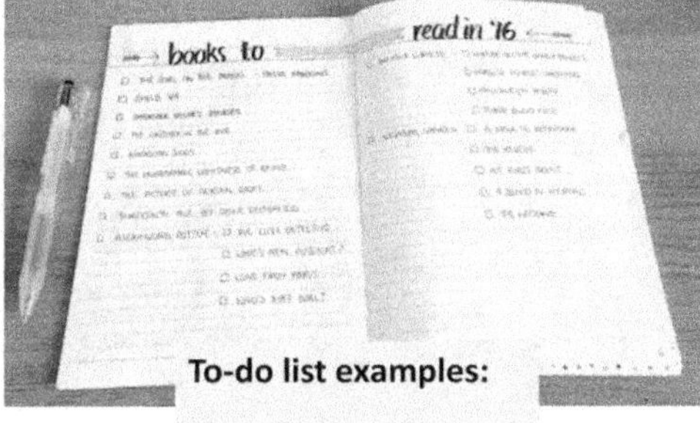

**To-do list examples:**

Projects to do
Books to read
Movies to watch
Places to visit
Restaurants to go
...

# Project Definition: A3

## Objectives

1. Understand the *importance* of project *planning* and *documentation*.
2. Understand A3 key elements.
3. Learn how to *create* an A3 in a simple way, to quickly *document* projects for an executive summary.

## Content

I. Background
II. What is an A3?
III. Benefits
IV. Elements and Procedure
V. Example

## I. Background

- Projects are the way we tactically execute strategy

- Almost every company implements projects

- Project pitfalls:

  - Not linked to their business strategies and have team members who do not fully understand the projects' benefits

  - Not  define them correctly from the start

- Proper project definition is the foundation for successful project execution

## What is meant by project definition?

- During initial project planning and documentation, we should clearly define the project's *objectives, problems* to be solved, *scope,* and the *expected results.*

- When we define a project, we should establish the elements we want to use to compare the *current* state with the *future* deliverables and results.

- Unless we correctly define the project in the beginning, we have no formal way to determine if the results are what we targeted from the start.



**LSSI**
LEAN SIX SIGMA INSTITUTE

## II. What is an A3?

- An **A3** is used to document and provide an executive summary of each improvement project.

- It is a simple and well-structured way to present a report.

## Origins of A3

- **A3** is an international standard name for the paper size: 11" x 17". It is called Tabloid or Ledger.

- The concept was developed by Toyota to describe the process of reducing report-writing to just one page.

- An **A3** is the integration of developing a one-page report and the thinking process applied to problem-solving.

## Applications of A3

Initially, A3s were only used for simple and common problems. Now we use A3s for:

- Strategic projects

- Simple projects

- Problem-solving

- Kaizen implementation

- Lean Six Sigma implementation

## III. Benefits

- Improvement projects are aligned with, and prioritized according to the company's strategies.

- Provides a standardized data-driven method to identify improvement projects.

- Project definition ensures that the number of projects assigned to an area or department does not exceed the resources available for their implementation.

**LSSI**
LEAN SIX SIGMA INSTITUTE

# Why use an A3?

- An A3 provides team members, at all levels, a structure and methodology for effective problem-solving.

- An A3 helps managers understand the need to develop their employees' skills and get everyone actively involved in the problem-solving process in order to achieve the organization's goals and objectives.

## IV. Elements and Procedure

1. Title: Identifies the name of the problem, theme or issue
2. Control reference: Number or code for document tracking
3. Owner: Identifies who owns the problem or situation
4. Date: Date of issue and latest revision
5. Background: Establishes the business case or context
6. Current conditions: Describes the current situation and known information about the problem
7. Goals/Targets: Identifies the desired outcome
8. Analysis: Analyzes the current state and root cause of the problem
9. Proposed countermeasures: Proposes corrective or improvement actions to reach the goals/targets
10. Plan: Presents the action plan and schedule required to reach each goal
11. Follow-up: Establishes follow-up meetings to ensure results, identify problems, develop new countermeasures and communicate improvements

## Main elements and procedure

Control Reference
Owner
Date

Title:

| **1. Background** |
| Why is the problem important? |

| **2. Current Conditions** |
| What is the problem? |

| **3. Scope / Baseline / Objectives** |
| What specific outcomes are required? |

| **4. Analysis** |
| What is the root cause(s) of the problem? |

**Left side: Current State**

| **5. Recommendations** |
| What is/are our proposed countermeasure(s)? |

| **6. Plan** |
| What activities will be required for implementation, and who will be responsible for what and when? |

| **7. Results and Follow-up** |
| How will we know if the implemented actions have reached the goals? What remaining issues can we expect? |

**Right side: Future State**

# 1. Background: define the business case or problem statement

| **1. Background** |
| Business Case |

- Developing a **"Business Case"** helps us identify our company's problems or areas of opportunity.

- It provides a summarized description of the characteristics of a situation or problem.

- It is used to estimate the potential value of implementing a project.

**LSSI**
LEAN SIX SIGMA INSTITUTE

A Business Case is a general definition of the area of opportunity assigned to the project team.

> As a company, the performance of ______________ in the area of__________ is not meeting __________. This is causing problems resulting in ______________ (problems), which cost us approximately______________ per year.

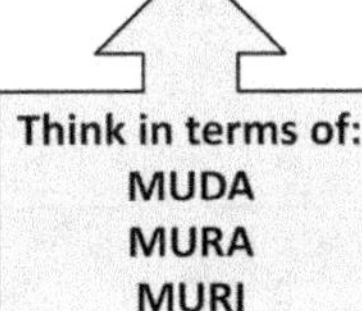


## Business case examples

As a company, the performance of **accounts receivable** in the area of **invoicing** is not meeting **our goal of 47 payment days**. This is causing problems resulting in **lack of liquidity and exceeding the established budget,** which cost us approximately **$4 million** per year.

As a company, the performance of **quality** in the **assembly** area is not meeting **our goal of 97% quality**. This is causing problems resulting in **insufficient floor space, late deliveries and high quality costs**, which cost us approximately **$1 million** per year.

As a company, the performance of **on-time deliveries** in the area of **medical products** is not meeting **our production schedule or budgeted operating costs**. This is causing problems resulting in **loss of customers and contracts, and decreased sales**, which cost us approximately **$850,000** per year.

## Main elements and procedure

Control Reference
Owner
Date

Title:

| 1. Background | 5. Recommendations |
| --- | --- |

**2. Current Conditions**

*What is the problem?*

**3. Scope/Baseline/Objectives**

**4. Analysis**

**6. Plan**

**7. Results and Follow-up**

This topic was taught in the Problem Solving Methodology

**Left side: Current State**

**Right side: Future State**

## 3. Establish the scope, baseline and objectives

**3. Scope / Baseline / Objectives**

*What specific outcomes are required?*

### For projects with poorly defined scopes like "Eliminating world hunger"

- The scope is so big and ambiguous that it is impossible to manage, and the team may become discouraged.

- It is difficult to relate the project results to the activities.

### Characteristics of projects with appropriate scopes:

- The project is large enough that it is challenging for all the participants.

- The team believes that the solution is achievable and within their area of responsibility.



**LSSI**
LEAN SIX SIGMA INSTITUTE

## What is a CTQ?

CTQ  Critical to Quality

A CTQ is a characteristic of a product or service
that must meet a critical customer requirement.

CTQs are identified by conducting a Voice of the Customer (VOC)
analysis and  documenting it as a function of the business case.

## Establish the project baseline and objectives

### Baseline

- At this step, we should have an idea of the magnitude of the problem or opportunity.
- The magnitude should be expressed in units:
  - Hours, orders, percent late, etc.
- Next, we determine the current performance levels (baselines) and desired performance levels (objectives/goals).
- It is important that we verify that we are using long-term information when estimating the baseline.

### Objectives

Each project objective should be written as a specific statement of the expected project results. Here are some examples:

- Improve lead time from 20 days to 5 days by December.
- Improve on-time delivery from 67% to 75% by March.
- Increase quality from 90% to 95% by January.
- Reduce the price from $5.00 to $ 4.85 by July.

## Scope, baseline and objectives

| BUSINESS CASE | SCOPE | CTQ´s | BASELINE | OBJECTIVE | SAVINGS |
|---|---|---|---|---|---|
| As a company, the performance of on-time deliveries in the area of medical products is not meeting our production schedule or budgeted operating costs. This is causing problems resulting in loss of customers and contracts, and decreased sales, which costs us approximately $850,000 per year. | Family of blood pressure monitors | On-Time Deliveries | 85% | 95% | $ 800,000 |
| | | Reasonable Prices | $ 120.00 | $ 100.00 | |

# Voice of the Customer

## Main elements and procedure

Control Reference
Owner
Date

Title:

**1. Background**

**2. Current Conditions**

**3. Scope / Baseline / Objectives**

**4. Analysis**

*What is the root cause(s) of the problem? Choose the simplest problem-analysis tool that clearly shows the cause-and-effect relationship.*

**e.g., Current VSM, FMEA, Balance Chart, Spaghetti Diagram, 5 Why's Fishbone Diagram, CRT, etc.**

**Left side: Current State**

**5. Recommendations**

**6. Plan**

**7. Results and Follow-up**

**Right side: Future State**



**LSSI**
LEAN SIX SIGMA INSTITUTE

Title: [    ]

Control Reference
Owner
Date

**1. Background**

**2. Current Conditions**

**3. Scope / Baseline / Objectives**

**4. Analysis**

**Left side: Current State**

**5. Recommendations**

*What is/are our proposed countermeasure(s)?*

**e.g., Future VSM, TPM, Kanban, Continuous Flow, SMED, etc.**

**6. Plan**

*What activities will be required for implementation, and who will be responsible for what and when?*

**Gantt Chart**

**7. Results and Follow-up**

*How will we know if the implemented actions have reached the goals? What remaining issues can we expect?*

*Gemba Walks/Box Score*

**Right side: Future State**

# What is a Gantt Chart?

- A Gantt Chart is a project planning tool that graphically depicts the tasks that need to be completed in a project.

- It was invented by Henry L. Gantt in 1917.

- The Gantt Chart also provides a graphical way of assessing project progress.

**A Gantt Chart allows you to:**

- Schedule project activities and tasks

- Quickly evaluate project progress at any time

- Monitor a project's completion with respect to time and activities

- Assign team member project responsibilities (i.e., tasks and activities)

# Elements

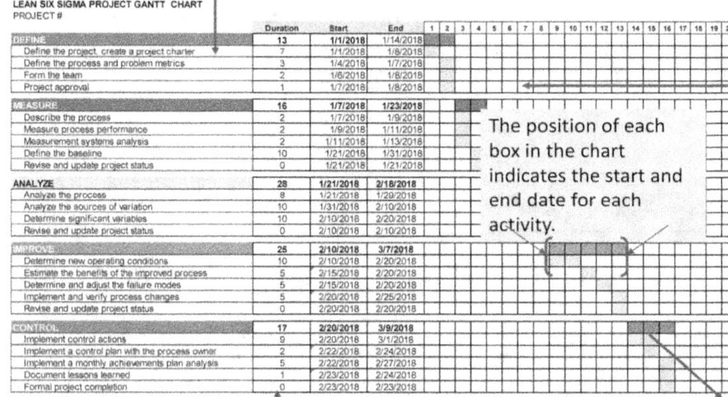


| | Duration | Start | End |
|---|---|---|---|
| **DEFINE** | 13 | 1/1/2018 | 1/14/2018 |
| Define the project, create a project charter | 7 | 1/1/2018 | 1/8/2018 |
| Define the process and problem metrics | 3 | 1/4/2018 | 1/7/2018 |
| Form the team | 2 | 1/6/2018 | 1/8/2018 |
| Project approval | 1 | 1/7/2018 | 1/8/2018 |
| **MEASURE** | 16 | 1/7/2018 | 1/23/2018 |
| Describe the process | 2 | 1/7/2018 | 1/9/2018 |
| Measure process performance | 2 | 1/9/2018 | 1/11/2018 |
| Measurement systems analysis | 2 | 1/11/2018 | 1/13/2018 |
| Define the baseline | 10 | 1/21/2018 | 1/31/2018 |
| Revise and update project status | 0 | 1/21/2018 | 1/21/2018 |
| **ANALYZE** | 28 | 1/21/2018 | 2/18/2018 |
| Analyze the process | 8 | 1/21/2018 | 1/29/2018 |
| Analyze the sources of variation | 10 | 1/31/2018 | 2/10/2018 |
| Determine significant variables | 10 | 2/10/2018 | 2/20/2018 |
| Revise and update project status | 0 | 2/10/2018 | 2/10/2018 |
| **IMPROVE** | 25 | 2/10/2018 | 3/7/2018 |
| Determine new operating conditions | 10 | 2/10/2018 | 2/20/2018 |
| Estimate the benefits of the improved process | 5 | 2/15/2018 | 2/20/2018 |
| Determine and adjust the failure modes | 5 | 2/15/2018 | 2/20/2018 |
| Implement and verify process changes | 5 | 2/20/2018 | 2/25/2018 |
| Revise and update project status | 0 | 2/20/2018 | 2/20/2018 |
| **CONTROL** | 17 | 2/20/2018 | 3/9/2018 |
| Implement control actions | 9 | 2/20/2018 | 3/1/2018 |
| Implement a control plan with the process owner | 2 | 2/22/2018 | 2/24/2018 |
| Implement a monthly achievements plan analysis | 5 | 2/22/2018 | 2/27/2018 |
| Document lessons learned | 1 | 2/23/2018 | 2/24/2018 |
| Formal project completion | 0 | 2/23/2018 | 2/23/2018 |

Horizontal axis: Calendar or timeline with units of measure that are most appropriate for the project: e.g., hours, days, weeks, months, etc.

The position of each box in the chart indicates the start and end date for each activity.

Add the number of days expected to complete each activity.

Each activity is represented by a box. The length of the box indicates the activity's duration.

# V. Example

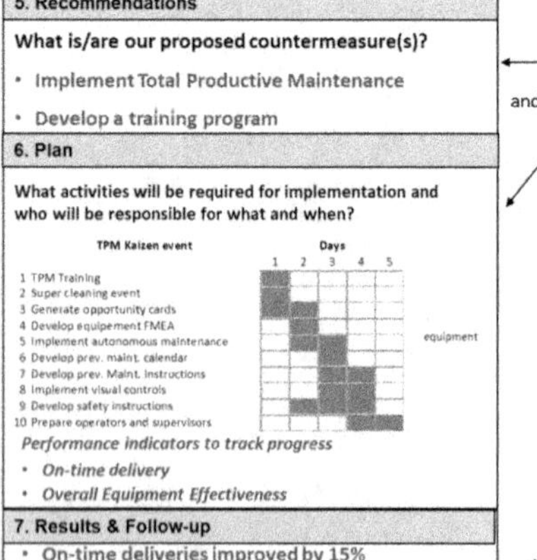


**Background:** Situation around the problem

**Current problem and impact**

**Causes:** Definition of causes from the fishbone diagram, the 5 whys and current reality tree

**Actions:** Activities, responsible and commitment dates

**Follow-up:** Verify results, actions and prevention

## How to fold an A3

- Since an **A3** paper is larger than the most commonly used office paper, it is difficult to file and add to report binders.

- Toyota adopted a specific way of folding an **A3** report that resulted in an 8.5" by 11" paper so that it could be placed in regular binders.

1. Fold in half from right to left

2. Fold in half from left to right

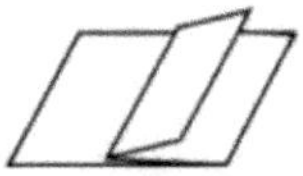

3. It is ready to file in a binder

# Measure the Voice of the Customer

### Objectives

Clearly establish what the Customers *need* and, on that basis, develop a consistent *strategy* and *projects* that really have an impact on the expectations of the services we offer.

### Content

I.   Introduction
II.  NPS: Net Promoter Score
III. Classify the Needs: Kano Model
IV.  Customer Needs Map

### I. Introduction

**Everything begins and ends with the Customer**
They are the ones who define and set expectations

**There's no business without Customers**

- Our Customers do not always express their needs and specific requirements fully and correctly.

- Companies generally assume what Customers want and do not make sure to write down mutual agreements determining what their Customers will receive.

- This creates problems throughout the service process since activities are simply carried out without a direct connection to what our Customers need.



LSSI
LEAN SIX SIGMA INSTITUTE

## Customer-Supplier Focus

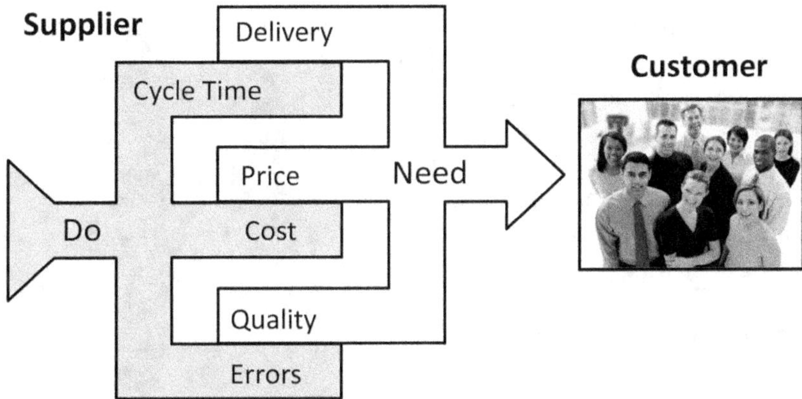


The Supplier looks for performance in Cycle Time, Cost and Errors to meet Customer expectations in Delivery, Price and Quality.

## Could we answer... ?

1. Who are my Customers?

2. What services does my Customer need that I am not delivering?

3. What do I give my Customer that he doesn't need?

4. What critical requirements do my Customers have?

5. In which activities and/or deliverables is the perceived value?

6. What am I doing differently from my competition to exceed my Customers' expectations?

7. Am I really delivering a service EXPERIENCE?

## II. NPS: Net Promoter Score

- In the past, a lot of resources were devoted to interviews, surveys, etc., to find out the Customer's perception, their needs and expectations.

- From the resulting surveys, we do not always know how to turn these responses into solid initiatives that support our strategies and projects.

- Marketing does not always convey the Customer's feelings correctly to the areas of design, sales, processes, finances, quality, etc.

## NPS Background

- Professor Fred Reicheld of Harvard University developed a method to understand Customer needs in a simple and very effective way.

- Instead of asking so many questions, classifying the responses and generally making plans without a clear path into the future, he discovered that it is no longer enough to meet the needs or delight the Customer.

- Now more than that is needed and also to understand them in a simple and practical way: **Ready for action**.



**LSSI**
LEAN SIX SIGMA INSTITUTE

## NPS = Net Promoter Score

- Now we need Promoter Customers.

- It has been proven that the best marketing is done by word of mouth.

- And social networks make this communication system 10,000 times more powerful.

- That's why we need to ask our Customers just one question:

### How willing would you be to recommend my product or service?

## NPS Procedure

1. Ask in writing: **How willing would you be to recommend my service to a friend or colleague?**

2. Ask the Customer to respond on a scale of 1 to 10.

3. Ask a second question: **What would you recommend I do to score a 10?**

4. Classify the responses:

   - From 1 to 6 as Detractor Customers.
   - 7 or 8 as Passive Customers.
   - 9 or 10 as Promoter Customers.

5. Get the percentages from each category.

6. Calculate the NPS = % Promoters - % Detractors

## Survey Format

- Apply this survey to as many of your Customers as possible.

- Ask for them to have some privacy so as not to be intimidated by employees.

- They do not need to give their name.

- Evaluate the NPS preferably after they have gone through the whole experience of the service provided.

Print and cut out survey

Survey

| How willing would you be to recommend our service? |
| --- |
| 1   2   3   4   5   6   7   8   9   10 |
| |
| What would you recommend we do to improve your experience (score a 10)? |

## Example

- A hotel carried out a satisfaction survey of 200 Customers, obtaining the following information:
  - 60% of Customers responded 9 or 10
  - 30% responded 7 or 8
  - 10% responded from 1 to 6

- Customer suggestions to score a 10:

  | | |
  | --- | --- |
  | Clean bedroom | 4 Customers |
  | Disinfected bathroom | 2 Customers |
  | More varied breakfast menu | 12 Customers |
  | High speed internet in rooms | 2 Customers |
  | Provide toothbrushes if left at home | 1 Customer |
  | Free airport shuttle | 3 Customers |

- **NPS:**
  - % Promotors – % Detractors
  - 60 % – 10 % = 50 %

▸ Only 60% are willing to recommend hotel services. Only a rating of 10 is considered a real service **experience**.

▸ A 50% in recommendation could mean expected business growth of around 50%, provided there is capacity to cater to it.

▸ 30% of Customers who answered 7 or 8 (passive) might change to another hotel if given the option so we must see how to elevate this type of Customer to promoters.

## NPS Graph

- The results of the NPS can be plotted continuously to assess trends:

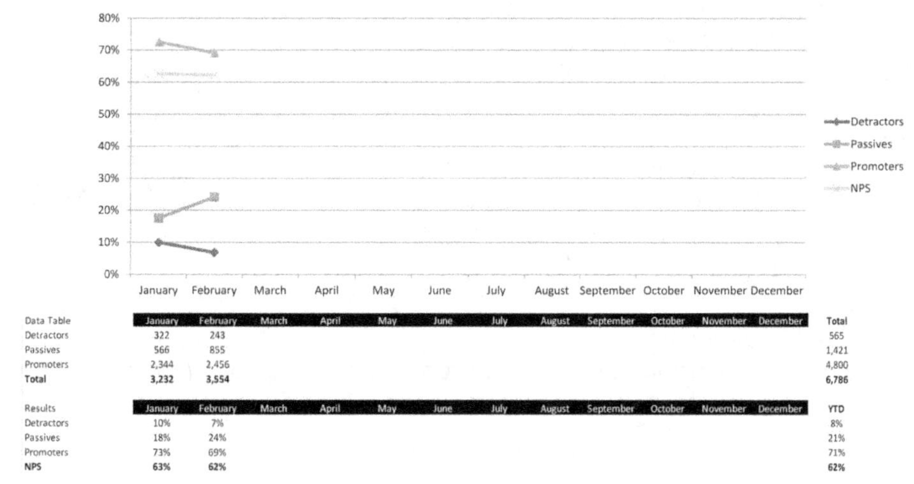

| Data Table | January | February | March | April | May | June | July | August | September | October | November | December | Total |
|---|---|---|---|---|---|---|---|---|---|---|---|---|---|
| Detractors | 322 | 243 | | | | | | | | | | | 565 |
| Passives | 566 | 855 | | | | | | | | | | | 1,421 |
| Promoters | 2,344 | 2,456 | | | | | | | | | | | 4,800 |
| **Total** | **3,232** | **3,554** | | | | | | | | | | | **6,786** |

| Results | January | February | March | April | May | June | July | August | September | October | November | December | YTD |
|---|---|---|---|---|---|---|---|---|---|---|---|---|---|
| Detractors | 10% | 7% | | | | | | | | | | | 8% |
| Passives | 18% | 24% | | | | | | | | | | | 21% |
| Promoters | 73% | 69% | | | | | | | | | | | 71% |
| **NPS** | **63%** | **62%** | | | | | | | | | | | **62%** |

## Exercise

- ABC Café applied the evaluations and obtained the following information:

  - 40 % Promotors
  - 20 % Detractors
  - 40 % Passives

- Calculate NPS

## III. Classify the Needs: Kano Model

Professor Noriaki Kano from Rika University in Tokyo developed this model by refining Herzberg's study on the theory of hygienic motivators.

**Uses:**
Identify Customer needs.
Development of new products and services.
Determine functional requirements.
Comparative analysis of services.

Quality dimensions:
The performance level of a product or service: low →high
The level of user satisfaction: low →high

## Kano Model

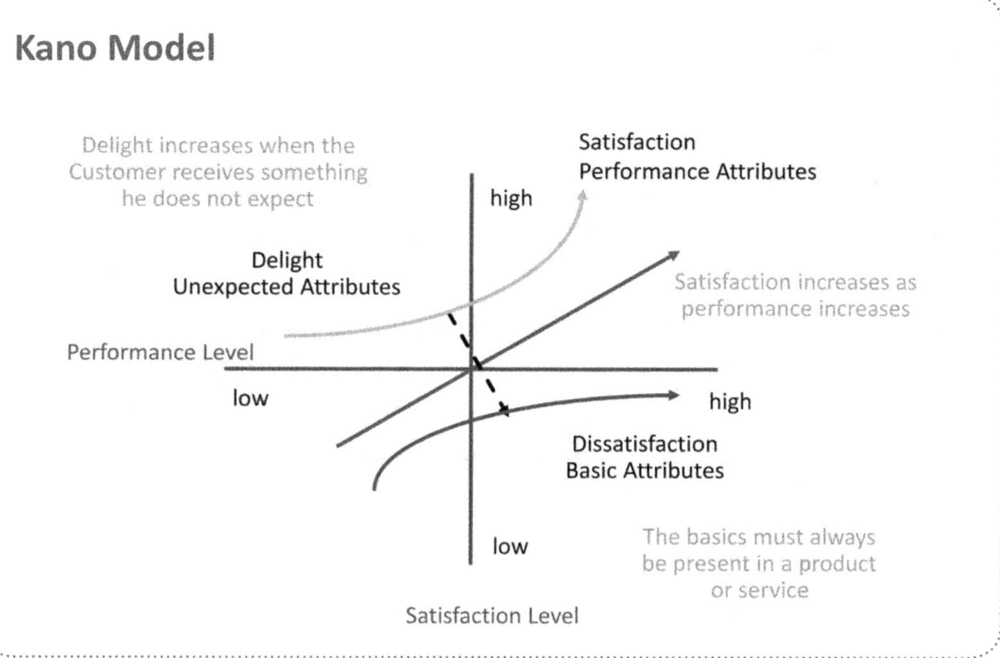


## Kano Model Procedure

1. Collect information from different media to identify Customer needs.
2. List the potential needs identified.
3. For each potential need, ask your Customers the following questions:
   What is your satisfaction level if the product or service has this attribute (potential need)?
   What is your satisfaction level if the product or service does NOT have this attribute (potential need)?
4. The Customer or user has the following response options:
   - Satisfied.
   - Neutral (it's the way I expect it - expectation).
   - It doesn't worry me.
   - Dissatisfied.

## Kano Model

**Classify the responses like attributes:** Basic, Performance or Unexpected.

The Basic attributes generally respond Neutral to question 1 and respond Dissatisfied to question 2.

The Performance attributes generally respond to the question "How much more would you be willing to pay for this attribute or for more of this attribute?" They respond Satisfied to question 1 and Dissatisfied to 2.

The Unexpected attributes generally respond Satisfied to question 1 and at the same time respond It doesn't worry me to question 2.

## Example

- The Customer responded with the following needs both in the NPS measurement as well as to some of the improvement team's suggestions:

|  | WRITE DOWN THE NEEDS | Satisfaction level if the Service has this attribute | Satisfaction level if the Service does NOT have this attribute | TYPE OF NECESSITY |
|---|---|---|---|---|
| Instructions | Clean bedroom | Neutral | Dissatisfied | BASIC |
|  | Disinfected bathroom | Neutral | Dissatisfied | BASIC |
| Capture the needs | More varied breakfast menu | Satisfied | Dissatisfied | PERFORMANCE |
|  | High speed internet in rooms | Satisfied | Dissatisfied | PERFORMANCE |
| Capture the responses that | Toothbrushes available in case left at home | Satisfied | Doesn't worry me | UNEXPECTED |
| are repeated most in each | Free airport shuttle | Satisfied | Doesn't worry me | UNEXPECTED |
| question (mode) | Cable Television | Satisfied | Dissatisfied | PERFORMANCE |

Choose the Response

**Note:** If any of these combinations are not fulfilled, check there are no inconsistencies in the responses.

## Kano Model Example

- **Basic**
  - Clean bedroom.
  - Disinfected bathroom.
- **Performance**
  - High speed internet in rooms.
  - Cable Television.
  - More varied breakfast menu.
- **Unexpected**
  - Free airport shuttle.
  - Courtesy toothbrush.

**Note**: The unexpected attributes tend to turn into performance attributes and later even become basic ones.

## IV. Customer Needs Map

The Customer Needs Map is a tool used to identify Customer CTQs (Critical To Quality).

- The needs map must contain **all** the requirements the Customer wishes for.

- The needs map could contain information on Customer needs collected from **NPS** measurements as well as the **Kano Model**.

## Needs Map Procedure

**1.** Brainstorm the Customer requirements after the interview

**2.** Group the requirements by categories

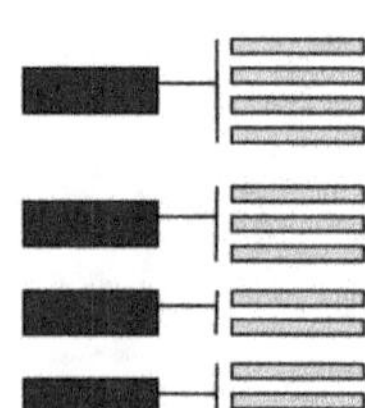

**3.** Classify them according to the level of importance for the Customer

Classification:
5 - Critical
4 - Important
3 - Would be good to have
2 - Not very important
1 - Doesn't matter

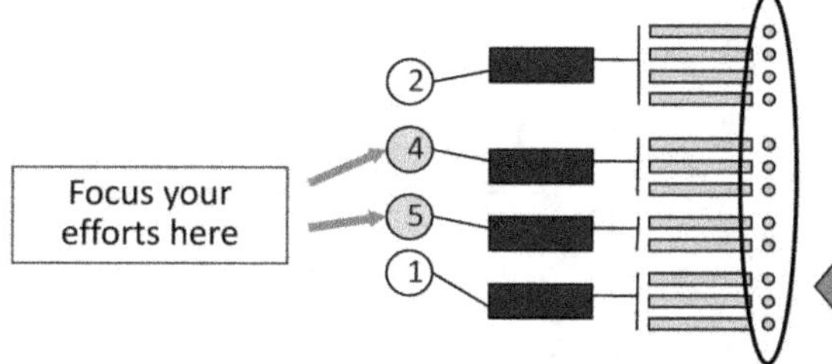


Note for numerical conclusions: If the data is inconclusive or there are too many categories, have the Customer classify the CTQ's obtained in this first CNM.

## Example: Needs Map

**Room** — **Level of importance**
- Clean bedroom — 5
- Disinfected bathroom — 5
- High speed internet in rooms — 4
- Cable Television — 3

**Food and drinks**
- Room service — 3
- More varied menu — 3

**Others**
- Free airport shuttle — 4
- Toothbrushes — 2

Those with a value of 5 are Critical to Quality, that is, they cannot be missing. Those with values of 3 and 4 must be seriously considered in order to make a difference.

# Measurement of Services

**9**

## Objectives

1. Develop a *measurement system* that allows the value generated for the Customer, owners and employees of a business to be understood.
2. Realize that measurements provide a means to *understand* better what we are doing and *challenge* our actions *continuously*.
3. Understand how we measure the *intensity* with which life experiences are provided to our Customers in a service.

## Content

I. Background
II. Measurements of Services
III. Box Score
IV. 4 Quadrant Analysis

## I. Background

- These days, despite the great technological advances and the extensive experience accumulated by the service companies, we are still not clear on how to evaluate services and companies.

- Measurements have mainly been related to the performance of the departments rather than the performance of the process.

- And the process is where the Customer experiences the deficiencies or the advantages of a company!

## If we were to ask...

If we had the opportunity to bring together the owners, directors, managers, supervisors and ask them if they knew:

- What is the Customer's perception of quality?
- Are our costs within budget?
- What are the real costs of the service?
- What is the demand and capacity?
- Are we delivering our services on time?
- Are we winning or losing?

**How many could answer all the questions correctly?**

## II. Measurements of Services

**Quality, Cost, Delivery, Safety, and Motivation Measurements**

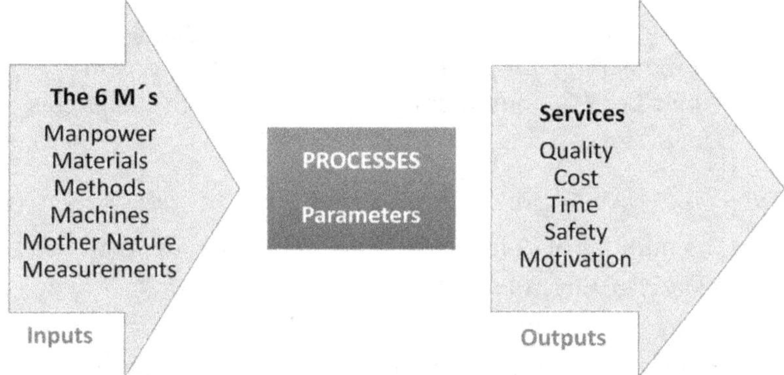


In a service it is necessary to measure the performance in terms of what we deliver to our Customers, that is, the outputs. We should also assess the critical processes and inputs to find out the real performance of the system.

## Quality in Services

- Net Recommendation Index (NPS)

    - This shows us the Customer loyalty ratio, not only to determine if we meet their requirements or delight them, but also whether they are willing to recommend us given their service experience.

    - NPS = % Promoters - % Detractors
    - % Promoters = 75%, % Detractors = 11%
    - NPS = 75% - 11%
    - NPS = 64%

A service requires high levels of **warmth** and that is achieved when Customers give a score of 10 in NPS recommendability.

- **<u>Defects (or Errors) per Million Opportunities</u>**
  - Six Sigma seeks to achieve perfection and that is achieved by measuring our performance no longer in percent (units per 100) but in units per million, which challenges our system.

**DPMO is:**
- The number of defects observed per million opportunities.
- A key measurement in Six Sigma.
- A corporate standard for counting defects and errors.
- A means to quantify the impact of our improvements.
- A means to amplify the urgency of problems.

## DPMOs: Example

$$DPMO = \frac{Defects}{Units \times Opportunities} \times 1{,}000{,}000$$

**Example: Beauty Salon**

- We had 35 services with some kind of complaint or rework.

- We performed 450 services in that period.

- Each service has 4 opportunities for failure: Late Appointment, Wrong Color, Wrong Cut, Wrong Charge.

$$DPMO = \frac{35}{450 \times 4} \times 1{,}000{,}000 = 19{,}444$$

## Sigma Level

| Sigma Level | Defect per million opportunities (DPMO) | Yield |
|---|---|---|
| 6 | 3 | 99.9997% |
| 5 | 233 | 99.997% |
| 4 | 6,210 | 99.379% |
| 3 | 66,807 | 93.32% |
| 2 | 308,537 | 69.20% |
| 1 | 690,000 | 31% |

19,444 defects per million opportunities places this Beauty Salon at a level between 3 and 4 sigma, which puts it at a disadvantage over any other one that works at levels of 5 or 6 sigma, that is, with a **higher performance**!

## Cost

- **Productivity:**

  Transactions or services carried out over a period divided by the resources used. Example:

    - 500 orders were made and there are 50 people on the payroll

    - Productivity per person = 10 Orders / Person

- **Cost per Service:**

  Sum of Conversion Cost + Material or Variable Cost divided by the Number of Services. Example:

    - Total Cost of Services = $ 10,000

    - 100 Services rendered

    - Cost per Service = $ 10 / Service

## Cost of Poor Quality

- **Cost of Poor Quality=**

  **Prevention + Appraisal + Internal Errors + External Errors**

**PREVENTION**
- Training + Consultancy + Audits + Calibration + Preventive Maintenance
- Salaries of Managers and Quality Engineers

**APPRAISAL**
- Tests + Inspector Salaries + Stationery

**EXTERNAL ERRORS**
- Returns + Delays + Claims + Lost Sales

**INTERNAL ERRORS**
- Waste + Rework + Overtime + Accidents + Corrective Maintenance
- Financial cost of Inventory

## Cost of Poor Quality: Example

- **Cost of Poor Quality=**

  **Prevention ($ 550) + Appraisal ($ 645) + Internal Failures ($ 255) + External Failures ($ 60)**

**PREVENTION**
- Training ($ 100) + Consultancy ($ 150) + Audits + Calibration
- Preventive Maintenance and Quality Salaries ($ 300)

**APPRAISAL**
- Tests ($ 120) + Inspector Salaries ($ 500) + Stationery ($ 25)

**EXTERNAL FAULTS**
- Returns ($ 135) + Delays + Claims ($ 120) + Lost Sales

**INTERNAL FAULTS**
- Waste ($ 10) + Rework + Overtime ($ 50) + Accidents + Corrective Maintenance
- Financial cost of Inventory

# Delivery

- Service Response Time:
    - Time from when the order is received until the service is paid for

- **Paint a house**
    - Make the appointment    1 day
    - Prepare the service    0.5 days
    - Perform the service    3 days
    - Collect payment    2 days

    - Total time    6.5 days

# Safety

- Safety should be the priority for any company, both the safety of the workers and of the Customers who use its services.

- Security Indicators:

    - Accidents
    - Injuries
    - Risk level (This will be seen in more detail in AMEF)

- Safety indicators will be scored weekly or monthly according to the counts of accidents, injuries, risks, etc.

## Demand and Capacity

- **Takt Time:** Available time / Number of services requested
- **Capacity:** Available time / Speed of slowest resource
- **Available Capacity:** Capacity - Demand

**Example:**
- **Daily Available Time:** 8 hours minus 30 minutes for lunch
- **Number of Services Requested (Demand):** 10 per day
- **Speed of Slowest Resource:** 20 minutes

- **Takt Time:** 450 minutes / 10 services = 45 minutes per service
- **Capacity:** 450 minutes / 20 min per service = 22 services per day
- **Available capacity:** 22 - 10 = 12 daily services

## Financial Measurements

- **Income:** Billing for the Period.
- **Material Cost:** Cost of the material associated with the billing.
- **Conversion Cost:** All costs for the period, except materials.
- **Margin / Profit:** Income - Material and Conversion Costs.

**Example:**

The carpet cleaning services company had the following results in week 45 of the year:

| | | |
|---|---|---|
| Income: | $ 120,000 | Billing for the week |
| Material cost: | $ 30,000 | Material required |
| Conversion cost | $ 50,000 | Salaries, rent, gasoline, etc. |
| Margin: | $ 40,000 | Income - Costs |

## III. Box Score

Now we need a location to place our results in order to evaluate them weekly, to be able to fully understand the process and realized what we have achieved as a team.

|  | BOX SCORE | Objective | 1 07-jan | 2 14-jan | 3 21-jan | 4 28-jan | 5 04-feb | 6 11-feb | 7 18-feb | 8 25-feb | 9 04-mar | 10 11-mar |
|---|---|---|---|---|---|---|---|---|---|---|---|---|
| Quality | NPS | | | | | | | | | | | |
| Quality | Quality at first | | | | | | | | | | | |
| Quality | DPMO | | | | | | | | | | | |
| Cost | Cost of non quality | | | | | | | | | | | |
| Cost | Average cost of service | | | | | | | | | | | |
| Cost | Units per person | | | | | | | | | | | |
| Delivery | Shipments on time | | | | | | | | | | | |
| Delivery | Delivery time (days) | | | | | | | | | | | |
| Sec. | Accidents | | | | | | | | | | | |
| Mot. | Evaluation 5 S's | | | | | | | | | | | |
| Mot. | NPS of employees | | | | | | | | | | | |
| Speed | Takt time (service demand) | | | | | | | | | | | |
| Speed | Service capacity | | | | | | | | | | | |
| Speed | Available capacity | | | | | | | | | | | |
| Finances | Income | | | | | | | | | | | |
| Finances | Material Cost | | | | | | | | | | | |
| Finances | Conversion Cost | | | | | | | | | | | |
| Finances | Gross Profit of Value Stream | | | | | | | | | | | |
| Finances | Chain return | | | | | | | | | | | |

The Box Score must be analyzed by the team weekly to determine the Lean Six Sigma Projects or actions that should be done.

# What is the relationship between the Box Score and Hoshin Kanri?

At Hoshin Kanri we express the What's and How's in Strategies and Projects and set the Indicators

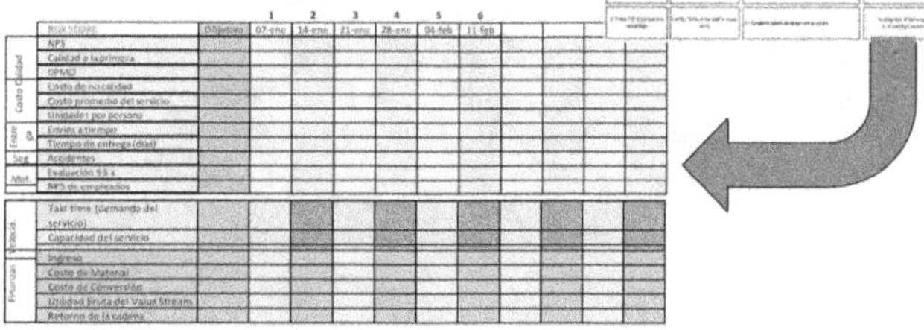

In the Box Score we continuously measure the results achieved.

**The Box Score works continuously, not only for a specific LSS Project.**

## IV. 4 Quadrant Analysis

Each indicator contained in the Box Score will have a level of detailed analysis that can be seen in the 4 Q's or Four Quadrants in which we will present :

- A Trend Chart
- A Pareto Chart
- An Ishikawa Graph
- A Table of Activities to be carried out

**Every KPI from the Box Score should be linked to a 4Q report in order to visually understand any situation in more depth, at any time.**

## What is a 4-Quadrant analysis?

- A 4-Quadrant analysis is a lean method used to support agile decision making.

- It involves analyzing root causes and their impact to objectively understand any situation.

**LSSI**
LEAN SIX SIGMA INSTITUTE

## Benefits

- On-the-spot problem solving

- Better understanding of any metric or indicator

- Focus on the most important aspects of an operation

- Improved decision-making based on data

## Key elements

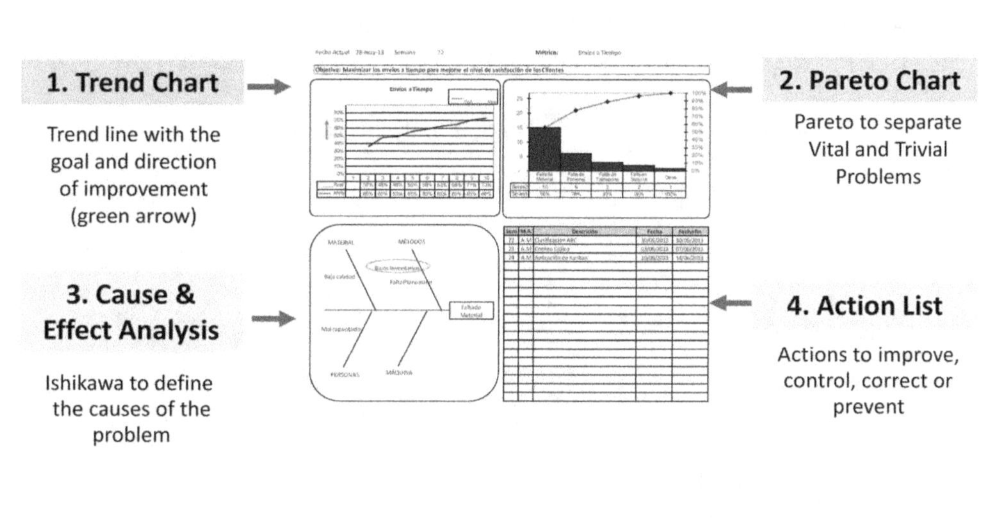

### 1. Trend Chart

Trend line with the goal and direction of improvement (green arrow)

### 2. Pareto Chart

Pareto to separate Vital and Trivial Problems

### 3. Cause & Effect Analysis

Ishikawa to define the causes of the problem

### 4. Action List

Actions to improve, control, correct or prevent

## Procedure

1. What is the current status of a KPI (Trend chart)?

   - What is the problem?
   - What are the historical results?

2. What is the most important aspect of the KPI that needs to be evaluated (Pareto chart)?

   - What **20%** of the issues generate **80%** of the results?
   - What are the 2 or 3 categories that we need to focus on?

3. What is the root cause of the problem (Cause and Effect)?

4. What needs to be **improved, prevented or controlled** (Action items)?

## 1. Trend chart

A trend chart is a graphical tool used to understand the behavior of a KPI (data) by showing its trend during any period of time.

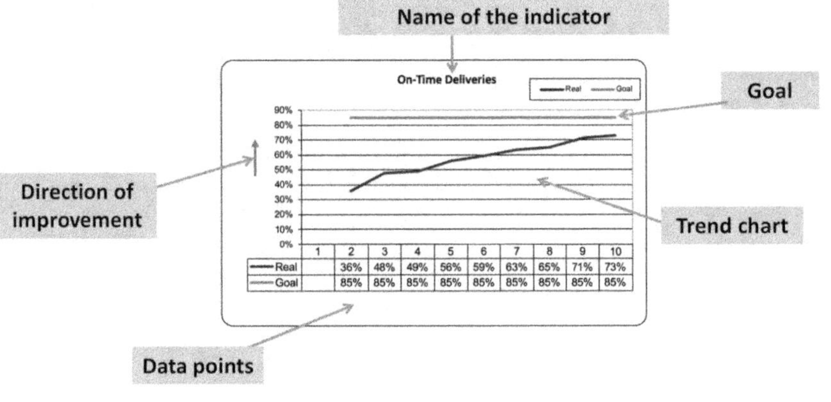

# What does a trend chart tell us?

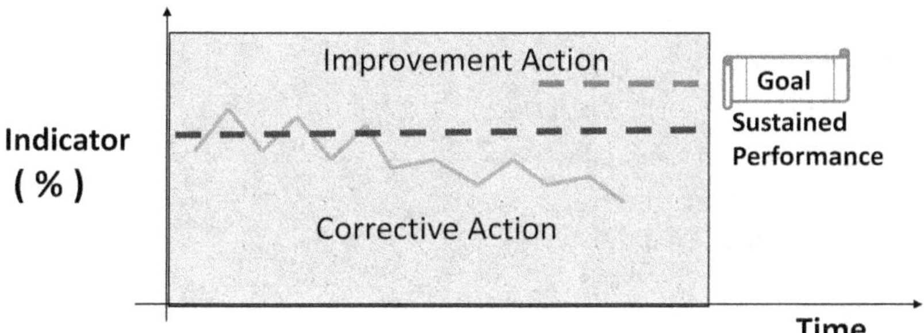


Preventive actions prevent *OCCURRENCE.*

Corrective actions prevent *RECURRENCE.*

Improvement actions *SURPASS* an already sustained performance level.

Control actions *MAINTAIN* what has been gained.

# 2. Pareto chart

- A Pareto Chart is used for counting and categorizing data, in which the categories (represented by bars), are plotted based on occurrences and in descending order, to show the importance of each category.

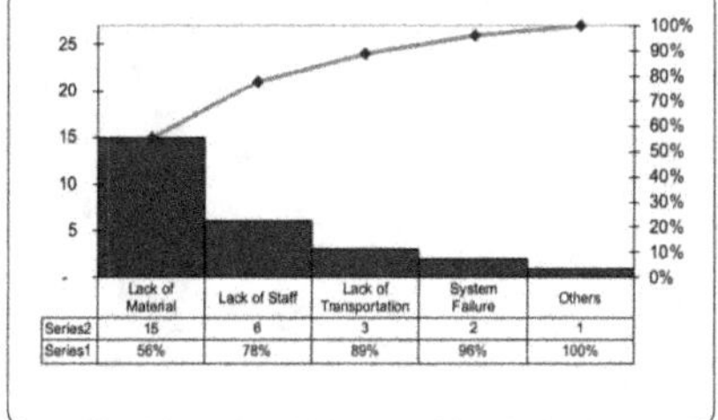

| | Lack of Material | Lack of Staff | Lack of Transportation | System Failure | Others |
|---|---|---|---|---|---|
| Series2 | 15 | 6 | 3 | 2 | 1 |
| Series1 | 56% | 78% | 89% | 96% | 100% |

- Pareto charts are used during the **Define and Analyze** phases to focus on the most vital resources in the organization (e.g., products, departments, problems, defects, causes, etc.) to help optimize performance.

*Vital few and the trivial many*

*Dr. Joseph Juran*

## 3. Cause and effect analysis: Fishbone diagram

**Fishbone Diagram**

- The result or effect is usually expressed as a problem statement instead of a desired condition, which makes the brainstorming session easier.

- Once the main causes have been identified, circle or highlight them in red.

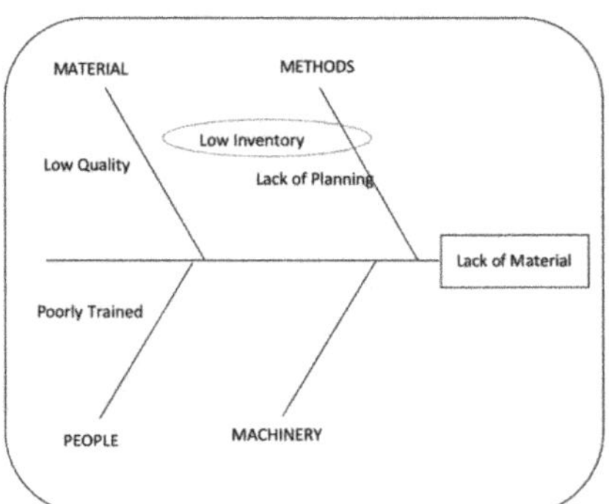


## 4. Action items

Results

Type of Action

**Corrective**
**Preventive**
**Improvement**
**Innovation**

Action

Methods & Tools

**Implement**
**Document**
**Teach**

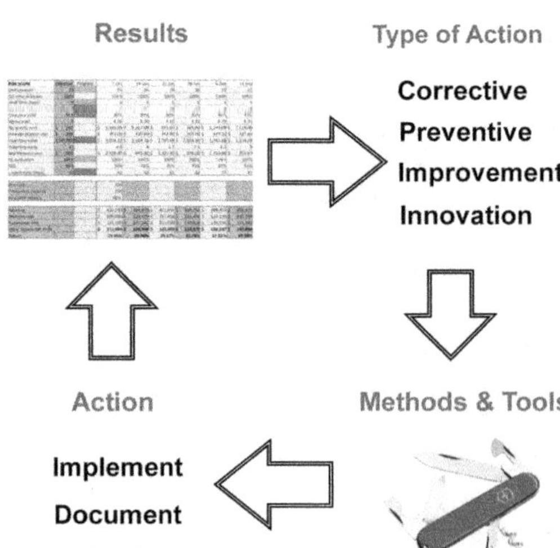

| Improvement Methodology | Tool Box | | |
| --- | --- | --- | --- |
| | White Belt | Yellow Belt | Green Belt |
| Define | | A3 | QFD<br>Needs Tree<br>Kano Model |
| Measure and Map | Trend chart | Data Collection<br>OEE<br>VSM | SIPOC<br>Basic Statistics<br>Sampling<br>MSA (R&R) |
| Analyze | 5 Whys | Spaghetti Diag.<br>Balance Chart<br>Trend Chart<br>Pareto Chart | Histogram<br>Sigma Level<br>Cp & Cpk<br>Correlation<br>Hypothesis Test<br>Box Plots<br>Conf. Intervals<br>Variance<br>Multi-Vari |
| Improve or Design | 5 S<br>Visual Management<br>(Andon) | Continuous Flow<br>Kanban<br>Quick Changes<br>(SMED)<br>TPM | Experiments |
| Control or Validate | Standard Work<br>Mistake Proofing<br>(Poka Yoke) | Checklist | Statistical Control<br>Control Plan |

DMAIC



**LSSI**
LEAN SIX SIGMA INSTITUTE

# Action Items → Kata Boards

- The most important use of any type of analysis is to make the best improvement decisions, solve a problem or control a situation.
- During Kata Cycles, the 4-Quadrant Analysis process will contribute to the formulation of a hypothesis and the generation of experiment ideas.

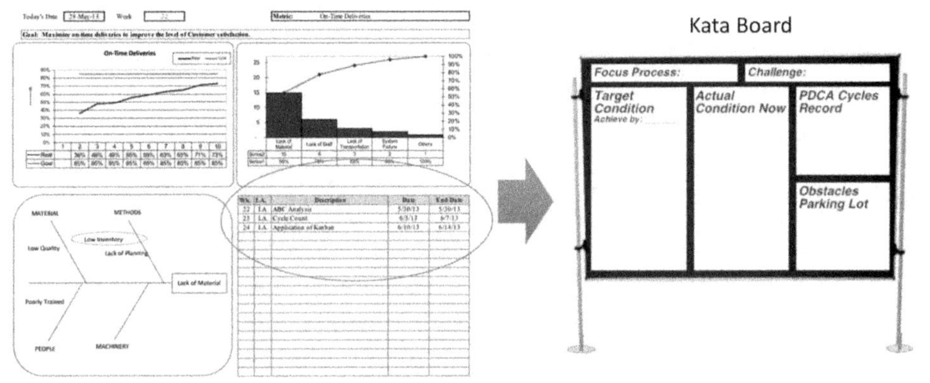

Kata Board

# Map the Service



Whenever there is a product or service for a client, there is a Value Stream. The challenge is to see it

## Objectives

1. Understand the importance of *developing* a Value Stream Map for *each* end-to-end process to be improved.
2. Know the general procedure to *obtain the information*.
3. Learn the general procedure to *map* any kind of process.
4. Identify the most *critical* areas and *bottlenecks* that require the implementation of improvements.

## Content

I. Background
II. Cross-Functional Flowchart
III. Data Collection
IV. What is a current state Value Stream Map?

### I. Background

One of the main reasons why Lean Six Sigma fails is:

- Implement tools **everywhere** and at the same time, without establishing a precise **focus** that considers the business needs.

We call it "Popcorn kaizen"

Very few people in any organization are able to respond all the following questions correctly:

1. What is the current demand for our products or services?

2. What is our current capacity?

3. What are the bottlenecks in our system? Where are these restrictions located?

4. What is the cost for each of our products or services?

5. Are we making or losing money?

## II. Cross-Functional Flowchart

Provides a graphical representation of the steps in a process, with an emphasis on interdepartmental relationships and responsibilities.

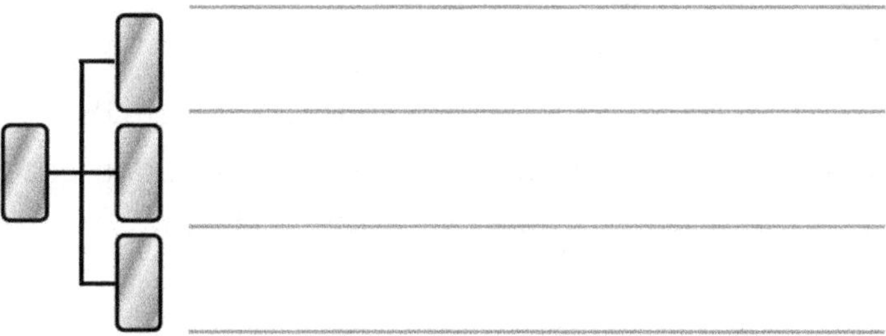

# When is a Cross-Functional Flowchart used?

- When you want to know the existing relationships and responsibilities between departments in a process.

- When you want to identify the possible causes of an existing problem between departments or individuals.

- When you want to delineate and delegate responsibilities to the areas involved in a process.

## Cross-Functional Flowchart Procedure

1. Identify the steps or activities in a process.

2. Define the person/people and/or department(s) responsible for the process.

3. Arrange the sequence of process activities according to the person/people and/or department(s) responsible with respect to time.

4. Validate the cross-functional flowchart.

## Cross-Functional Flowchart Example

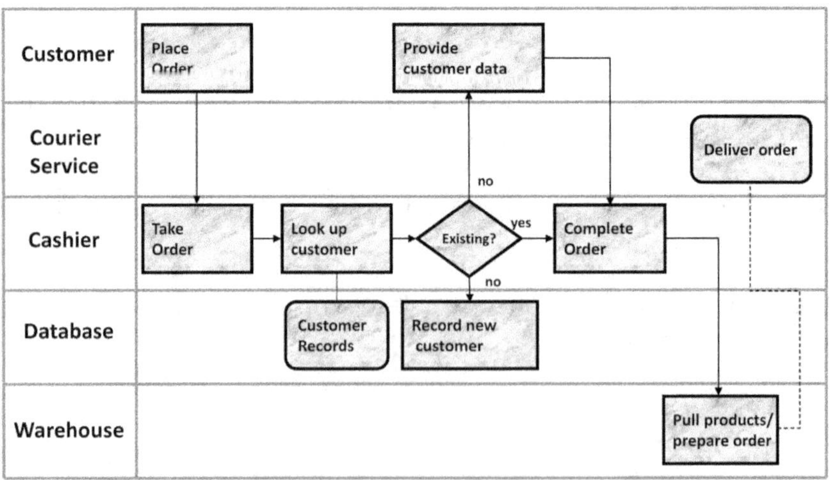

## III. Data Collection

### Data gathering

- In Lean Six Sigma, data is the basis for quality decision-making.

- Data gathering has to be as clear and simple as possible to prevent errors.

## Common data collection errors

- **Measurement:** errors following procedure of instruments' calibration.

- **Operational:** failure to follow instruction manuals, lack of training, missing data, and errors collecting data.

- **Influence from interaction:** the process of measuring could have a negative effect over the performance of a given operation.

- **Perception/Bias:** those who collect the data tend to see what they want to see.

- **Sampling:** the data collected does not represent the entire process.

## Benefits

- Effective knowledge of those data elements that are relevant to establish current state conditions.

- The acquisition of wider knowledge about the process and the personnel in charge through the data collection allows for a more efficient project execution.

- Recognize potential opportunities to improve the quality of the data generated in processes and verify that the data collected is accurate.

## Data Collection Procedure

1. Identify the data sources

2. Collect the data

# 1. Identify the data sources

| Information flow | Service / Material Flow |
| --- | --- |

Examples:
- Monthly or weekly demand
- Forecasts
- Order confirmations
- Etc.

Examples:
- Cycle times for each operation (C/T)
- Setup times (C/O)
- Overall Equipment Effectiveness (OEE)
- EPE* (Production batch sizes)
  "Every part every________"
- Number of workers
- Work in process (WIP) Inventory levels
  (i.e., the most common quantities)
- Transportation methods between suppliers, operations, and clients
- Scrap rate

# 2. Collect the data

In its different forms, data collection allows to obtain data in a more reliable fashion that will be analyzed later with more sophisticated tools.

Types:
1. Post-its
2. Time studies sheet
3. Photos and videos

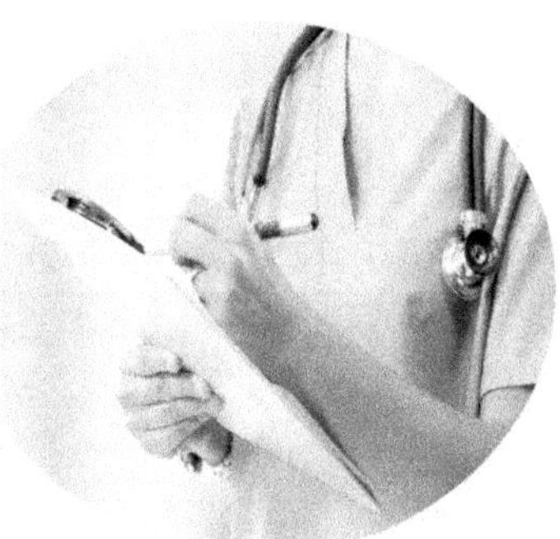

## Using Post-its to collect data

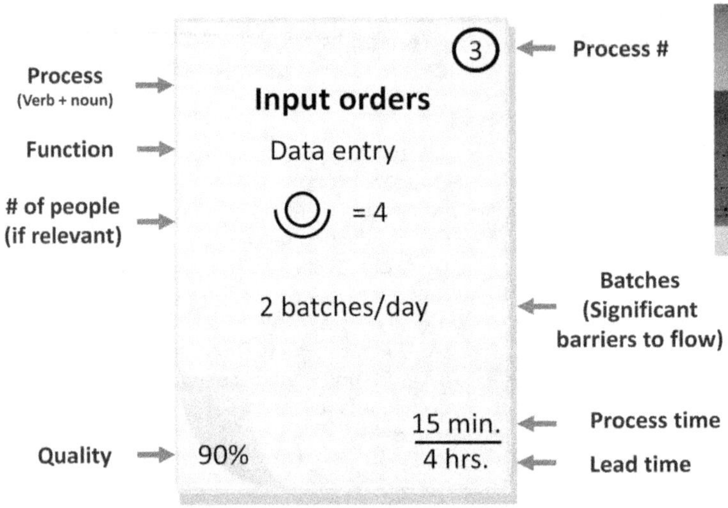

## Time study - data collection sheet

| Process | LSSI LEAN SIX SIGMA INSTITUTE | TIME STUDY DATA COLLECTION SHEET | | Date | | | Process # | | | |
| --- | --- | --- | --- | --- | --- | --- | --- | --- | --- | --- |
| | | | | Time | | | Observer | | | |

| No. | Work elementS | Measure point | 1 | 2 | 3 | 4 | 5 | 6 | 7 | 8 | 9 | 10 | 11 | 12 | 13 | 14 | 15 | Lowest repeated time |
| --- | --- | --- | --- | --- | --- | --- | --- | --- | --- | --- | --- | --- | --- | --- | --- | --- | --- | --- |
| | | | | | | | | | | | | | | | | | | |
| | | | | | | | | | | | | | | | | | | |
| | | | | | | | | | | | | | | | | | | |
| | | | | | | | | | | | | | | | | | | |
| | | | | | | | | | | | | | | | | | | |
| | | | | | | | | | | | | | | | | | | |
| | | | | | | | | | | | | | | | | | | |
| | | | | | | | | | | | | | | | | | | |
| | | | | | | | | | | | | | | | | | | |
| | | | | | | | | | | | | | | | | | | |
| | | | | | | | | | | | | | | | | | | |
| | | | | | | | | | | | | | | | | | | |
| Cycle Time | | | | | | | | | | | | | | | | | | |

## Data collection tips

- Collect new and factual data. Do not use historical records.

- Walk around the production floor or office. Use a stopwatch to time each step of the process. Trust what you measure, not what you are told.

- The inventory data stored in information systems is not always reliable. Make sure to perform physical counts of the raw materials, work-in-process and finished goods inventory. Do not count units. Instead, count containers, pallets, boxes, etc.

## IV. What is a current state Value Stream Map?

It is a graphical representation of the steps of the process and the information flow. This tool allows to understand the process flow and identify waste, with the purpose to develop improvement plans.

A Value Stream includes all activities required to satisfy customer requests, from the customer order to delivery.

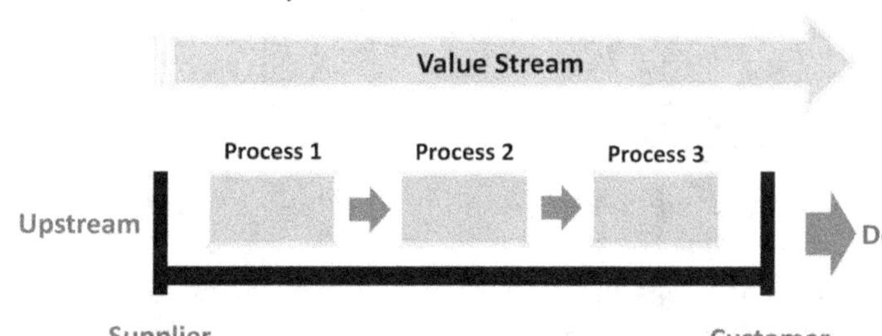

## Types of maps

### Current State VSM

- A current state VSM is a reference document used to identify the most critical forms of waste as well as the improvement opportunity areas.

### Future State VSM

- A future state VSM defines the best short-to mid-term solution for the operation, proposing the improvements to be incorporated into the productive system.

## VSM provides a general overview of the end-to-end business process

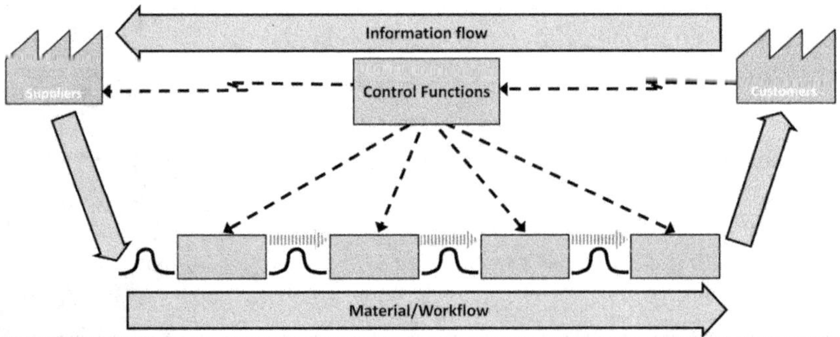


- Establishes the interaction between the material/workflow and the information flow.
- Provides a common visual language to understand a complex system.
- Helps identify those operations that add value to products and services



LSSI
LEAN SIX SIGMA INSTITUTE

## Material / workflow and information flow

- The material/workflow represents the movement of diverse elements throughout a system with the purpose to generate products or services.

- The information flow tells each process step what to do next and what to produce.

- For Lean production, information flow is considered as important as the material/workflow.

## Different process levels in an organization

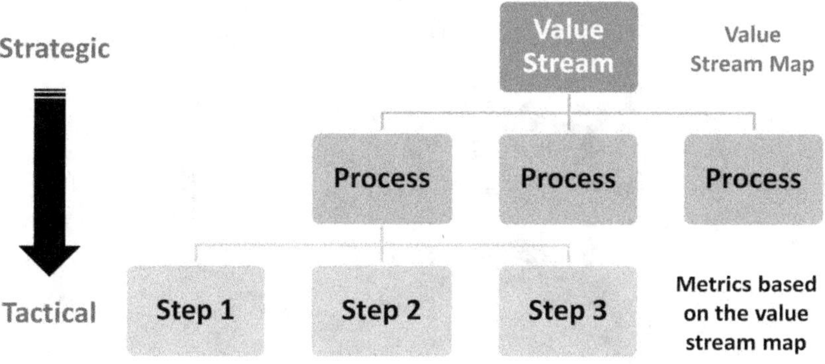

## VSM Benefits

- Provides a graphical method to understand the entire supply chain in one document

- Helps in the development of an improvement strategy for the value stream before implementing changes

- Reveals the process flow and the sources of waste

- Establishes a common language for process analysis

- Promotes a model to create flow and implement Lean Six Sigma methods and tools

- Support in the detection of bottlenecks and improvement areas

## Why create a VSM?

- Further the complete understanding of the full process from the customer's perspective
- Identify activities that **DO NOT** add value
- Identify activities that **ADD** value

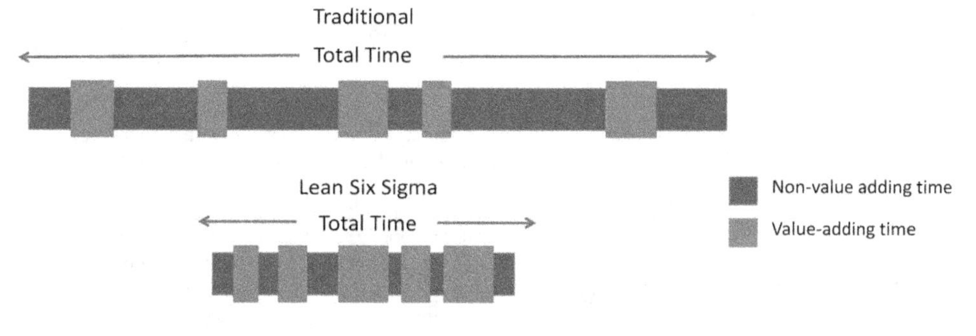


## Key elements: Value Stream Mapping symbols

| Symbol | Name | Description |
|---|---|---|
|  | **Process Box** | Represents a process or operation through which work or material flows. We typically do not include detailed process steps unless there is significant accumulation of inventory or batching between process steps. |
|  | **External Sources** | Represents both suppliers and customers. The supplier is the starting point and is typically located on the upper left-hand corner of the map. The customer is the end point and is typically located on the upper right-hand corner of the map. |
|  | **Shipments** | Represents the transportation of either receiving materials from an external supplier or delivering finished products or services to the customer. |

| Symbol | Name | Description |
|---|---|---|
|  | Data Box | This symbol is located under other symbols to present critical data/information. Normally, it will show data such as shipment frequency, lot size, material information, etc. When it is located under a process box, it typically shows information such as cycle time, changeover time, activity time, lead time, available capacity, batch size, yield, etc. |
|  | Inventory | Represents the inventory level before and after each process. The inventory level is shown under the symbol. |
|  | Employees | Represents one or multiple employees. The number of employees is shown under the symbol. |
|  | Push Arrow | Represents the movement of material from one process to another. It is used when the previous process "pushes" materials to the next process, independently of what is truly needed by the next process. |
|  | Material Receipts and Shipments | Represents the movement of finished goods or services to the customer. It can also be used to represent movement of raw materials from suppliers to the facility. |
|  | Electronic Information Flow | Represents the flow of electronic information or data. |
|  | Manual Information Flow | Represents the flow of manual information. |
|  | Go See | Refers to confirming something visually during the process. "Go See" scheduling is a manual count of the inventory to make schedule adjustments. |
|  | Timeline (Value-Adding Activities) | Represents a timeline when an activity adds value. |
|  | Timeline (Non-Value Adding Activities) | Represents a timeline when an activity does not add value. |

| Symbol | Name | Description |
|---|---|---|
| | **Withdrawal arrow** | Represents the withdrawal of material from the preceding process. |
| -FIFO→ | **FIFO** | Represents a "First-in First-out" inventory system. |
| | **Withdrawal Kanban** | Used to signal the withdrawal of parts from a supermarket. |
| | **Production Kanban** | Used to signal a previous process to produce parts for a downstream process. It is usually in a predefined quantity. |
| | **Kanban Post** | Represents the location where Kanban cards are kept. |
| | **Signal Kanban** | Used to signal a process to change and start the production of a specific part or service. This is normally used when the inventory level in the supermarket goes below the minimum required level. |
| | **Supermarket** | Represents a predetermined inventory level which the next process or customer can use or pull from whenever necessary. The supplier process will replenish the supermarket inventory once it is consumed by the next process. |
| | **Buffer/ Safety Stock** | Represents the safety stock required to continue production whenever the process encounters issues related to fluctuations in demand or production inactivity. It is a buffer for internal issues and a safety stock for external issues. |
| OXOX | **Load Leveling** | Used to level the production volume and mix. |
| | **Kaizen** | Depicts areas of opportunity and the execution of kaizen events to achieve the future state. |

## Common mistakes when mapping

- Not preparing Current and Future Value Stream Maps before Kaizen events.

- Creating maps without collecting enough data.

- Developing Value Stream Maps with the incorrect team members or no team at all.

## Value Stream Mapping stages



**The cycle to develop Value Stream Maps for each of your product/service families is to be performed twice or thrice per year, depending on the specific needs of the organization.**

## Procedure

### PHASE 1: Define Families

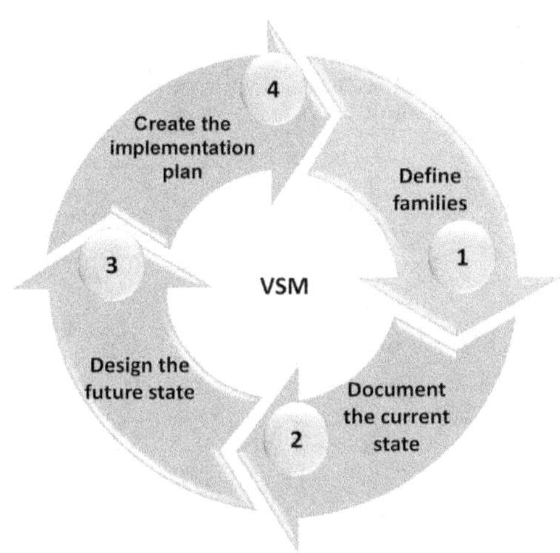



**1.1** Define the scope of the problem

**1.2** Define the service family

**1.3** Complete the process mapping charter

## 1.1 Define the scope of the problem: office/service

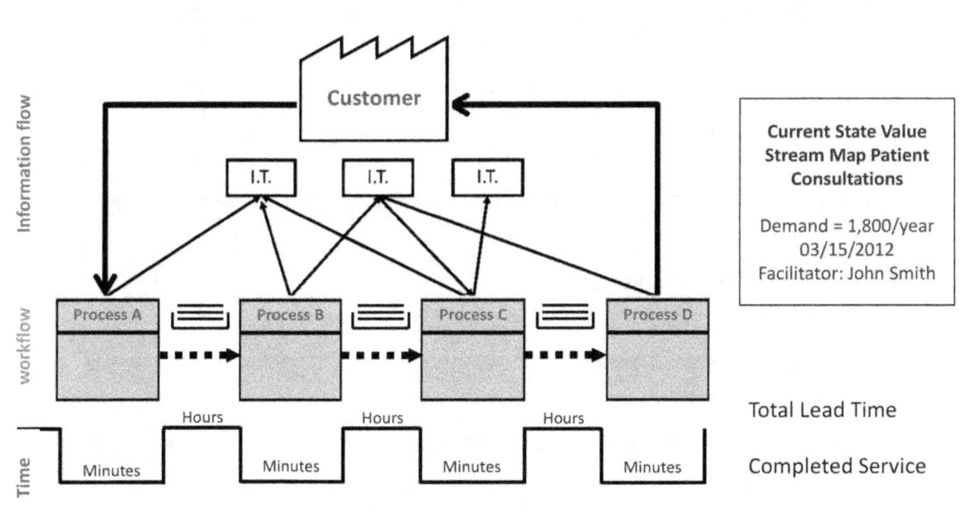

## 1.2 Define the service family

Group service families based on processes, steps/sequence, and similar equipment.

| Services | Process Steps and Equipment | | | | | | Qty. |
|---|---|---|---|---|---|---|---|
| | Step 1 | Step 2 | Step 3 | Step 4 | Step 5 | Step 6 | |
| Service A | X | X | X | | X | X | 500 |
| Service B | X | X | X | | X | X | 730 |
| Service C | | X | | X | X | | 20 |
| Service D | X | | X | | X | | 50 |
| Service E | | X | | X | X | | 150 |
| Service F | X | X | | | | X | 120 |
| Service G | X | X | X | X | X | X | 10 |

## 1.3 Complete the Process Mapping charter

### Process Mapping Charter

| Scope | | Accountable Parties | | Logistical Information | |
|---|---|---|---|---|---|
| Value Stream | What is the value stream being improved? | Executive Sponsor | Required: VP or C-level | Event Dates and Times | 3 days typically; Consecutive days are best. 6 hrs. per day minimum; 7 or 8 hours is best. |
| Specific Conditions | What circumstances are included/excluded? (e.g. Customer type, geographic location, etc.) | Value Stream Champion | If Needed: Director or Manager level | | |
| Demand Rate | How many times is this done per wk., qtr., or mo.? | Facilitator | Required: objective person leading the activity | Location | On-site, ample wall space, quiet/private |
| Trigger | What initiates the process? | | | | |
| First Step | Task on first process block | Logistics Coordinator | Not always needed | Meals Provided | Yes or no? Keeps team from wandering |
| Last Step | Task on last process block | | | | |
| Boundaries & Limitations | What is the team NOT authorized to change? | Briefing Attendees | List all people who are required to attend the briefings | Briefing Dates and Times | Typically last 30 min. or 1 hour of the day |
| Improvement Timeframe | Typically 3-6 months | | | | |

| Current State Problems & Business Needs | | Team | | | |
|---|---|---|---|---|---|
| 1 | What's driving the need for improvement? | | Function/Title | Name | Contact Info |
| 2 | | 1 | | | |
| 3 | | 2 | | | |
| 4 | | 3 | | | |
| 5 | | 4 | | | |
| Measurable Target Condition | | 5 | | | |
| 1 | Reduce <defined metric> from X to Y (Z% improvement). | 6 | | | |
| 2 | Increase <defined metric> from X to Y (Z% improvement). | 7 | | | |
| 3 | | 8 | | | |
| 4 | | 9 | | | |
| 5 | | 10 | | | |
| Benefits to Customer & Business | | On-Call Support | | | |
| 1 | How will the business, internal and external customers, and | | Function | Name | Contact Info |
| 2 | internal/external suppliers benefit from improvement? | 1 | | | |
| 3 | | 2 | | | |
| 4 | | 3 | | | |
| 5 | | 4 | | | |
| Relevant Data | | Agreement | | | |
| 1 | What data is required to understand current state issues? | | Executive Sponsor | Value Stream Champion | Facilitator |
| 2 | Examples: work volume & variation, process quality & | | | | |
| 3 | effectiveness, market trends, customer satisfaction, employee | | Signature: | Signature: | Signature: |
| 4 | engagement, financials, lead time, safety records, etc. | | Date: | Date: | Date: |

## Procedure

### PHASE 2: Document the Current State

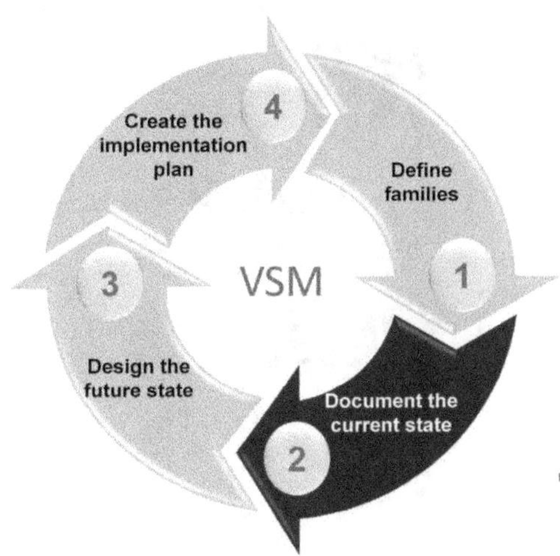


**2.1** Create a Spaghetti Diagram.

**2.2** Draw the Current State VSM.

**2.3** Calculate Takt Time.

**2.4** Create a Balance Chart to identify the bottleneck.

**2.5** Document all forms of waste.

**2.6** Quantify the current state.

- **Note:** This procedure will be explained later using an example.

## Example: Wilson Retail

Wilson is a business selling home appliances.

## Process Information

### Process Steps

The processes for Wilson Retail are:

1. Take the order

2. Confirm inventory

3. Pick order

4. Pack and check order

5. Ship order

### Customer Requirements

Customers place 8,400 orders a year.

### Time available at Wilson Retail

- 20 days a month.
- An 8 hour shift.
- A 30 minute break.

**Functions**

- Customers send their 30-day forecasts.

- Customers confirm their orders every week.

- Planning department sends its 8-week purchase program to goods suppliers.

- Orders are confirmed weekly to suppliers by fax.

- A weekly order program is generated for the billing, warehouse and shipping areas.

**1. Take the order**

- One person

- Cycle time: 5 minutes

- Orders waiting to be captured = 10

- Orders in queue for the following process = 9

### 2. Confirm inventory

- One person

- Cycle time: 8 minutes

- Orders in queue for the following process = 18

### 3. Pick Order

- One person

- Cycle time: 17 minutes

- Orders in queue for the following process = 7

### 4. Pack and check order

- One person

- Cycle time: 8 minutes

- Orders in queue for the following process = 12

### 5. Ship order

- One person

- Cycle time: 7 minutes

## Spaghetti diagram

A Spaghetti Diagram is a graphical tool used to represent the movement of people, materials and information in any type of process (e.g., manufacturing, service, administrative, etc.)

**It is an effective tool to identify:**

- **Unnecessary movements**
- **Unnecessary transports**

## Spaghetti Diagram benefits

- Provides a structured method to identify the movement of people, materials, and information in a process

- Quantifies the travel distances of items and people that are part of any process

- Prompts layout modifications aimed to reduce or even eliminate unnecessary transport and movement.

## 2.1 Create a Spaghetti Diagram

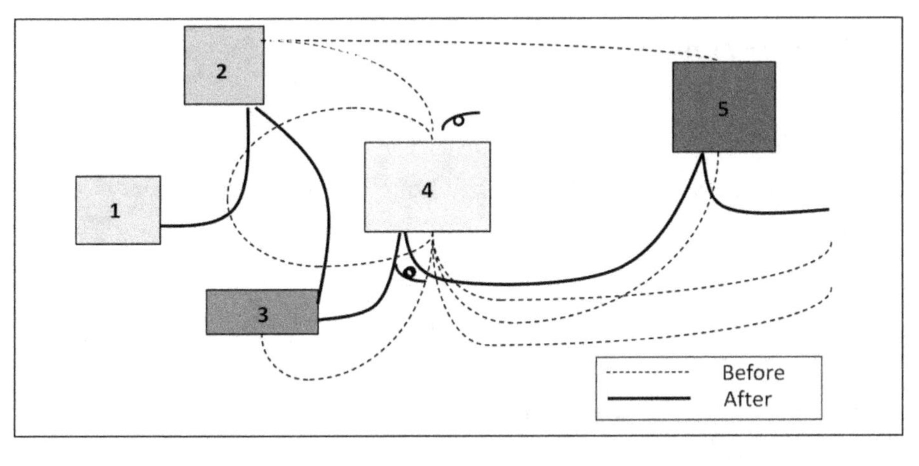


## 2.2 Draw the Current State VSM

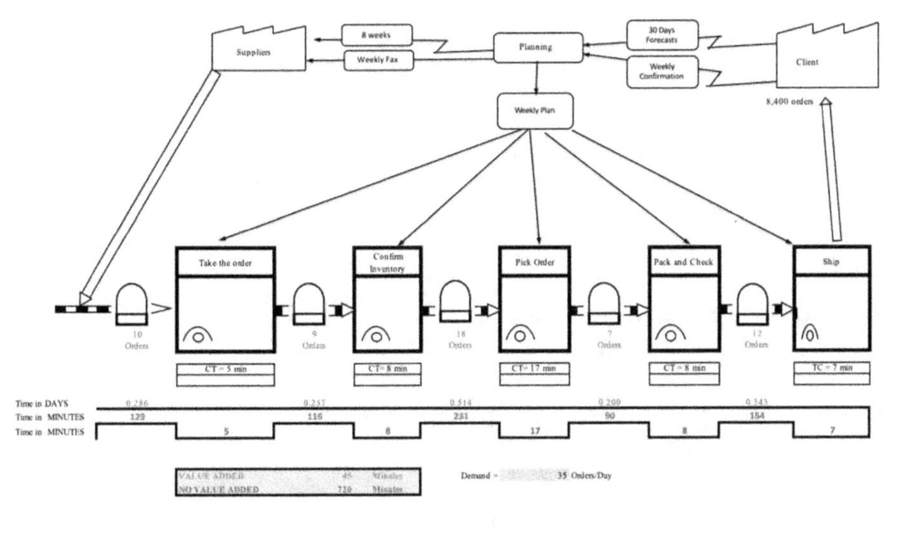

## 2.3 Calculate Takt Time (speed of demand)

- Takt time = Available Time / Demand

- Available Time:
    - 7.5 hours / day x 60 minutes / hour = 450 minutes / day

- Demand:
    - 8,400 / 12 / 20 = 35 orders / day

- Takt time = 450 / 35 = 12.9 minutes / order

## 2.4 Create a Balance Chart

- A Balance Chart is an effective graphical tool to identify:

    - Muda - Waste
    - Muri - Overburden
    - Mura - Variability

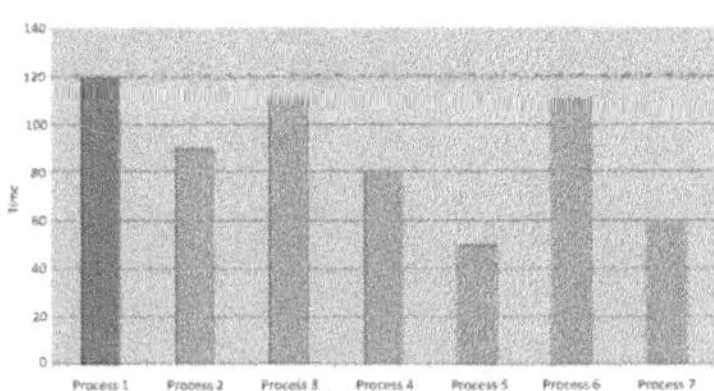


- Used to compare each worker's cycle time against the Takt Time.

- Allows to visualize, contrast and balance the workloads of every employee in a cell/pod.



**LSSI**
LEAN SIX SIGMA INSTITUTE

- The Balance Chart summarizes the real cycle times for each process.

|   |                  | Cicle Time | Takt time |
|---|------------------|-----------|-----------|
| 1 | Take the order   | 5         | 12.9      |
| 2 | Confirm inventory| 8         | 12.9      |
| 3 | Pick order       | 17        | 12.9      |
| 4 | Pack and Check   | 8         | 12.9      |
| 5 | Ship order       | 7         | 12.9      |

| Available Time | 450  | Minutes/Day |
|----------------|------|-------------|
| Demand         | 35   | Orders/Day  |
| **TAKT TIME**  | 12.9 | Minutes/Day |

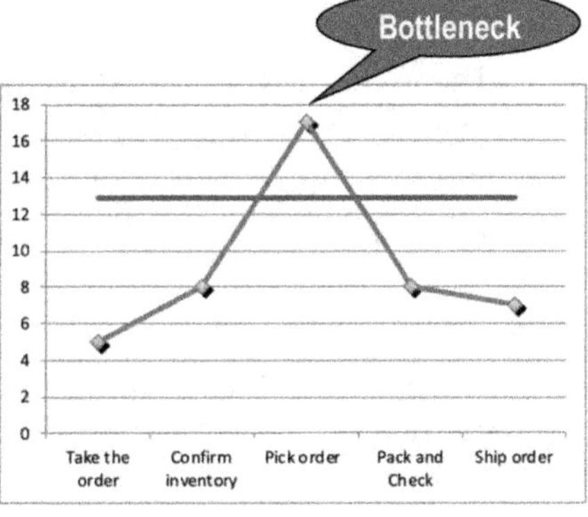


## 2.5 Document Waste, Overload and Variability

| Form of Waste | Notes | Opportunity | Proposed Actions |
|---|---|---|---|
| Overprocessing | | | |
| Overstock | | | |
| Defects or errors | | | |
| Movements | | | |
| Unnecessary activities | | | |
| Waits | | | |
| Transportation | | | |
| Talent without action | | | |
| Energy Waste | | | |
| Pollution / Contamination | | | |
| Variation | | | |
| Overload | | | |

# Which activities add value to the process?

## Identify value-adding and non-value adding activities

### Value-adding activities

- These are activities that change or transform a product or service.
- The customer is willing to pay for these activities.

### Non-value adding activities

- These are activities that consume time and resources, but do not add value to the product or service.
- The customer is not willing to pay for these activities.

### Value-adding window

Adds Value?

|            | Yes | No |
|------------|-----|-----|
| **Needed? Yes** | IMPROVE | MINIMIZE |
| **Needed? No**  | SELL TO CLIENT | ELIMINATE |

# 2.6 Quantify the current state

| Metric | Current State | Future State (Goal) | % Improvement |
|--------|---------------|---------------------|---------------|
| Value-Adding Time | 5.88% | | |
| Required Space | 15,000 Sq. ft | | |
| Quality | 80% | | |
| Lead time | 765 minutes | | |
| Conversion Cost | $125,000 | | |
| Number of Employees | 5 | | |

# Limitations to Productivity

## Objectives

1. Be able to identify the *waste, variability* and *overload* of the service that is going to be improved.
2. Identify the most important *areas of opportunity.*

## Content

I. LSS eliminates Waste, Variability and Overload
II. Opportunity Analysis
III. Procedure

## I. LSS eliminates Waste, Variability and Overload

- **Overprocessing / Overproduction**
  - Filling out and/or sending the same document several times.
  - Entering the same information in multiple documents.
  - Ineffective meetings.
  - Too much unnecessary analysis.
  - Producing reports that are not used.

- **LSS tools to eliminate and reduce Overprocessing:**
  - VSM, Balance Analysis.
  - Standard work.
  - Continuous Flow of Services.
  - Effective meetings.

- **Overstock:**
  - Purchasing excess materials or supplies for services.
  - Filling out unnecessary or excessive service forms.
  - Keeping too many copies of reports.
  - Requiring too many signatures to provide or approve a service.
  - Waiting for others to finish preliminary stages of service.

- **LSS tools to eliminate and reduce overstock:**
  - Standard work.
  - 5 S's.
  - Continuous Flow of Services.
  - Kanban.
  - Process Mapping (VSM, SIPOC, Cross Functional).

- **Defects or Errors:**
  - Errors while capturing service orders.
  - Losing documents: results, reports, invoices, etc.
  - Issuing incorrect information.
  - Errors while providing a service poorly.

- **LSS tools to eliminate and reduce Defects and Errors:**
  - Standard work.
  - 5 S's.
  - Voice of the Customer.
  - Andon: Visual Controls.
  - Continuous Flow of Services.
  - Problem solving.
  - Poka Yoke (Fail-safe).

- **Movements**
  - To search for people / documents.
  - Departmentalization - Movement between departments.
  - Movements of Customers to perform their service.
  - Movement of people who have to perform services.

- **LSS tools to eliminate and reduce Movements:**
  - Standardized work.
  - 5 S's.
  - Continuous Flow of Services.
  - Workers Balance Chart.
  - Spaguetti diagram.

- **Unnecessary activities:**
  - Duplicating reports or providing more detailed information than necessary.
  - Entering the same information in different systems.
  - Allocating too many resources / people when not required.
  - Providing more activities than necessary in a service.

- **LSS tools to eliminate and reduce unnecessary Activities:**
  - Standard work.
  - 5 S's.
  - Andon.
  - Continuous Flow of Services.
  - Poka Yoke (Fail-safe).
  - Process Mapping (VSM, Cross Functional).

- **Waits:**
  - Waits at reception.
  - Slow service attention lines.
  - Waits to get approvals.
  - Waits to access services.

- **LSS tools to eliminate and reduce Waits:**
  - VSM, Balance Analysis.
  - 5 S's.
  - "Runners."
  - Visual Controls.
  - Continuous flow.
  - Standard work.

- **Transportation**
  - Transporting Customers unnecessarily.
  - Transporting documents / materials excessively.
  - Transporting information excessively or unnecessarily.
  - Transporting materials or information when we do not know that unnecessary.

- **LSS tools to eliminate and reduce transport:**
  - Standard work.
  - Value Stream Map.
  - 5 S's.
  - Continuous Flow of Services.
  - Value Offices.
  - Spaguetti diagram.

- **Talent without action:**
  - Not listening carefully to employee suggestions.
  - Work imbalance in a department or team.
  - High absenteeism and rotation.
  - Hiring people without the necessary skills.
  - Impossible to devote time to value-added activities due to emergencies.

- **LSS tools to take advantage of Talent:**
  - Standard work.
  - 5 S's.
  - Value Offices.
  - Continuous Flow.
  - Cells
  - Talent Development
  - Effective Meetings.
  - Time Management.

- **Variation**
  - Variation in the time the service is performed.
  - Work imbalance in a department or team.
  - Inability to perform services when staff are missing.
  - Variability in the service due to lack of training.
  - Variation in the cost of services.

- **LSS tools to reduce Variation:**
  - Standard work.
  - 5 S's.
  - Teamwork.
  - Kanban
  - Talent Development.
  - Lean Accounting

- **Overload:**
  - Overtime to cover services.
  - Little planning time, too many emergencies.
  - Long workdays.
  - Too much stress at work.
  - Risky / heavy work.

- **LSS tools to reduce Overload:**
  - Standard Work.
  - 5 S's.
  - Teamwork / Value Offices.
  - Time Management.
  - Talent Development.

## II. Opportunity Analysis

It is recommended that the Work Team analyze all the improvement opportunities that exist in the area where waste, variation and overload may be revealed.

| IDENTIFICATION OF WASTE, VARIATION AND OVERLOAD | | | |
|---|---|---|---|
| AREA<br>TEAM<br>RESPONSABLE: | | DATE:<br>PAGE:     OF: | |
| MUDA, MURA, MURI | OBSERVATIONS | DESIRED CHANGES | OBSTACLES |
| OVERPROCESSING | | | |
| OVERSTOCK | | | |
| DEFECTS OR ERRORS | | | |
| MOVEMENTS | | | |
| UNNECESARY ACTIVITIES | | | |
| WAITS | | | |
| TRANSPORTATION | | | |
| TALENT WITHOUT ACTION | | | |
| ENERGY WASTE | | | |
| POLLUTION / CONTAMINATIO | | | |
| VARIATION | | | |
| OVERLOAD | | | |

## III. Procedure

1. Walk through the mapped process together with the team.

2. Using the opportunity sheet discuss the possible opportunities found.

3. Document all those that are found on the opportunity sheet and see that everyone agrees on them.

# Failure Mode and Effects Analysis (FMEA)

**Detecting Potential Problems and their Effects**

## Objectives

1. Know how to use FMEA to *prevent* any kind of problem.
2. Know how to *identify* potential problems (errors) in a system and determine their possible effects.
3. Understand how to use this information to quickly *prioritize* and *focus improvement* efforts on prevention, supervision and response plans.

## Content

## I. Introduction

In regard to the problems that we often have had to face, we also know they could have been avoided by taking preventive action.

- We are all exposed to risks in every day life.

- Throughout every process of service there are several types of risk. However, the process that can lead to these risks is often times not analyzed in detail using an organized method.

- Thanks to AMEF, risks of various types have been prevented from becoming actual problems.

# Failure Mode and Effects Analysis



- FMEA was first used in the 1940s by the U.S. military and later in the 1960s by the aerospace industry during the Apollo mission.

- At the end of the 1970's, the automotive industry began to use FMEA when high costs and liability claims affected some companies.

- Ford was the first American company that implemented the use of FMEA in its quality management systems.

- In 1993 Chrysler, Ford and GM created the document "Potential Failure Mode and Effects Analysis", which covered the two most current types of FMEA. This document was part of the QS 9000 guidelines (today ISO/TS 16949).

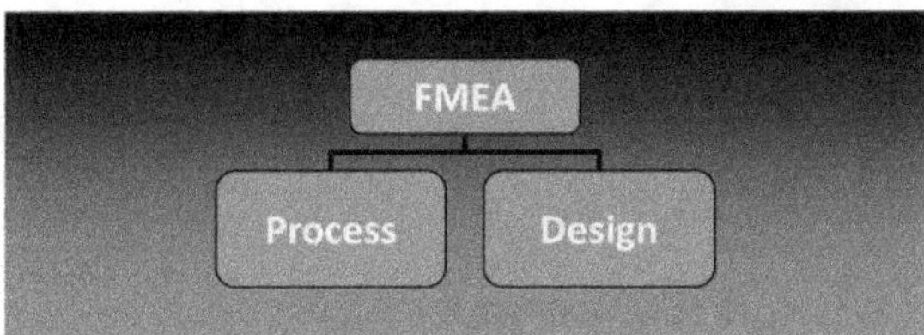

## III. What is FMEA?

It is a formal, analytic and preventive method to:

1. Recognize and evaluate potential failures of services and the effects of such failures.

2. Identify actions to reduce the probability of potential failures.

3. Document the entire process and maintain the "know-how."

4. Serve as a knowledge bank for the entire company.

## IV. Benefits

- Used to identify service functions and requirements
- Used to identify all potential failure modes caused by service deficiencies
- Helps in understanding the effects of possible failure modes on customers
- Used to identify process variables that need to be controlled in order to improve problem detection and reduce occurrences
- Helps us develop a priority list of potential failure modes to establish preventive or corrective actions
- A source for contributing to the development of control plans
- Helps reduce waste and rework
- Helps provide more reliable services

## V. When is FMEA used?

- After we solve a problem, and we want to prevent reoccurrence

- When we want to prevent a problem from happening

- When we want to understand a process in detail

- When we want to understand what steps in a process need improvement

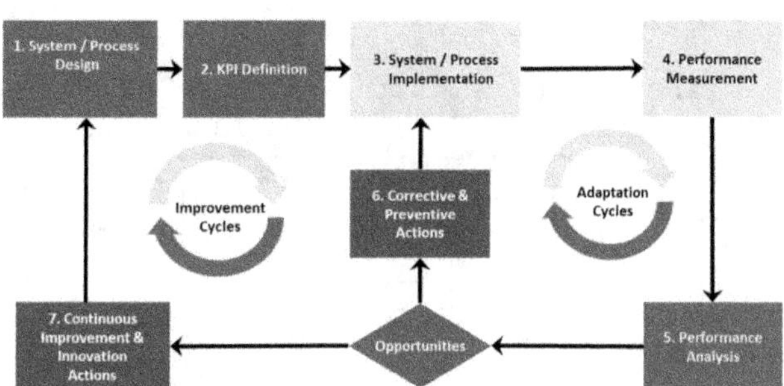


## VI. FMEA content

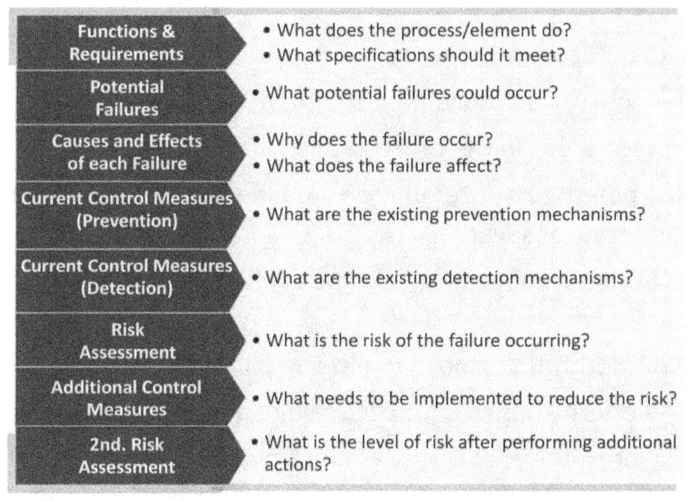

| Functions & Requirements | • What does the process/element do?<br>• What specifications should it meet? |
|---|---|
| Potential Failures | • What potential failures could occur? |
| Causes and Effects of each Failure | • Why does the failure occur?<br>• What does the failure affect? |
| Current Control Measures (Prevention) | • What are the existing prevention mechanisms? |
| Current Control Measures (Detection) | • What are the existing detection mechanisms? |
| Risk Assessment | • What is the risk of the failure occurring? |
| Additional Control Measures | • What needs to be implemented to reduce the risk? |
| 2nd. Risk Assessment | • What is the level of risk after performing additional actions? |

## FMEA Template

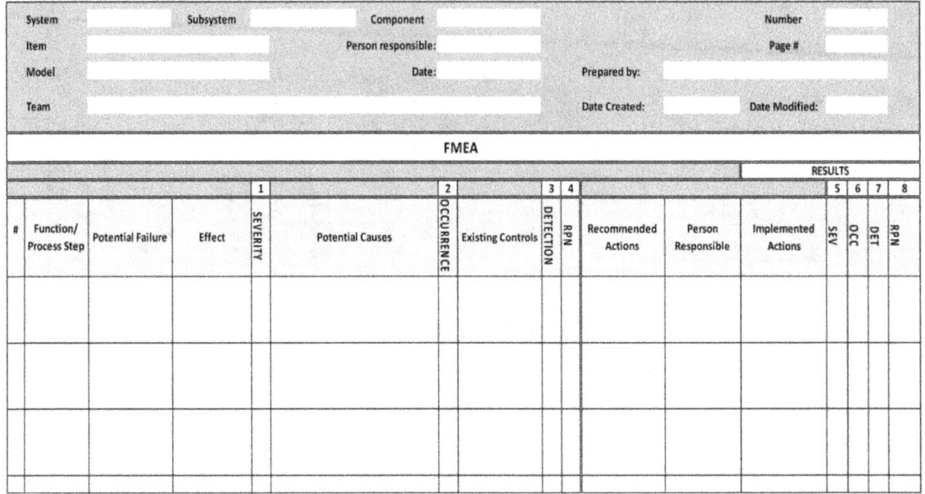



> ## VII. FMEA procedure

1. Develop the process map.
2. Form a work team and document the service process.
3. Choose critical steps in the process.
4. Determine potential failures in each step, define effects of the failures and assess their level of severity.
5. Indicate the causes of each failure and evaluate the occurrence of the failures.
6. Indicate the controls you have to detect failures and evaluate them.
7. Obtain the priority number for each failure and make decisions.
8. Undertake preventive, corrective or improvement actions.

## Severity

- Severity is the numerical value of the seriousness of the effect from the Customer's point of view.

- The severity can be estimated on a scale from 1 to 10, where 10 would be the most severe. Each effect would have a severity value. The characteristics that affect safety or the breach of governmental norms should have a value of 9 to 10.

| Score | Severity |
|---|---|
| 1 | **Minor**  (customer doesn't notice) |
| 2 | **Low** (light customer discomfort, probably will |
| 3 | notice small deterioration) |
| 4 | **Medium** (some customer dissatisfaction, notices |
| 5 | deterioration of product performance) |
| 6 | |
| 7 | **High** (High customer dissatisfaction, makes the |
| 8 | product useless) |
| 9 | **Very High** (Upset customer, unsafe product) |
| 10 | |

## Occurrence

Occurrence is a numerical value for the frequency with which the failure can occur as a result of the specific cause. Each cause has an occurrence value on a scale of 1 to 10 as shown in the table.

| Score | Occurrence (ppm's) |
|---|---|
| 1 | $x < 1$ ppm |
| 2 | $1 < x < 250$ |
| 3 | |
| 4 | $250 < x < 12,500$ |
| 5 | |
| 6 | |
| 7 | $12,500 < x < 50,000$ |
| 8 | |
| 9 | $50,000 < x$ |
| 10 | |

## Controls

- The controls describe how the fault will be prevented or detected.

- Detection generally occurs by way of a preventive inspection which may use some type of control in the service.

- The inspection may be in the next operation as long as it happens before the Customer finds it.

## Detection

- Detection is a numerical value for the difficulty in detecting the fault.

- A scale of 1 to 10 is used. The higher the probability of not detecting the fault with the controls, the higher the value of the detection.

| Score | Detection |
|---|---|
| 1 | **Very High**  probability of detecting the defect |
| 2 | |
| 3 | **High**  probability of detecting the defect (almost |
| 4 | always) |
| 5 | **Moderate** (the defect may be detected) |
| 6 | |
| 7 | |
| 8 | **Low** (the defect probably won't be detected) |
| 9 | |
| 10 | Cannot be detected |

# Obtain the Risk Priority Number (RPN) for each Failure and make Decisions

- The **Risk Priority Number (RPN)** is the product of the multiplication of Severity x Occurrence x Detectability and is a number between 1 and 1,000 which indicates the attention priority for each failure that the improvement and prevention team must work on reducing.

**FMEA RPN = S x O x D (Severity x Occurrence x Detection)**

- For RPNs (Risk Priority Number) greater than 100, prevention or correction actions must be taken to prevent failures from occurring. RPNs greater than 30 and less than 100 should be considered as second priority attention.

- The preferred method for reducing occurrence and/or detection is to implement **Poka Yoke**, **Six Sigma** and **Standardize Work**.

## VIII. Example

| Service | Reservations | | | Design Manager | J. Martinez | | | Page | 1 |
|---|---|---|---|---|---|---|---|---|---|
| Area | Hotel Paraiso - Reception | | | Date | 2/23/13 | Prepared by: | | | |
| Team | | | | | | Created: | | Modified: | |

**Process FMEA**

| | | | | | | | | | | | | | | RESULT OF ACTIONS | | | |
| | | | | 1 | | | 2 | | 3 | 4 | | | | 5 | 6 | 7 | 8 |
|---|---|---|---|---|---|---|---|---|---|---|---|---|---|---|---|---|---|
| No. | Function | Potential Failure | Effect | SEV | Potential Causes | OCC | Current Controls | DET | RPN | Recommended Actions | Managers | Actions Taken | SEV | OCC | DET | RPN |
| 1 | Reserve room | Reservation not found | Customer annoyed | 6 | Telephonist Carelessness | 5 | Nonexistent | 10 | 300 | Confirmation System Training | HR Manager | 100% Training of Receptionists | 6 | 1 | 1 | 6 |
| | | | | | System Failure | 3 | Nonexistent | 10 | 180 | Poka Yoke to avoid deletion of reservations | Information Systems | Backups every two hours | 6 | 1 | 1 | 6 |

# 5S Housekeeping

**A Discipline for Productivity**



## Objectives

1. Understand the *benefits* of working in a *clean* and *orderly* environment.
2. Learn how to *implement* the 5S discipline.

## Content

I. Background
II. What is 5S Housekeeping?
III. Benefits
IV. Procedure
V. Examples

## I. Background

Why is order important?

**I cannot find my keys!**

**Where did I put that document?**

**Where are those materials?**

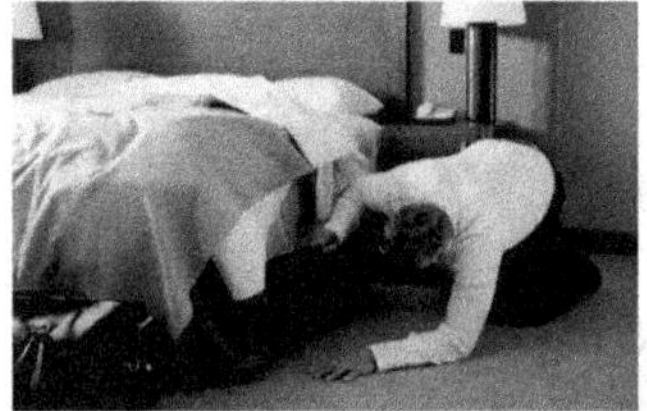  

- <u>Culture</u> and <u>habits</u> are the most important elements of agile thinking (Lean Thinking).

- 5S was developed by Hiroyuki Hirano and is considered a stepping stone to other improvement tools or systems.

- Therefore, it is said that a good improvement event is one that starts with 5S.

**Hiroyuki Hirano**



**LSSI**
LEAN SIX SIGMA INSTITUTE

## Origin of the 5Ss

**1950**

- Ford Motor Company developed the CANDO program.
- The Japanese, who visited the Ford Michigan plants, adopted it (Hiroyuki Hirano).

| | | |
|---|---|---|
| **C** | leaning up | = Seiri |
| **A** | rranging | = Seiton |
| **N** | eatness | = Seiso |
| **D** | iscipline | = Shitsuke |
| **O** | ngoing Improvement | = Seiketsu |

## II. What is 5S Housekeeping?

5S is a *discipline* that improves productivity in the workplace by standardizing *housekeeping habits* (orderliness and cleanliness).

**What is NOT 5S Housekeeping?**

- A methodology that is only applicable to manufacturing environments.
- A program to impress visitors and customers.
- A spring cleaning event.
- A system that has little impact on efficiency and customer satisfaction.

## III. Benefits

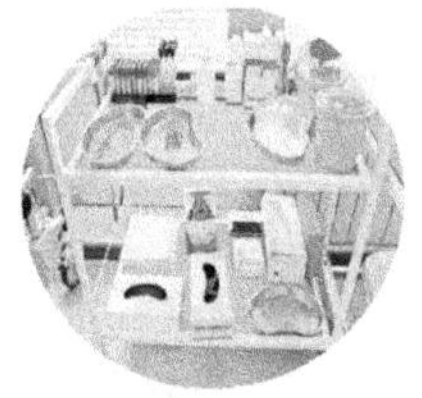

- Find anything in less than 30 seconds

- Improved employee productivity

- Improved personal satisfaction

- Safer work environment

- Higher Quality

## IV. Procedure

A **5S program** is well-developed with the successful completion of the following steps:

| Sort | Straighten | Shine | Standardize | Sustain |
|---|---|---|---|---|
| Separate the necessary items from the unnecessary items. | Organize the necessary work items by establishing a specific place for each item. | Clean the workspace and keep it clean. | Define methods to ensure that the procedures and activities are implemented consistently. | Make a habit out of 5S activities to ensure that work areas are more productive. |

## Sort – Seiri

| Sort | Straighten | Shine | Standardize | Sustain |

*Sort:* Remove all the items from the workplace that are not necessary for performing productive operations.

### Sorting process:

1. Recognize areas of opportunity
2. Define the selection criteria
3. Identify the selected items
4. Make the selected items available

## Recognize areas of opportunity

- Warehouses
- Common areas
- Offices
- Briefcases
- Binders
- Computers

## Selection criteria

You must decide what to do with the items that are **not needed**.

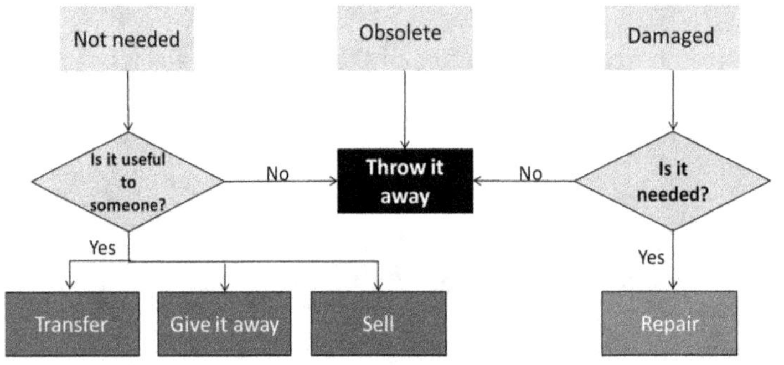


- Select what is not needed.

- Go through all work areas, shelves, drawers, etc. Keep only essential items. Store or discard everything else.

## Identify selected items

- The items categorized as **not needed** must be clearly labeled and confined in a quarantine area.

## Principle Seiri

*"Only what is needed, only the amount needed and only when you need it."*

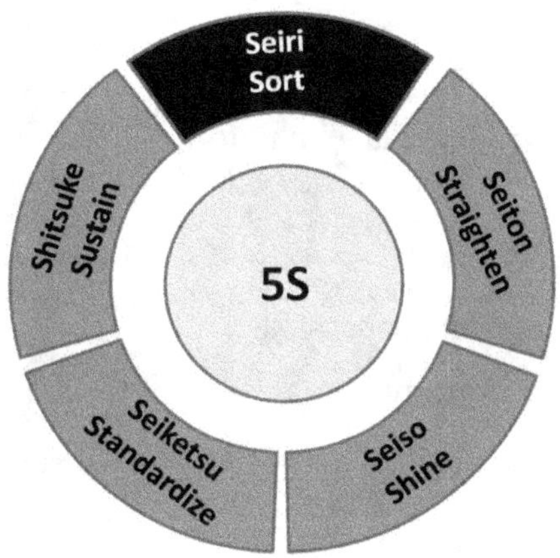



## Straighten – Seiton

| Sort | Straighten | Shine | Standardize | Sustain |
|------|-----------|-------|-------------|---------|

*Straighten:* Organize necessary work items and establish a specific place for each item. This will facilitate item identification, location, availability and return after use.

**Straightening process:**

1. Prepare the work area
2. Establish a specific place for each item
3. Establish rules and follow them

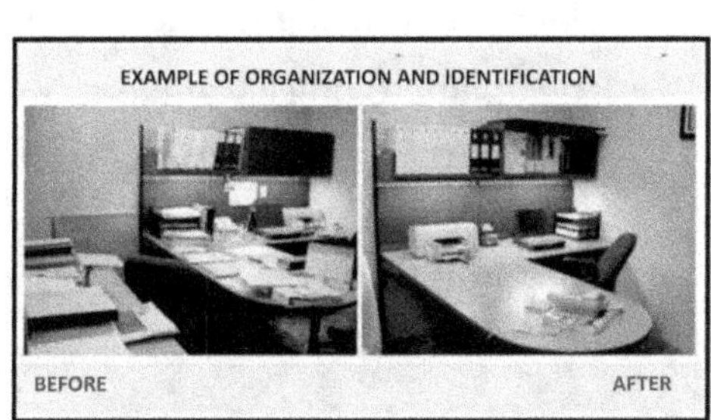

## Straighten

### Key elements

- All needed items have a designated location.
- The need to search for items is eliminated.

### Value

- Everything is organized and accessible.
- There is a place for everything.
- After use, items are returned to where they belong.

- Determine how long it takes to find the items.
    - Can you find any item in less than 30 seconds?

- When organizing, focus on:
    - Defining the location for the parts, tools, supplies and materials based on their function.
    - Clearly identifying the items' names and locations.
    - The ability to quickly and easily retrieve the items.

- **DELIVERABLE:**
    - A list of necessary items, where they can be found and locations that are clearly marked.

# 1. Prepare the work area

- **Color Codes for 5S**

# 2. Establish a specific place for each item

**"Anyone" can immediately see, retrieve and return any item.**

| Question | Answers |
|---|---|
| What? | Define which items are necessary (select) |
| | Identify the items |
| Where? | Define their correct location |
| | Mark their locations to make them identifiable |
| How many? | Define the quantity of items |
| | Identify the number of items needed |

## Straighten the work area

### What?

- Define which items are required.

- Use removable labels to clearly identify an item and use another label to specify where it should be kept.

- Provide specific and accessible locations for each item.

Define specific locations for each item so that it is accessible.

### Where?

- Store all items that are used together in the same location.

- Store items with similar functions together.

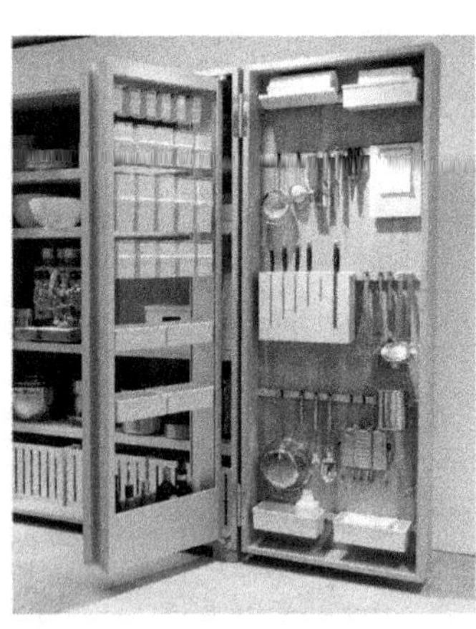

*Avoid storing items in enclosed spaces.*

### Where?

**Cabinet Identification**

- Use letters to identify cabinets
- Arrange the cabinets in rows and columns
- Name files and folders

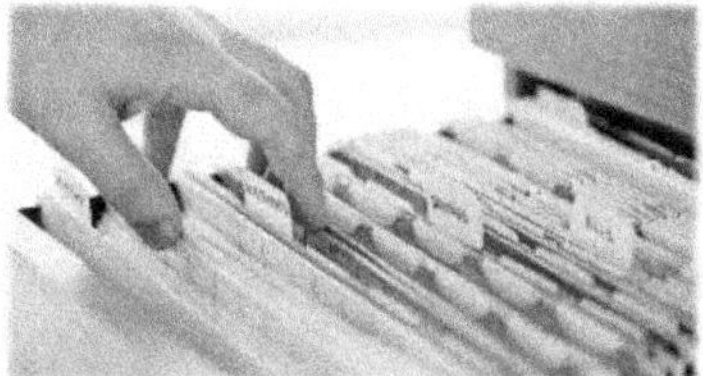

### How many?

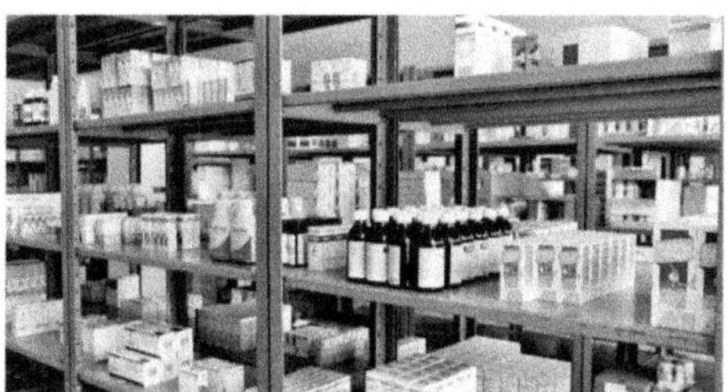

## Principle Seiton

*"A place for everything and everything in its place."*

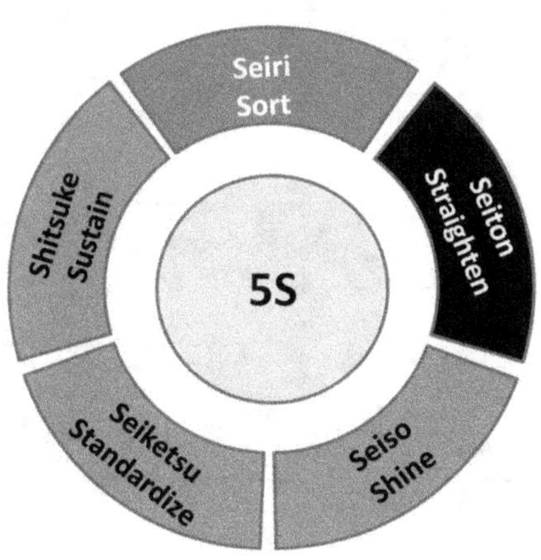

## Shine – Seiso

Sort > Straighten > **Shine** > Standardize > Sustain

_Shine_: Very simple. Clean the workspace! Remove all the dirt.

### Cleaning process:

1. Create a cleaning schedule
2. Define cleaning methods
3. Develop discipline

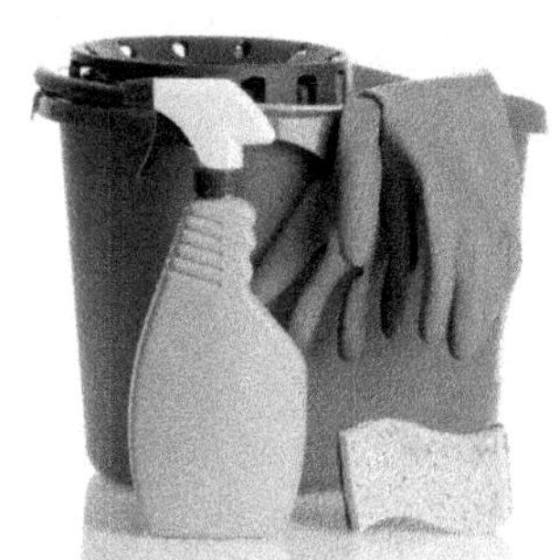

## Cleaning process

- To create a cleaning schedule, start by determining what must be cleaned.

- A good method for organizing activities is to use a map of the entire work area.

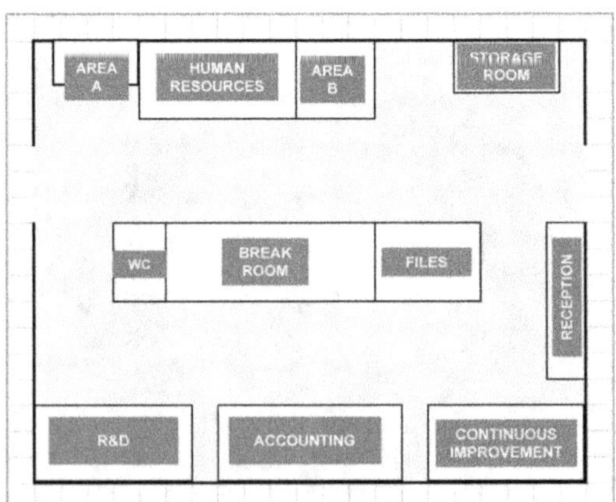

## Shine - useful tips

- Identify sources of dirt

- Always inspect while cleaning

- Repair leaks to prevent soiling

- Paint areas, equipment, floors, walls and ceilings

- Improve lighting in the work areas

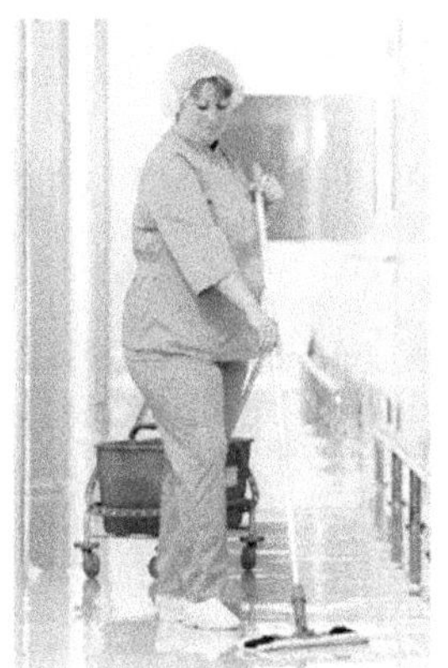

## 1. Create a cleaning schedule

Determine who is responsible for the cleaning activities, and define when and how often each activity should take place.

| Cleaning Schedule | | | | |
|---|---|---|---|---|
| *Area* | *Items* | *Responsible* | *Shift* | *Frequency* |
| Reception | Floors | J. Hobbs | 1st | Daily |
| | Desks | M. Hilton | 2nd | Weekly |
| | Lamps | H. Patrick | 3rd | Weekly |
| | Bathroom | J. Chase | 2nd | Daily |

## 2. Define cleaning methods

- Make a list of all cleaning activities

- Make a list of the items, supplies and equipment needed

- Document the cleaning activities

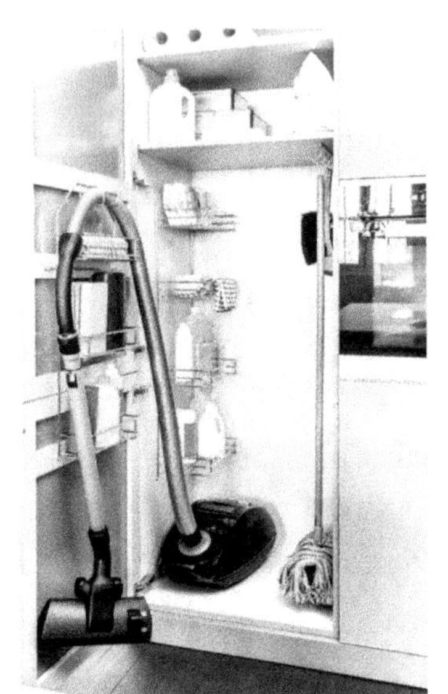

## 3-Step approach to cleaning

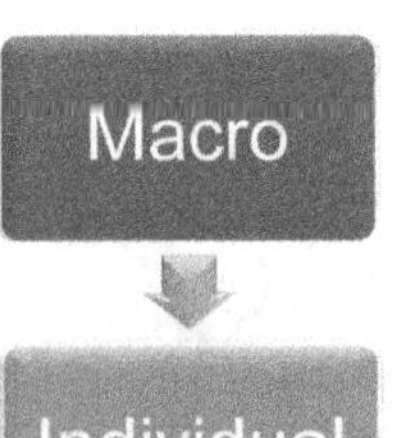


**Common areas:** surfaces, walls, ceilings, lights, storage areas, bathrooms, shelves, filing cabinets, etc.

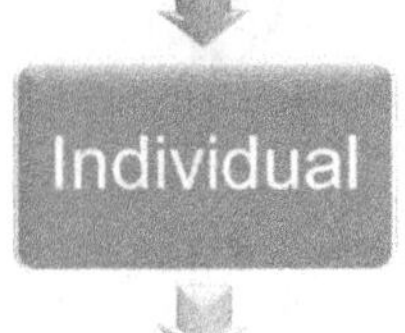


**Individual work stations:** chairs, drawers, computers, shelves, etc. Clean things under your table!

**Measuring instruments:** micrometers, calibrators, Vernier calipers, microscopes, etc.

## Principle Seiso

*"The cleanest place is not the one cleaned the most, but the one that gets dirty the least."*

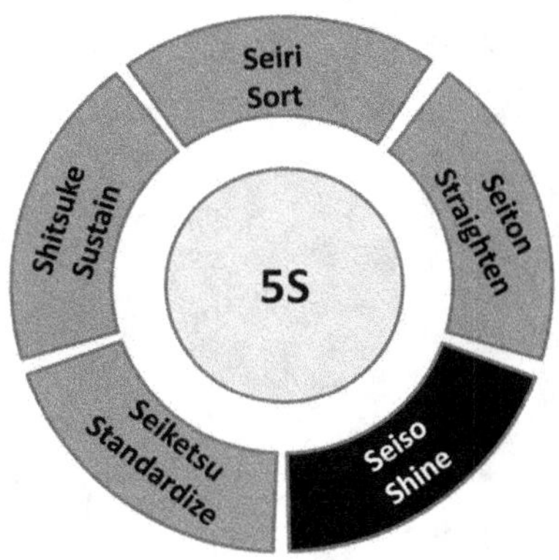


## Standardize – Seiketsu

Sort  >  Straighten  >  Shine  >  Standardize  >  Sustain

**Standardize:** Ensure that procedures, practices and activities are implemented consistently and on a regular basis. Ensure that the *Sort*, *Straighten* and *Shine* stages are maintained in the work areas.

Standardize process:

1. Integrate the 5S activities into your regular work day
2. Evaluate the results

# Integrate the 5S activities into your regular work day

- Establish procedures

- Develop a standardization manual

- Perform inspections

## Evaluation

**5S Audit**

| AREA AUDITED | AUDITING TEAM | SIGNATURES |
|---|---|---|
| DATE | AUDITED TEAM | SIGNATURES |

| | | AUDIT ITEMS | SCORE |
|---|---|---|---|
| SORT | 1.1 | There is a list of required items in the work area | |
| | 1.2 | The quantity of required items in the work area has been established | |
| | 1.3 | The required items are in good condition for use | |
| | 1.4 | The list of required items matches what is actually in the work area | |
| | 1.5 | The aisles and work areas are free of obstacles and unnecesary items | |
| | 1.6 | Unnecesary items were either sent to the quarantine area, thrown away, relocated or sold | |
| | | Total | |
| STRAIGHTEN | 2.1 | Location codes have been established for each item in the list of required items | |
| | 2.2 | Locations have been established for each item (equipment, tools, materials, etc.) | |
| | 2.3 | Identification methods have been established and standardized (color coding, location codes, organization and labeling of racks and tools) | |
| | 2.4 | Areas have been taped off according to color codes | |
| | 2.5 | The locations and codes are respected for each item (the required items are properly identified and in their place) | |
| | 2.6 | There is visual information that communicates the organization of areas, objects and required items | |
| | 2.7 | The information which is posted is up to date | |
| | 2.8 | It is possible to identify when something is out of place | |
| | 2.9 | It is possible to find any item in 30 seconds or less | |
| | | Total | |
| SHINE | 3.1 | Work areas are clean | |
| | 3.2 | Tools and required items are clean | |
| | 3.3 | Methods have been established to prevent areas/items from getting dirty | |
| | 3.4 | Cleaning schedules have been established and cleaning activities are documented | |
| | 3.5 | The required cleaning supplies and equipment is available and in good conditions | |
| | 3.6 | The team members' appearance looks clean (Uniform, shoes, face, etc.) | |
| | | Total | |
| STANDARDIZE | 4.1 | Color coding, labels and written signs have been standardized | |
| | 4.2 | Furniture, tooling, work items, work materials, etc have been standardized | |
| | 4.3 | The use of safety equipment has been standardized (for those operations that require it) | |
| | 4.4 | A standardization manual has been established (5S rules, item locations, area layout, racks, etc.) | |
| | 4.5 | Completed last weeks' audit of the corresponding area in a timely manner | |
| | | Total | |

| OBSERVATIONS | Scoring Guide |
|---|---|
| | 0 = Implementation between 0 and 20% |
| | 1 = Implementation between 20 and 40 % |
| | 2 = Implementation between 40 and 60 % |
| | 3 = Implementation between 60 and 80 % |
| | 4 = Implementation between 80 and 90 % |
| | 5 = Implementation between 90 and 100 % |

## Evaluate the results

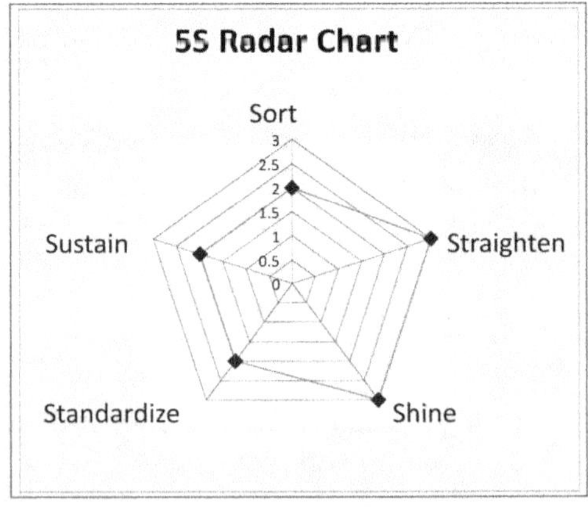


= Implementation between 20 and 40%



**LSSI** LEAN SIX SIGMA INSTITUTE

## Principle Seiketsu

*"Say what you do, do what you say and prove it."*

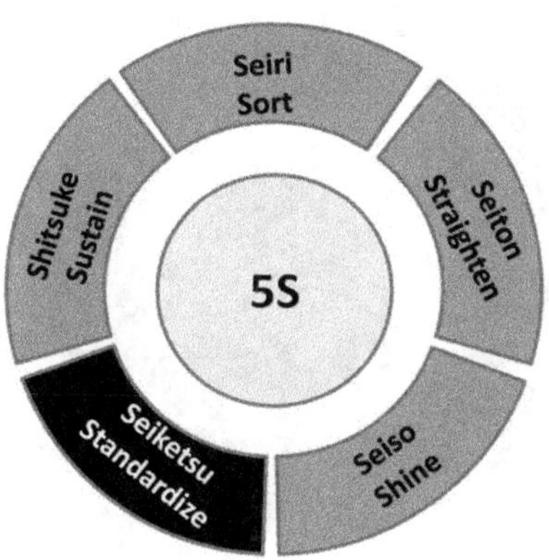


## Sustain – Shitsuke



- Have follow-up / monitoring meetings
- Improve standards
- Conduct Gemba Walks
- Invite people who are outside your area
- Have contests
- Publicly acknowledge the successes

## Principle Shitsuke

*" What is difficult is not getting there, but remaining there."*

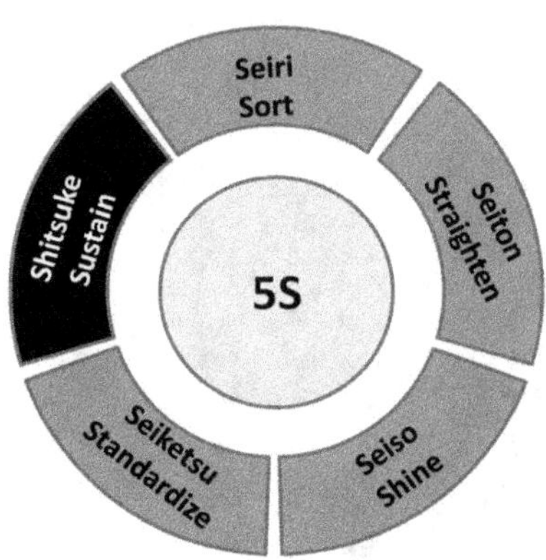


## Suggestions for implementation

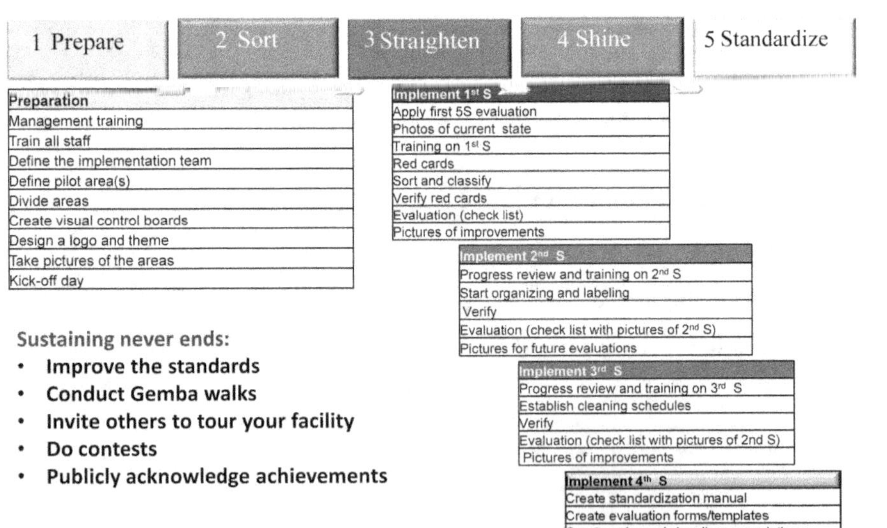

| 1 Prepare | 2 Sort | 3 Straighten | 4 Shine | 5 Standardize |
|---|---|---|---|---|

| Preparation |
|---|
| Management training |
| Train all staff |
| Define the implementation team |
| Define pilot area(s) |
| Divide areas |
| Create visual control boards |
| Design a logo and theme |
| Take pictures of the areas |
| Kick-off day |

| Implement 1st S |
|---|
| Apply first 5S evaluation |
| Photos of current state |
| Training on 1st S |
| Red cards |
| Sort and classify |
| Verify red cards |
| Evaluation (check list) |
| Pictures of improvements |

| Implement 2nd S |
|---|
| Progress review and training on 2nd S |
| Start organizing and labeling |
| Verify |
| Evaluation (check list with pictures of 2nd S) |
| Pictures for future evaluations |

| Implement 3rd S |
|---|
| Progress review and training on 3rd S |
| Establish cleaning schedules |
| Verify |
| Evaluation (check list with pictures of 2nd S) |
| Pictures of improvements |

| Implement 4th S |
|---|
| Create standardization manual |
| Create evaluation forms/templates |
| Create order and cleanliness regulations |

**Sustaining never ends:**

- **Improve the standards**
- **Conduct Gemba walks**
- **Invite others to tour your facility**
- **Do contests**
- **Publicly acknowledge achievements**

## V. Examples

## 5S Example: Pharmacy/Storage

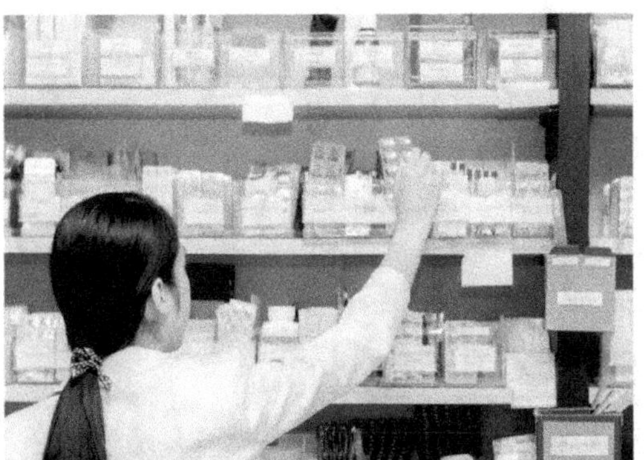

All materials are identified and in their designated places.
Wheels are installed under the storage units for easy movement.

## 5S Example: Laboratory

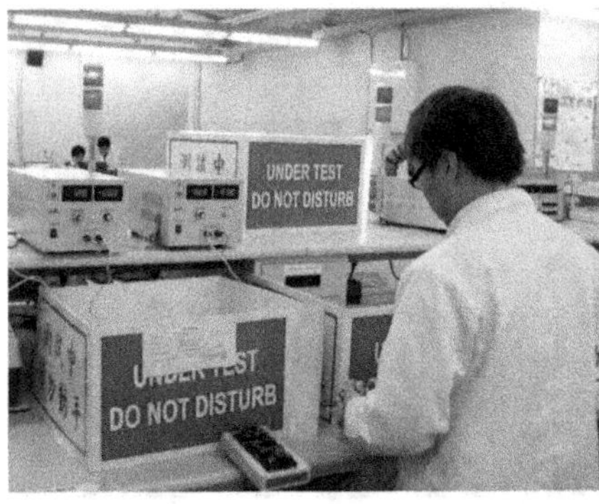

## 5S Example: Office

## 5S Example: Office

LSSI
LEAN SIX SIGMA INSTITUTE

# 14

# Andon

**Visual Management**

## Objectives

1. Understand how visual management works as an *essential* part of the Lean transformation.
2. Leverage visual tools to *improve* operational structure and stability, reduce variation and increase efficiency.
3. Apply visual tools in your *daily routines* to *improve efficiencies* in both your work and personal life.

## Content

I. Background
II. What is Andon?
III. Benefits
IV. Procedure
V. Examples
VI. Exercise

- Long ago, early humans painted on cave walls as a form of communication and establish a legacy.

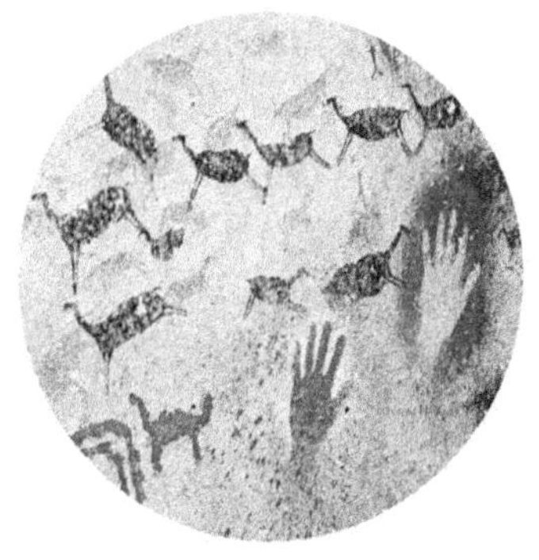

- Historically, armies recognized one another by their flags and uniforms.

## How do humans perceive information?

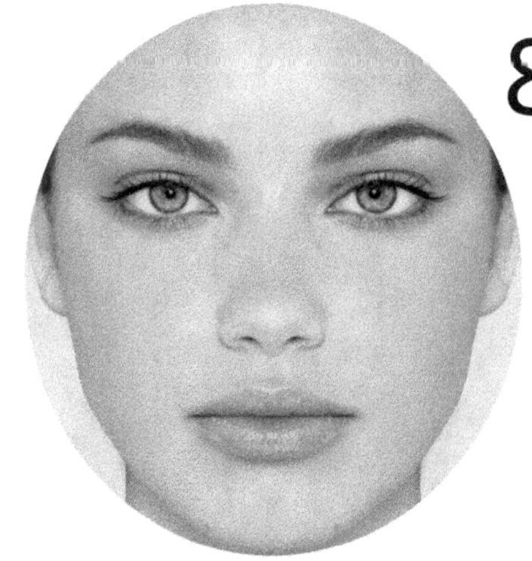

# 83 % By Sight

## 11% By Hearing

| | |
|---|---|
| 4% | **By Smell** |
| 1% | **By Touch** |
| 1% | **By Taste** |

## Origin of Andon

- In ancient Japan, an Andon was a lamp.

- It was made of sheets of paper placed around a base, with a candle inside.

- An Andon was used as a visual signal to communicate a message over long distance.

- Andon is a signal that incorporates visual, auditory and textual elements, and is used to notify people of quality issues or stoppages due to specific reasons.

- Information provided by these signals can be used to identify or indicate a regular or irregular condition at the workplace, which might require further action.

- Andon provides real-time information and feedback on the status of a process.

- These signals are efficient, self-regulating and managed by the operators.

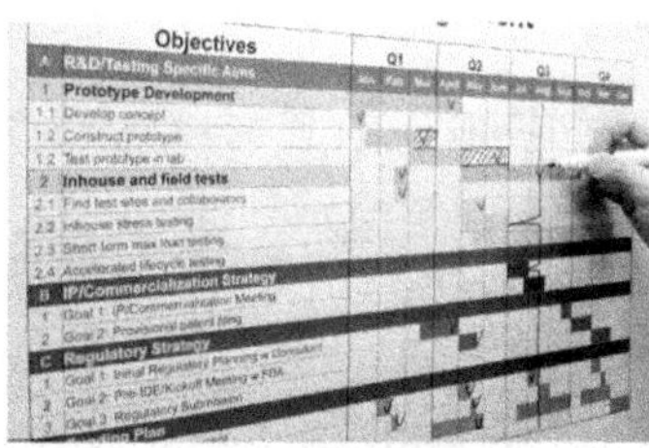

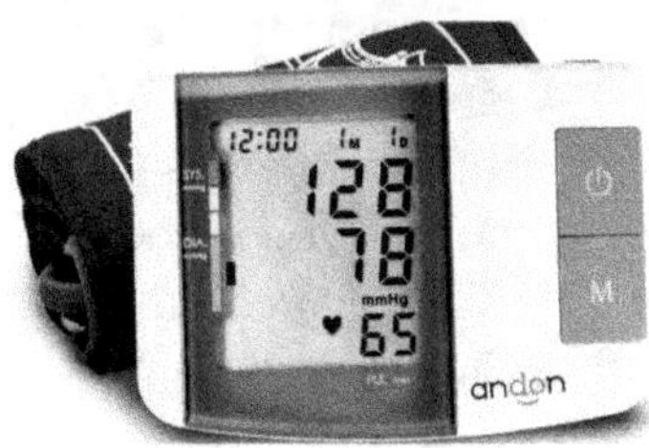

## What is NOT Andon?

- A presentation of screens and graphics to impress corporate visitors or customers

- An opportunity to fill up space on bare walls for decorative purposes

- A one-time effort, where  visual elements or information become obsolete over time

- An isolated application of Leader Standard Work

## Key Points

- Visual management is an essential part of a Lean management system.

- For visual management to be effective and sustainable, it must be integrated with:

  - Strategic management
  - Management follow-up (Gemba walks)
  - Situation analysis (Kata)
  - Standardized work
  - Project management
  - Daily management
  - Results management
  - 5S Housekeeping
  - Continuous flow
  - Quick preparations
  - Total Productive Maintenance
  - Kanban
  - Etc.

## Form of communication

A distinctive aspect of visual communication is that it helps to guide the activities of group members, so that everyone is working in the same direction.

**An Andon can be a:**

- signal
- sound
- label
- screen
- trend chart
- color scheme
- etc.

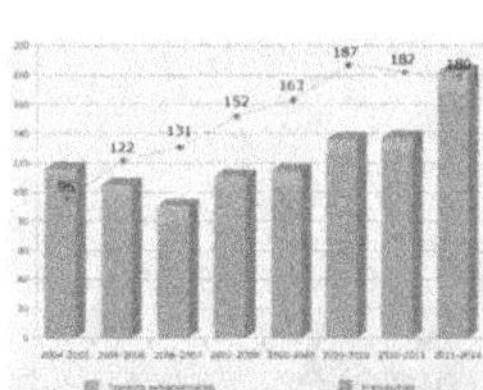

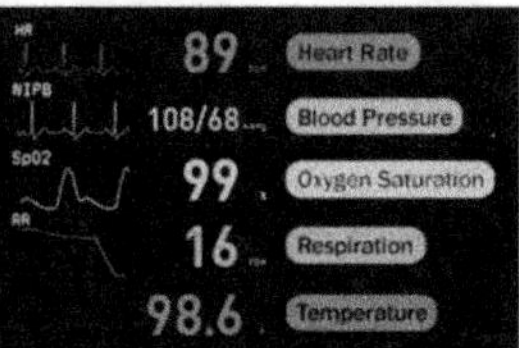


## Andon example - Turning off car lights

### Visual Control Levels combined with Poka-yoke

| | |
|---|---|
| 1) Share Information | Include instructions to "turn off the lights before turning off the engine" in the car's owner's manual. |
| 2) Share established standards | Write the instructions on the car's dashboard so that it is easy for the driver to see them: "The lights should be turned off before leaving the car." |
| 3) Incorporate standards in the workplace | Install a red light near the instructions so that both are easily seen by the driver. |
| 4) Notification of irregular condition | Install a bell that sounds immediately when you open the car door if the lights are on. |
| 5) Detection of irregular condition | Install a device that prevent the keys from being removed from the ignition if the lights are on. |
| 6) Prevent irregular condition | Install a device that automatically turns off the lights when the engine is turned off. |

## III. Benefits

- Improves Quality
- Reduces Costs
- Improves Response Time
- Improves Safety
- Improves Communication

- Provides a way to bring Immediate attention to a problem

- Offers a simple mechanism to communicate information

- Improves accountability

- Increases the speed and quality of decision-making

# Andon



1. Identify the information you want to know and the errors you want to avoid.
2. Design a simple visual way to guide and manage the activities of the group members.
3. Test the method – Seek feedback from the involved group members.
4. Train the entire group so that everyone is using the system.
5. Review and improve the system regularly.

## V. Example

Andon is widely applicable in both Services and Manufacturing.

- Hospitals and clinics
- Restaurants
- Laboratories
- Manufacturing facilities
- Logistics operations
- Etc.

# ANDON in Hospitals

Hospital Admissions

Dashboard

# ANDON in Product Family / Value Stream

- The Value Stream team meets to analyze results.

- Both the current state and future state VSMs for the next 2-4 months are shown.

- The strategies, structure and talent program are analyzed.

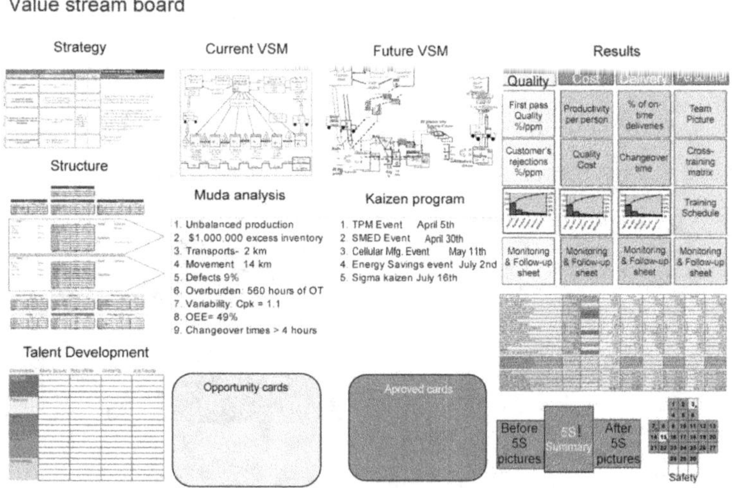




**LSSI**
LEAN SIX SIGMA INSTITUTE

## Tips for creating a visual space

- Mark all inventory areas.
- Mark the places where the equipment belongs with labels.
- Indicate visually the amount of paperwork allowed.
- Label all cabinets, shelves, etc., with their designated content.

Supplies

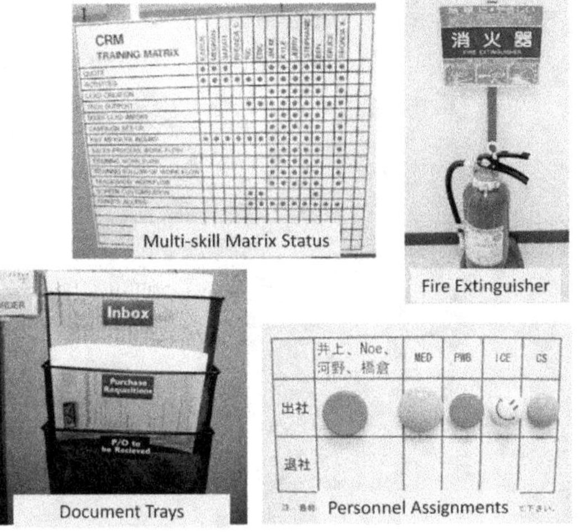
Multi-skill Matrix Status

Fire Extinguisher

Inbox

Document Trays

Personnel Assignments

## Visual signal Andons

- The visual warning sensors inform the operator that there is a problem.

- These sensors use colors, alarms and / or lights to get the workers' attention.

- They may be combined with a contact or energy sensor to get the workers' attention.

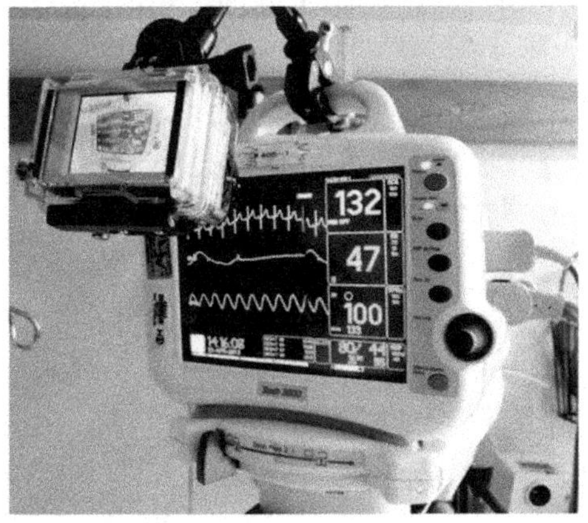

## Healthcare Andons

- Color-coded Andons indicate the status of different patient areas.

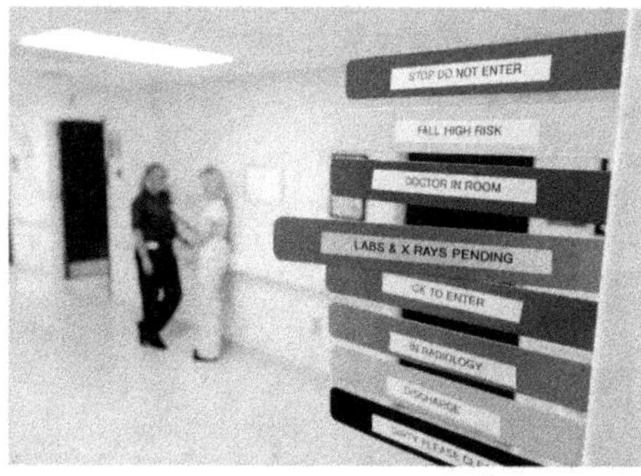


- An Andon used in a team meeting to help guide actions.

## VI. Exercise

1. In your work area, identify opportunities to apply visual management and the corresponding Andon types.

2. Design a simple visual way to show what you have learned in this session.

3. Test the method you develop. Seek feedback from others who are involved in the system.

# Total Productive Maintenance (TPM)



# 15

"When we fail to grasp the systemic source of problems, we are left to 'push on' symptoms  rather than eliminate underlying causes." *Peter Senge*

## Objectives

1. Understand the *importance* of having proper maintenance at any organization.
1. Understand the *key elements* of Total Productive Maintenance (TPM).
1. Learn the *procedure* to implement TPM.

## Content

I. Background
II. What is TPM?
III. Benefits
IV. Types of Maintenance
V. Pillars of TPM
VI. Procedure

### I. Background

- Maintenance is required by service and manufacturing companies.
- In our life, maintenance is also an important activity.

**Has this happened to you before?**

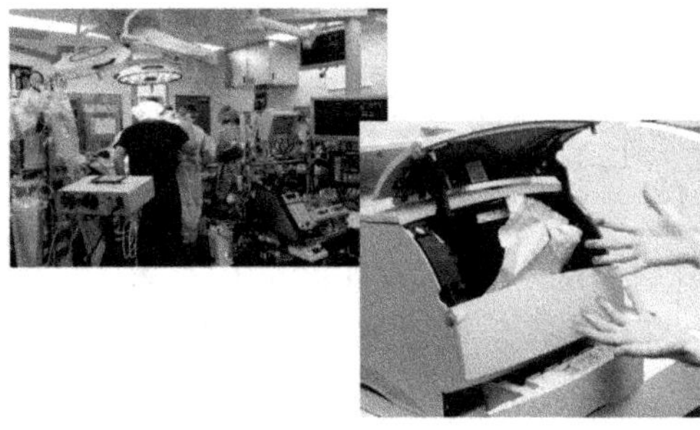

- Frequent stops due to repairs
- Failure to meet customers specifications
- High risks related with equipment
- Frequent challenges getting tasks done on time

## Origins of TPM

- Total Productive Maintenance has its origins in the United States where manufacturing companies applied practices to prevent untimely equipment failures.

- In the post-war period, Japanese business executives and engineers visited U.S. manufacturing plants to gain knowledge and apply what they learned at their own companies back in Japan.

- The concept of all company employees (not just maintenance staff) performing maintenance duties was first introduced by **Nippondenso**, one of Toyota's auto parts suppliers at the time.

*NIPPONDENSO*



LSSI
LEAN SIX SIGMA INSTITUTE

## Maintenance in Services

- Services cannot stop because the equipment breaks down or malfunctions.

- In a hospital they cannot stop operations because the equipment monitoring vital signs broke down.

- In a café the equipment cannot break down because it stops the sale of coffee.

- In a hotel they cannot stop serving the guests because the boiler broke down.

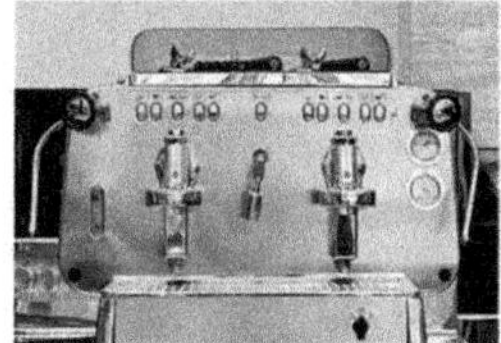

## Maintenance costs

- Maintenance costs typically account for about 15% to 40% of a company's total operating costs.

- Emergency repairs tend to be more than three times as expensive as planned repairs.

- Typically, about 58% of maintenance costs are due to the improper operation of equipment.

- About 17% of maintenance costs are due to poor equipment lubrication.

## Defect triangle

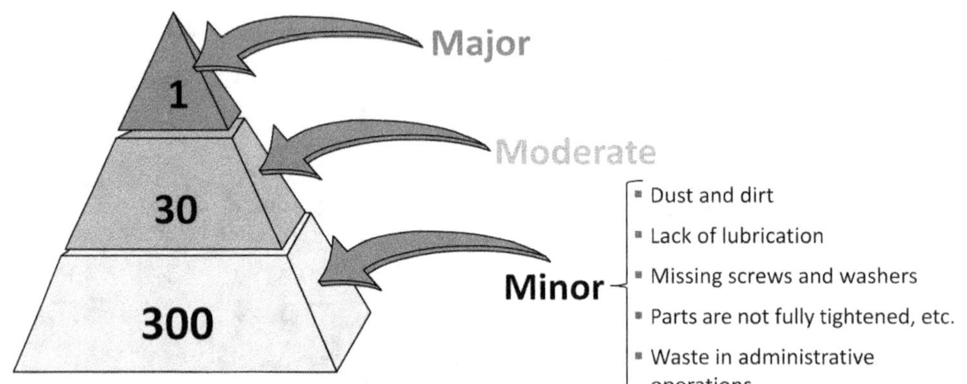


From statistical analyses of the root causes of problems, findings suggest that a certain proportion of minor and moderate issues must first occur before a major problem occurs.

## II. What is TPM?

Total Productive Maintenance (TPM) is a method to achieve optimal equipment effectiveness through the participation of all company employees. It allows the stability of services by means of the following concepts:

- Prevention
- Zero defects caused by machines or equipment
- Zero accidents
- Zero machinery stoppages
- Full participation of staff

**Leaders + Users + Maintenance**

## Definition

What is TPM?

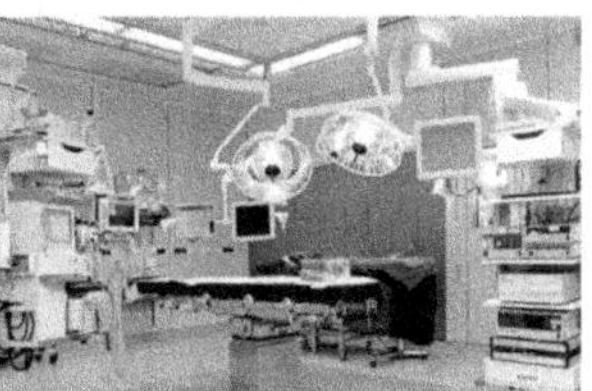

### TOTAL

- Refers to all departments, facilities and processes
- All employees are involved
- Aim is to eliminate all defects, breakdowns, accidents, etc.

### PRODUCTIVE

- Maximization of the efficiency of production/service systems
- Minimization of the productivity losses in any production or service process

### MAINTENANCE

- Establishes a complete system of preventive equipment maintenance
- Refers to the entire lifecycle of production/service systems

## III. Benefits

- Improved total equipment effectiveness

- Improved production quality

- Longer equipment life expectancy

- Reduced equipment lifecycle costs

- Converts reactive activities into proactive   activities

- Increased job safety and process reliability

## Focus of autonomous maintenance

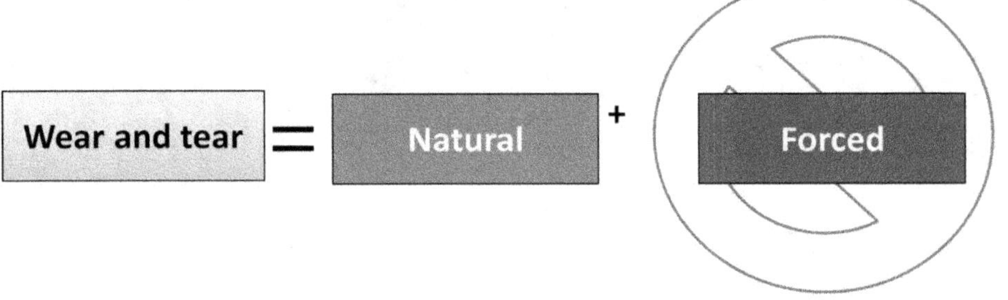


TPM helps **eliminate** forced wear and reduce natural wear.

## IV. Types of Maintenance

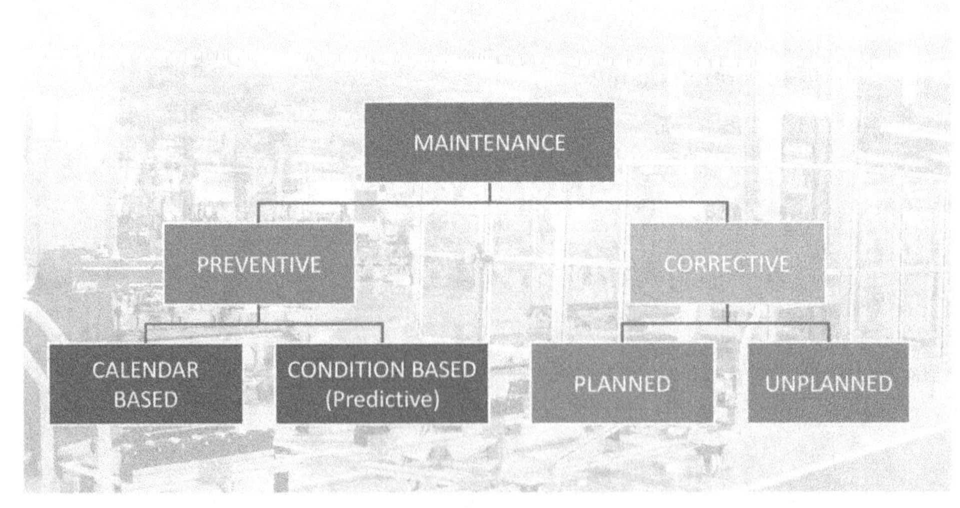

## V. Pillars of TPM

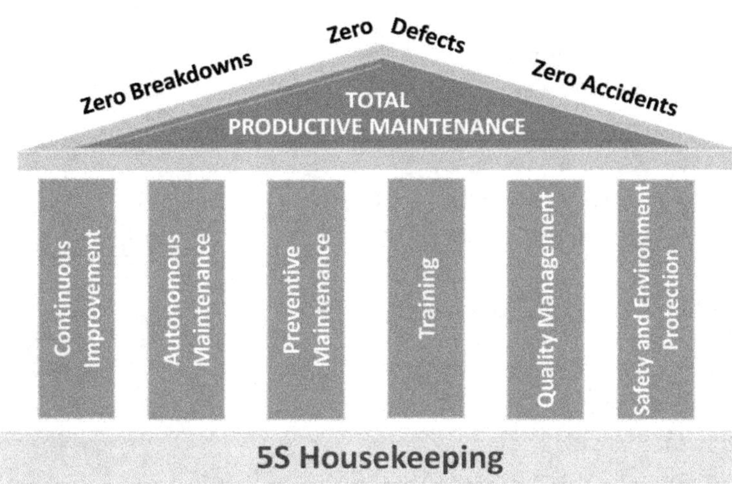


## VI. Procedure

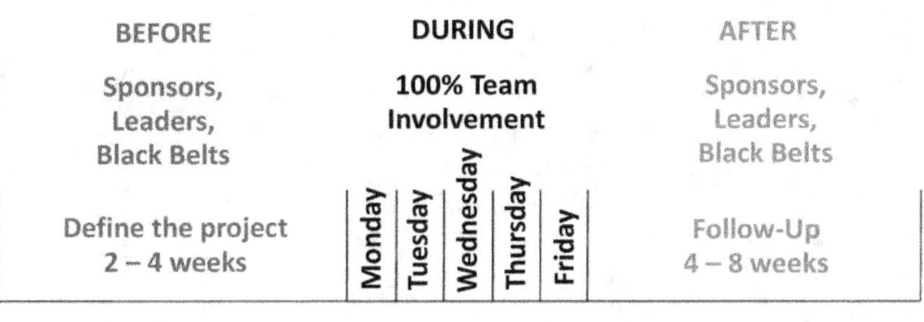

## TPM Kaizen event agenda

### Before the Event

- Define the project and team
- Implement 5S Housekeeping
- Select team members
- Perform TPM assessment
- Create Value Stream Map and Balance Chart
- Schedule the event date with the logistics and production staff
- Make sure that the following items are complete and available:
  - Cleaning supplies for super-cleaning activity
  - Opportunity cards
  - Equipment manuals
  - Documentation of Preventive Maintenance routines
  - TPM training materials

**OPPORTUNITY CARD**

| Date: | Number: |
|---|---|
| Area: | |
| Opportunity detected: (Muda, Muri, Mura) | |
| Activity to be performed: | Classification |
| Equipment: | |
| Observations: | |
| Date: | Folio: |
| Area: | |
| Opportunity detected: (Muda, Muri, Mura) | |
| Activity to be performed: | Caissification: |
| Equipment: | |

## Apply 5S Housekeeping to maintenance

LSSI
LEAN SIX SIGMA INSTITUTE

## TPM Kaizen event agenda

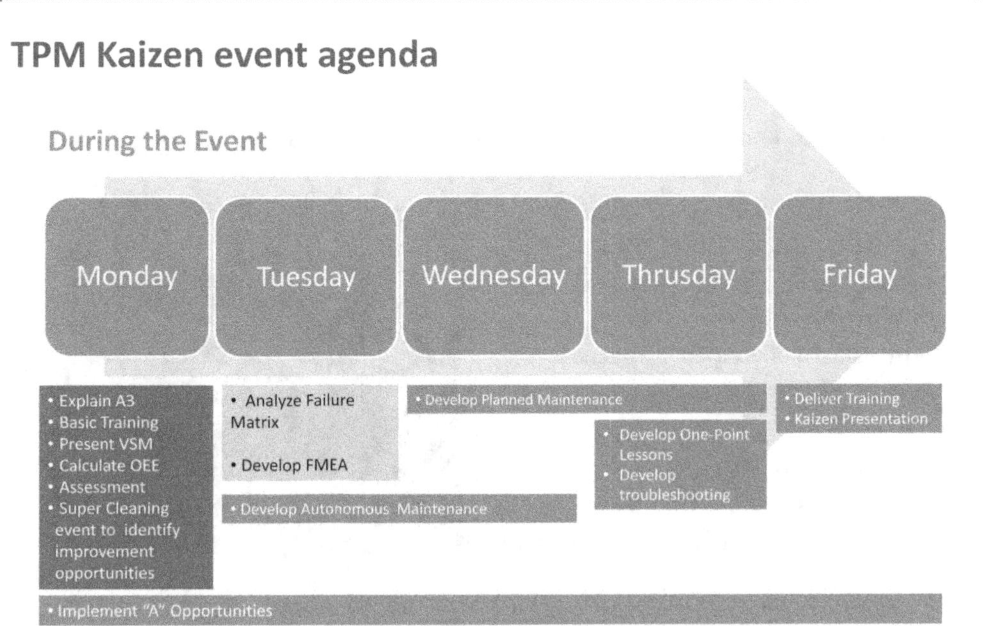


## TPM event launch - day one

- Explain A3
- Training (Approx. 1 hour)
  - What is TPM?
  - What is TPM for?
  - The 6 Pillars of TPM
  - Explain OEE and the 6 big losses
- Present VSM and Balance Chart
- Calculate OEE
- Present initial assessment

## Conduct super-cleaning event

The team really knows about the equipment and conditions when they:

- Superficially clean the machines
- Clean the equipment's interiors
- Identify leaks, loose parts and equipment, etc.
- Enthusiastically work in teams
- Document potential improvements on opportunity cards
- Identify anomalies
- Ask experts about anomalies
- Identify unsafe working conditions
- Take pictures

## Super-cleaning event

- Search for visible and hidden defects:
  - Heat
  - Vibration
  - Dirty Filters
  - Missing pieces
- Observe to determine ease-of-cleaning obstacles:
  - Improperly positioned lubrication points
  - Covers that are difficult to remove
  - Parts that are difficult to clean
- Ensure that all measuring instruments are working well.
- Investigate leaks/product spills (e.g., steam, water, oil, compressed air).
- Look for hidden problems such as corrosion and obstructions

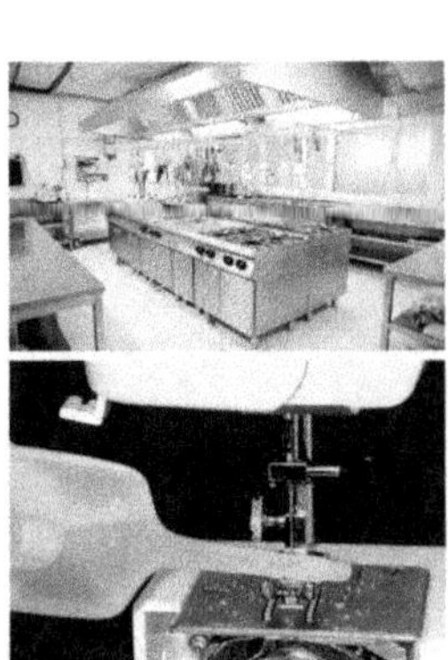

# TPM event

### Day two

- Continue working on opportunity cards
- Analyze opportunities found
- Analyze Failure Matrix
- Develop Failure Mode and Effect Analysis (FMEA)
- Conduct a cause and effect analysis (equipment-quality)
- Establish an action plan
- Develop an autonomous maintenance plan

### Day three

- Develop a preventive maintenance plan
- Develop instructions and training plan
- Move forward with "A" opportunities

# Autonomous maintenance plan

1. Set frequencies: before the shift, during and at the end of the shift.

2. Document the activities that require only a few minutes a day to check conditions, cleanliness, minor adjustments and lubrication in some cases.

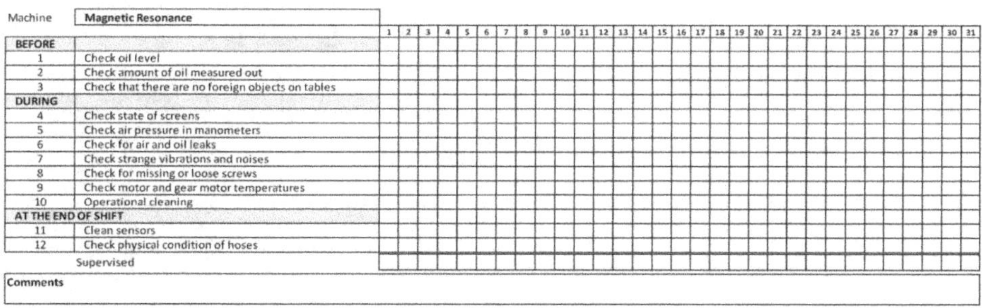

| Machine | Magnetic Resonance | 1 | 2 | 3 | 4 | 5 | 6 | 7 | 8 | 9 | 10 | 11 | 12 | 13 | 14 | 15 | 16 | 17 | 18 | 19 | 20 | 21 | 22 | 23 | 24 | 25 | 26 | 27 | 28 | 29 | 30 | 31 |
|---|---|---|---|---|---|---|---|---|---|---|---|---|---|---|---|---|---|---|---|---|---|---|---|---|---|---|---|---|---|---|---|---|
| **BEFORE** | | | | | | | | | | | | | | | | | | | | | | | | | | | | | | | | |
| 1 | Check oil level | | | | | | | | | | | | | | | | | | | | | | | | | | | | | | | |
| 2 | Check amount of oil measured out | | | | | | | | | | | | | | | | | | | | | | | | | | | | | | | |
| 3 | Check that there are no foreign objects on tables | | | | | | | | | | | | | | | | | | | | | | | | | | | | | | | |
| **DURING** | | | | | | | | | | | | | | | | | | | | | | | | | | | | | | | | |
| 4 | Check state of screens | | | | | | | | | | | | | | | | | | | | | | | | | | | | | | | |
| 5 | Check air pressure in manometers | | | | | | | | | | | | | | | | | | | | | | | | | | | | | | | |
| 6 | Check for air and oil leaks | | | | | | | | | | | | | | | | | | | | | | | | | | | | | | | |
| 7 | Check strange vibrations and noises | | | | | | | | | | | | | | | | | | | | | | | | | | | | | | | |
| 8 | Check for missing or loose screws | | | | | | | | | | | | | | | | | | | | | | | | | | | | | | | |
| 9 | Check motor and gear motor temperatures | | | | | | | | | | | | | | | | | | | | | | | | | | | | | | | |
| 10 | Operational cleaning | | | | | | | | | | | | | | | | | | | | | | | | | | | | | | | |
| **AT THE END OF SHIFT** | | | | | | | | | | | | | | | | | | | | | | | | | | | | | | | | |
| 11 | Clean sensors | | | | | | | | | | | | | | | | | | | | | | | | | | | | | | | |
| 12 | Check physical condition of hoses | | | | | | | | | | | | | | | | | | | | | | | | | | | | | | | |
| | Supervised | | | | | | | | | | | | | | | | | | | | | | | | | | | | | | | |
| Comments | | | | | | | | | | | | | | | | | | | | | | | | | | | | | | | | |

This plan is a check sheet that is filled out every day

# Preventive maintenance plan

1. Set the frequencies of preventive and predictive maintenance.
2. Set the activities to be carried out at each frequency.
3. Document them in the check sheet.
4. Have this plan in full view and near the equipment.

**Preventive and Predictive Maintenance Program**    Month ______

Machine: **Magnetic Resonance**

| No. | Activity | 1 | 2 | 3 | 4 | 5 | 6 | 7 | 8 | 9 | 10 | 11 | 12 | 13 | 14 | 15 | 16 | 17 | 18 | 19 | 20 | 21 | 22 | 23 | 24 | 25 | 26 | 27 | 28 | 29 | 30 | 31 |
|---|---|---|---|---|---|---|---|---|---|---|---|---|---|---|---|---|---|---|---|---|---|---|---|---|---|---|---|---|---|---|---|---|
| **WEEKLY** | | | | | | | | | | | | | | | | | | | | | | | | | | | | | | | | |
| 1 | Lubricate maintenance unit filters | | | | | X | | | | | | | X | | | | | | | X | | | | | | X | | | | | | |
| 2 | Grease vacuum cylinder | | | | | X | | | | | | | X | | | | | | | X | | | | | | X | | | | | | |
| 3 | Grease recording mechanism regulators | | | | | X | | | | | | | X | | | | | | | X | | | | | | X | | | | | | |
| 4 | Grease sliding base of frame | | | | | X | | | | | | | X | | | | | | | X | | | | | | X | | | | | | |
| **MONTHLY** | | | | | | | | | | | | | | | | | | | | | | | | | | | | | | | | |
| 5 | Identify abnormal noises | | | | | | | | | | | | | X | | | | | | | | | | | | | | | | | | |
| 6 | Check safety micros | | | | | | | | | | | | | | X | | | | | | | | | | | | | | | | | |
| 7 | Clean floor and refrigerant lines | | | | | | | | | | | | | | X | | | | | | | | | | | | | | | | | |
| 8 | Keep the area clean in general | | | | | | | | | | | | | | X | | | | | | | | | | | | | | | | | |
| **SIX-MONTHLY** | | | | | | | | | | | | | | | | | | | | | | | | | | | | | | | | |
| 9 | Check bearings | X | | | | | | | | | | | | | | | | | | | | | | | | | | | | | | |
| **ANNUAL** | | | | | | | | | | | | | | | | | | | | | | | | | | | | | | | | |
| 10 | Check connections | | | | | | | | | | | | X | | | | | | | | | | | | | | | | | | | |

Supervised

Comments

# Document the procedure in a manual

1. The manual is the same as we already saw in standard work.
2. Document all safety considerations.

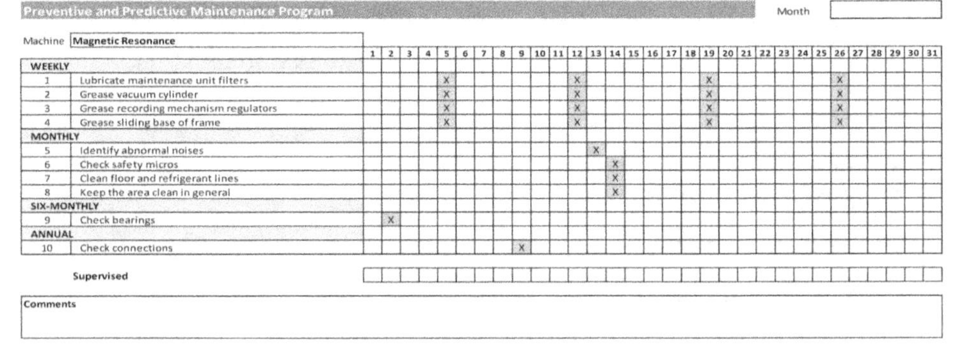

| No. | Activity | Specification | Requirement |
|---|---|---|---|
| **BEFORE** | | | |
| 1 | Check oil level | At 50% of the container capacity | Visual |
| 2 | Check height of safety stop in head cage | 1/4 inch below the nozzles | Level |
| 3 | Check cleanliness of conveyor and guide rails | Dust and oil free | Visual |
| 4 | Check amount of oil measured out | 1 drop per minute | Visual |
| 5 | Check that there are no foreign objects on patient table | Free of foreign objects | Visual |
| **DURING** | | | |
| 6 | Check style of screens | Whole and clean | Visual |
| 7 | Check air pressure in manometers | Pressure = 0.5 - 1.0 PSI | Visual |
| 8 | Check for air and oil leaks | No leakage | Visual and additive |
| 9 | Check speed of conveyor chain | 63 RPM | Visual |
| 10 | Check oil level in lubricating cup | Visible in the peephole | Visual |
| 11 | Check strange vibrations and noises | Pending determination of standard | Pen vibration meter |
| 12 | Check for missing or loose screws | Screws in place and tight | Visual |
| 13 | Check motor and gear motor temperatures | 40 - 45 °C | Thermometer |
| 14 | Operational cleaning | Equipment free of dust and excess grease | Visual |
| **AT THE END OF SHIFT** | | | |
| 15 | Clean sensors | Dust and oil free | Visual |
| 16 | Clean excess release agent lubricant | Equipment free of dust and excess grease | Visual |
| 17 | Change and clean mist recovery filter | Dust free | Visual |
| 18 | Check for air and oil leaks | No leakage | Visual and additive |
| 19 | Check physical condition of hoses | No leakage | Visual and additive |

| Notes and/or Precautions: | |
|---|---|
| Always wear gloves and safety glasses | |
| Lubricate with equipment turned off | |

| Conducted by: | Ismael Bueno |
|---|---|
| Completion date: | 11/05/2009 |
| Last inspection: | 11/05/2009 |
| Approved: | Eng. Alfonso Martínez |
| Version: | 1 |

## Day Four

- Develop one-point lessons (OPL)
- Develop troubleshooting charts
- Finish "A" opportunities

## One-Point lessons (OPL)

- Focused training
- 10 minutes
- Theory
- Practice
- Everyone participates
- Based on instructions

## Day five

- Deliver Training on:
  - Correct use of equipment
  - Autonomous maintenance
  - Planned maintenance
  - Equipment safety
- Present results (Kaizen picture)
  - Introduce the team
  - What was our initial situation?
  - What did we do?
  - What did we accomplish?
  - What's next?

## Follow-up agenda

### After the event

- Conduct daily or weekly analysis meetings
- Visit the equipment to analyze progress
- Continue working on "B" and "C" improvement opportunities
- Analyze OEE progress through daily or weekly box score
  - Review activities at the Gemba according to TPM instructions
- Apply acquired knowledge to improve other equipment

**LSSI**
LEAN SIX SIGMA INSTITUTE

## Sustain TPM

- Management teams walk the process (Gemba Walk)
- Employ qualified personnel
- Active guidance to implement TPM
- Celebrate successes
- Show appreciation
- Continuous improvement of Overall Equipment Effectiveness (OEE)
- Expand and implement to all processes that require the use of equipment (service and manufacturing)

# Continuous Flow

**A way for your product or service to flow continuously**

## Objectives

1. Learn how to design *uninterrupted* processes.
2. Understand the concept of *Work Cells* or *Office pods.*
3. Learn the *procedure* to develop Continuous Flow.

## Content

## I. Background

- In 1776, Adam Smith, a Scottish economist and philosopher, demonstrated that dividing labor into specific tasks would result in increased productivity.

- Frederick Taylor, the father of scientific management, agreed with this concept. He introduced the idea of dedicating specialized labor to repetitive tasks in order to achieve a more productive flow.

- The implementation of production lines, a concept developed by Henry Ford, who supported the idea of specialized labor by using large assembly lines.

- Today, demand and volume conditions have changed from large lot sizes of the same product to small lot sizes with a high mix of products. These changes make it difficult for companies to succeed using these early methods.

- As a result, beginning with Shigeo Shingo's first implementations at Toyota, Lean promotes continuous workflow as a core principle.

- It is a common practice to transfer workers from one value stream to another according with the demand.



**LSSI**
LEAN SIX SIGMA INSTITUTE

## II. What is Continuous Flow?

- **Continuous Flow** is a process concept designed to significantly improve a facility's layout and create uninterrupted work flow between operations.

- As a result, employees' skills and performances are optimized and response times are dramatically reduced.

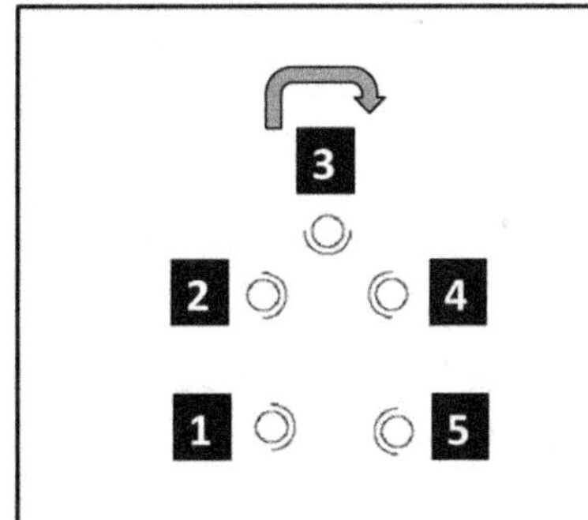


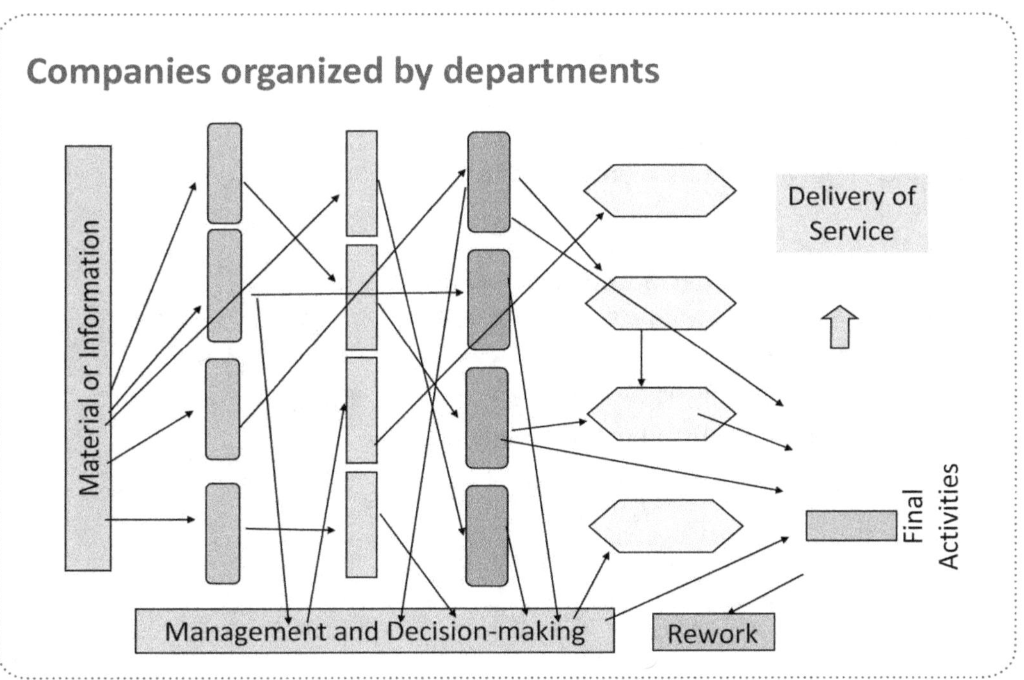

## Problems related to organization by departments

- Defects may not be detected until the service is performed or the product is finished.

- Material handling results in an increased number of defects.

- People and parts spend extensive waiting times between each phase of the process.

- Materials and product inventory consume too much space.

## What are Workcells or Pods?

In Lean methodology, **Continuous Flow** is applied through the implementation of Workcells and Pods.

Workcells and Pods are work structures that connect the activities of a process according to specific considerations:

- Workload balancing effectiveness
- Adaptation to customers requirements
- Enhancement of Process/Service capability
- Assurance of Continuous Flow
- Layout optimization

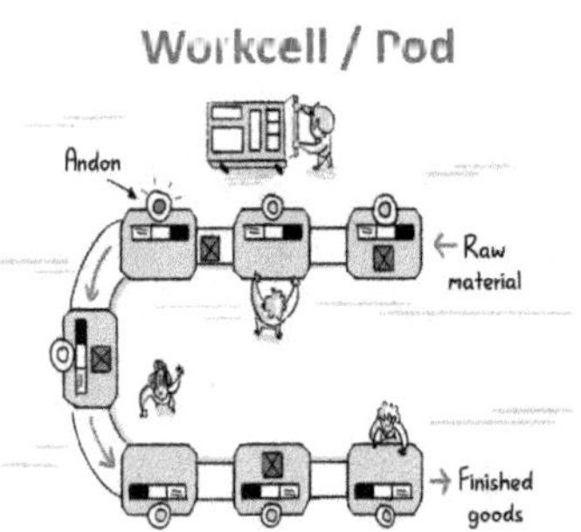

## Example of a Work Cell

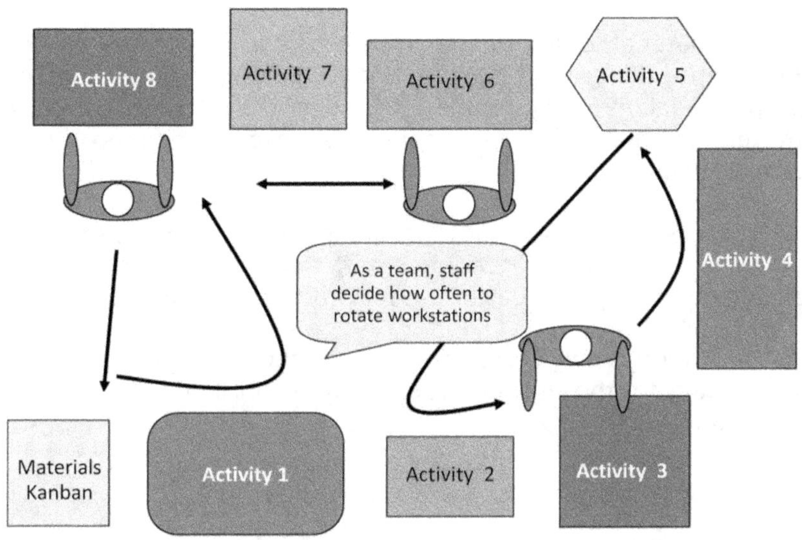




- Significant reduction in response time.

- Improves teamwork and communication – the team members are closer to each other and have better opportunities to help one another.

- Ensures a complete understanding of the entire work process.

- Promotes a work environment where team members feel a greater sense of control, ownership and responsibility for their activities.

- Leads to greater employee satisfaction.

### IV. Key elements: Layout waste

- **Transport:** Materials or information must travel to other areas where the next step in the process is located. Moving things around an office takes time and does not add value.  The longer the distance that things are moved, the more effort and resources are expended for no additional value.

- **Space:** There is also a cost associated with storing, managing and maintaining inventory; and it requires staff, time, funding and physical space that could be put to better use for other value-added activities.

- **Delays:** Batch processing causes delays while the first unit of service of the batch waits for the last unit of service to be finished before moving to the next process.

## Where does an increase in productivity come from?

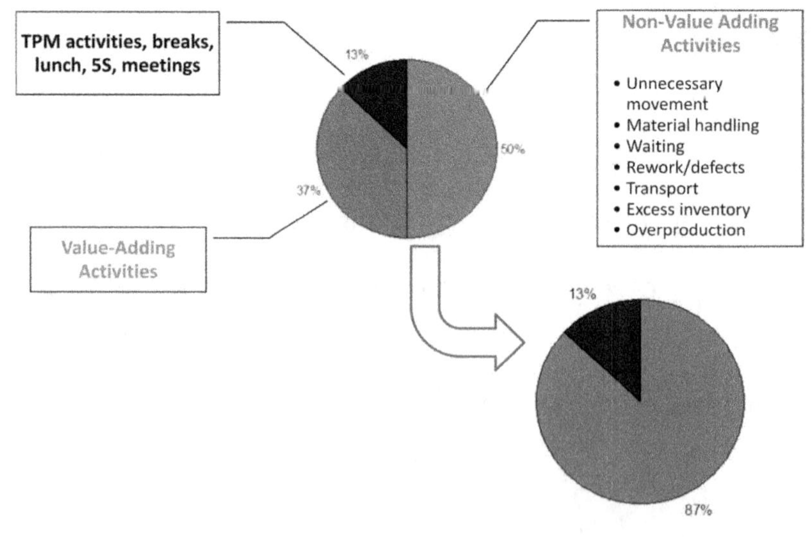

## Continuous Flow requirements

- Cells or pods are designed for every service family (they share the same or similar steps of the process and work teams)

  Flexible and multi-skilled employees

- 5 to 12 team members (at least 2 people working in the selected process)

- Maintenance personnel, if applicable

- Quality personnel

- Process engineers, if available

- Supervisors

- Cost accounting staff

- Trainers

## VI. When do we implement Continuous Flow?

- When lead time needs to be substantially reduced

- When we need to produce a higher-mix and lower volume of products or services

- When the demand for products or services is difficult to forecast

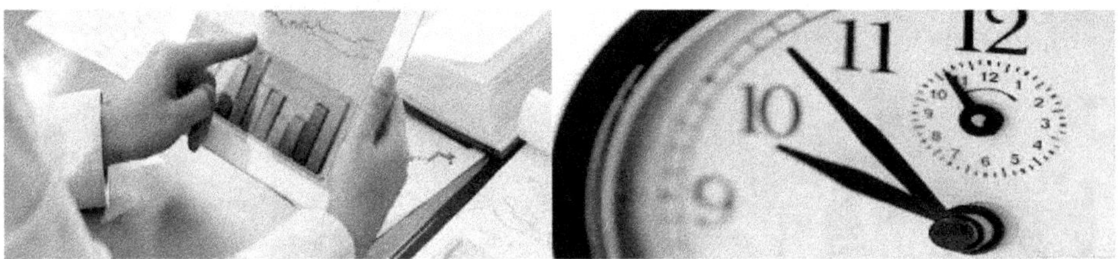

## VII. Kaizen event procedure

### Before the event

Kaizen events are planned with time in advance. During this planning phase, the following is accomplished:

1. Select a product or service family and draw a Value Stream Map (current and future).
2. The event opportunities are identified and proposed.
3. The team leader is selected.
4. The event sponsor is selected (this is a person who has authority and is capable of making decisions to support the teams' proposals).
5. The team is selected. Sometimes, customers and suppliers are invited to participate.
6. The event plan and logistics are prepared (e.g., meeting room, event area, tools, etc.).
7. The project documentation is prepared.

## During the event

1. Draw a Spaghetti Diagram and analyze waste (Muda) and identify opportunities.

2. Calculate takt time and capacity and determine the number of process employees.

3. Design and balance the work cells or Pods.

4. Simulate the different options with the team members in the workplace (use cardboard boxes, tape on the floor, etc.).

5. Implement the work cells or Pods.

6. Practice the operation with the team and make changes if necessary.

7. Apply ergonomics to the workstations' designs.

8. Document the new process and train the personnel.

## VIII. Example

A service company has a departmental structure. The management team has decided to transform the process into a Pod for a family of services. There are eight operations performed on the process (identified as codes A - H). The cycle times are shown below. The Takt Time for the family is **79** seconds.

| OPERATION CODE | CYCLE TIME (SECS.) |
|:---:|:---:|
| A | 32 |
| B | 35 |
| C | 40 |
| D | 42 |
| E | 20 |
| F | 42 |
| G | 160 |
| H | 15 |
| **TOTAL CYCLE TIME** | **386** |

## Determine the number of workers

- To determine the number of team members required, divide total cycle time (386 seconds) by the takt time (79 seconds), which equals **4.88** workers.

- Ideally, 5 team members combined will produce one unit of service every 79 seconds. This is considering a scenario where that there are no delays or interruptions, team members are utilized 100% of the time, and they are all contributing to multiple operations.

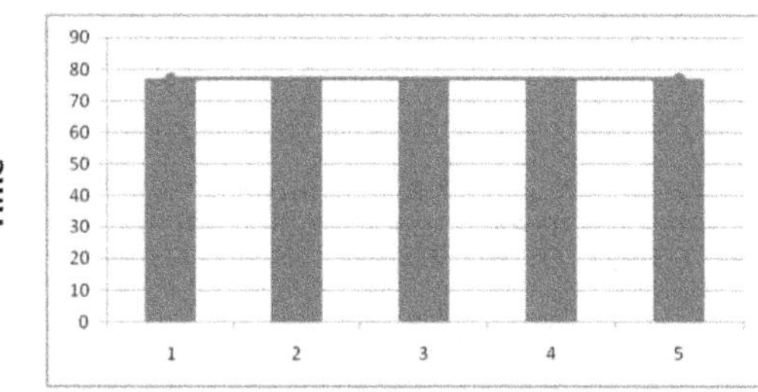


| Operator | Cycle Time | Takt Time |
|---|---|---|
| 1 | 77.2 | 79 |
| 2 | 77.2 | 79 |
| 3 | 77.2 | 79 |
| 4 | 77.2 | 79 |
| 5 | 77.2 | 79 |

## Balancing of operations

- When implementing **Continuous Flow**, some operations are reassigned in order to obtain the desired takt time.

| Operator | Time (Secs.) | Operation Code |
|---|---|---|
| 1 | 67 | A + B |
| 2 | 82 | C + D |
| 3 | 77 | E + F + part of G |
| 4 | 77 | Part of G |
| 5 | 83 | Part of G + H |
| Total Cycle Time | 386 | |

## Conclusions

- One or more operations are assigned to each team member to most efficiently use their time. However, process improvements should be implemented to reduce the time of team member 2 and 5 so that they can produce faster than the takt time.

- It is important to note that this first design is ideal, but that the operations should be further studied to determine the relative ease of combining operations.

Takt time = **79 sec.**

Redesign operations

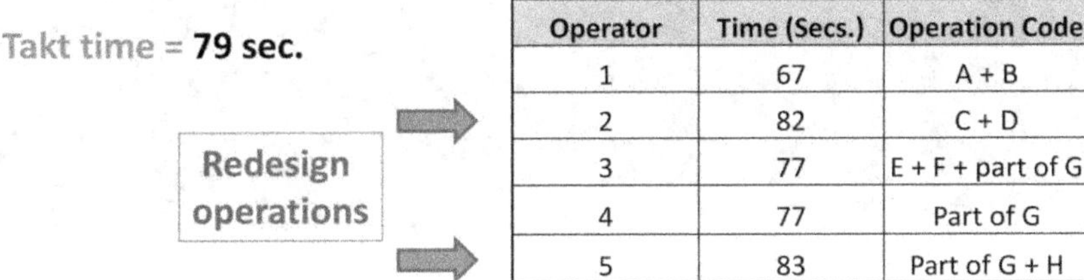

| Operator | Time (Secs.) | Operation Code |
|----------|--------------|----------------|
| 1 | 67 | A + B |
| 2 | 82 | C + D |
| 3 | 77 | E + F + part of G |
| 4 | 77 | Part of G |
| 5 | 83 | Part of G + H |

## Drawing a new Cell

- First draw the inner workstation area and then locate the first and last operation at each end of the U.

- Next, insert the second and second to last operations in succession, until the U is closed.

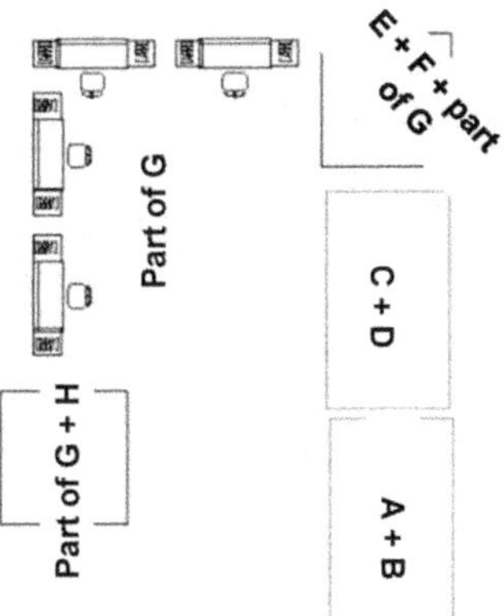

## Simulate

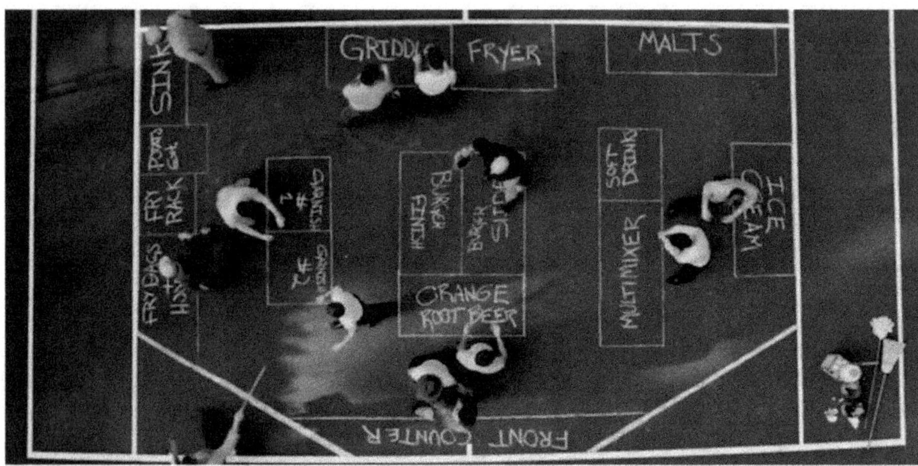


Source: Movie "Founder". Mc Donald's system

## Ergonomic design considerations

1. Height

2. Space available (reach)

3. Positioning of materials

4. Working below the heart

5. Visual fields

6. Illumination

7. Adjustable positions

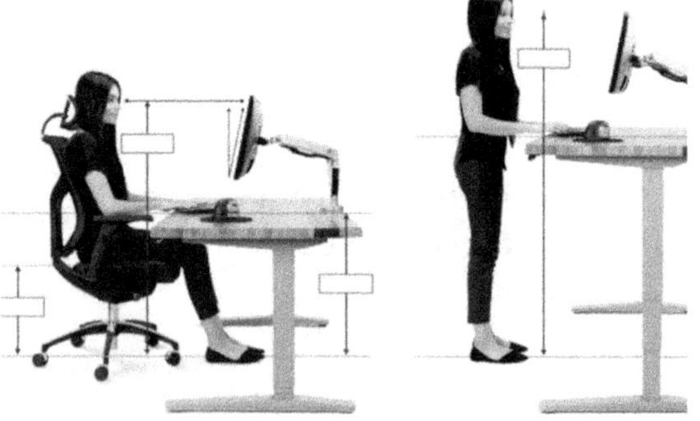

## Examples

**Office Cell ("Pod")**
Provides a complete service or process in a continuous flow.

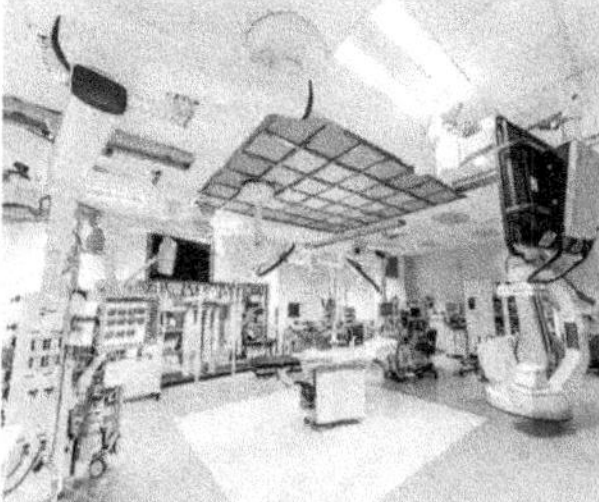

**Medical diagnostic and surgical services are performed in the same room.**

**Continuous flow at a Gymnasium.**

## Continuous Flow at a Restaurant

Kitchen process steps are aligned with the food order sequence.

Every kitchen pod prepares all dishes according to the current demand.

## Continuous Flow at a Car Rental Agency

Register and pay      Obtain insurance      Pick up, review and exit

# Quick Setups (SMED)

"Speed is everything. It is the indispensable ingredient in competitiveness." *Jack Welch*

## Objectives

1. Learn a method that *maximizes value-added* activities and *minimizes* non-value added activities by reducing setup times.
2. Understand the *benefits* of implementing SMED (Quick Setups).
3. Learn a *procedure* to develop a quick setup event.

## Content

I. Background
II. What is SMED/Quick Setups?
III. Benefits
IV. Important definitions
V. Procedure
VI. Example

### I. Background

- **Taiichi Ohno** joined Toyota in 1943 and later became Production Manager. He analyzed the North American Automotive industry and noticed that companies were using a large number of stamping presses to manufacture multiple vehicle models in order to avoid changing molds. **At that time, mold setup took more than 24 hours.**

- Because Toyota had a limited number of stamping presses, they were challenged to manufacture a wide variety of vehicles using less equipment than their competitors.

**Shigeo Shingo**

- In 1950, Shigeo Shingo studied mold changeovers at Mazda and later he was hired as a consultant at Toyota as well.

- His work led to:

  - Eliminating bottlenecks

  - By 1970, Shingo and Toyota managed to reduce changeover times on 1,000 ton stamping presses from 4 hours to 3 minutes.

  - Today, these changes are performed in 30 seconds.



LSSI
LEAN SIX SIGMA INSTITUTE

## II. What is SMED/Quick Setups?

- SMED (Single Minute Exchange of Die) is a Lean method used to reduce waste in any type of process. The phrase "single minute", referring to single digits, suggests that all setups should take less than 10 minutes.

- Quick setups employs this principle of quickly preparing processes (e.g., service, manufacturing, logistics, administrative, etc.) in order to maximize the ability to deliver products or services on time.

**Quick Setups (Changeovers) are similar to when race cars make pit stops to change tires, refuel, make inspections, perform cleaning, etc.**

https://youtu.be/9OUGbRGIl1k

## What is a SMED event?

- A **SMED or Quick Setup Event** is an improvement event that is performed by a cross-functional team to substantially reduce product or service setup times.

- The goal is to produce a high variety of products or services in the shortest time, using fewer resources.

- It is based on the principle that it is better to dedicate more time to effective processing and  less time to setup.

## III. Benefits

- The goal of quick setups is to substantially reduce the time it takes to deliver an order once it has been submitted by a customer.

- Minimizing setup times, provides companies with opportunities to produce a large variety of products or services using the same resources.

**Significant reduction in:**

- Delivery time

- Defects

- Service delays

**Significant increase in:**

- Flexibility to respond to customer demands

- Productivity

- Service capacity

## IV. Important definitions

- **Setup Time (service or office process):** Time it takes after finishing one task to prepare and complete the next task correctly.

- **Internal Setup Time:** Time spent on the setup when the machine or process is stopped.

- **External Setup Time:** Time spent on the setup when the machine or process is running.

## Prerequisites for Quick Setups

- Commitment from management

- Initial training for all participants

- Knowledge on how to conduct Kaizen events

- Creation of the necessary documentation

- 5S Housekeeping implementation is a requirement

- In-depth knowledge of setup processes and procedures

## V. Procedure

### Before the event

1. Draw a value stream map of the service process.
2. Evaluate the impact of the planned Kaizen event.
3. Determine which process you will focus on according to the bottleneck from the VSM.
4. Establish a cross-functional team.
5. Schedule the Kaizen event.
6. Create an agenda for the Kaizen event and share it with the team.
7. Record the changeover on video.
8. Train the team members on Quick Setups.

## Procedure during the event

| Steps | Before the stop | During the stop | After the stop |
|---|---|---|---|

1. Observe and measure total setup time.
2. Differentiate internal activities from external activities.
3. Convert internal activities to external activities and then practice them outside the stop.
4. Eliminate waste from internal activities.
5. Eliminate waste from external activities.
6. Standardize and maintain the new procedure.



## 1. Observe and measure total setup time

- Record the entire setup including all personnel movements associated with the setup. The rest of the team will look for improvement opportunities.

- **Note**: Activate the time display on the video

## Observe and measure total setup time

Video recording guidelines

- Identify everyone who is involved in the setup
- Be respectful if someone does not want to be filmed
- Record a panoramic view of the entire process
- Record hand movements (closely), tool handling and interactions with other processes
- Document the time and date of the video
- Record personnel comments since they often provide valuable information
- Watch the video with the people involved soon after the event
- Schedule and conduct meetings to review the video during the Kaizen event

## 2. Differentiate internal from external activities

- When analyzing the video, review every activity and complete the "Setup Analysis" form.
- Classify all activities:
  - External activities are those that can be performed while the process is still running.
  - Internal activities are those that can only be performed when the process is stopped.

Area:

| No. | Changeover activity | Workers 1 | 2 | 3 | 4 | 5 | Accumulated time | Time | Potential | Classification activity Internal | External | Waste |
|---|---|---|---|---|---|---|---|---|---|---|---|---|
| 1 | Pick up dirty dishes | X | | | | | 7:00:00 | | | X | | |
| 2 | Remove dirty tablecloth | X | | | | | 7:00:15 | 0:00:15 | | X | | |
| 3 | Gather plates and cutlery | X | | | | | 7:00:30 | 0:00:15 | 0:00:00 | | X | |
| 4 | Clean table | X | | | | | 7:02:30 | 0:02:00 | 0:00:30 | X | | |
| 5 | Place clean tablecloth | X | | | | | 7:02:35 | 0:00:05 | 0:00:05 | X | | |
| 6 | Place plates and cutlery | X | | | | | 7:02:50 | 0:00:15 | 0:00:07 | X | | |

## 3. Convert internal activities to external

In this step, activities performed during the stop will be analyzed, simplified and/or improved. To do this, consider the following activities.

Common external activities during a setup:

- Find and retrieve the materials needed for the setup.
- Collect information about next service.
- Communicate the need for a setup.
- Communication between people who are involved.
- Inspections and paperwork related to the setup.
- Schedule or contact the personnel ahead of time who will perform the setup.

Suggested activities for this step:

- Keep materials close by or in a designated setup cart.
- Implement an Andon System used to communicate when setups will take place.
- Standardize roles for every team member.
- Wait until process is running before doing the paperwork.
- Have a setup plan and follow it.

## 4. Eliminate waste from internal activities

- Reduce the number of operations

- Use a Spaguetti Diagram to eliminate or reduce walking and transportation

- Design standardized materials to simplify the setup

- Implement 5 S's to reduce searching times

- Relocate materials to an easy-to-find location to reduce time spent walking and searching

## 5. Eliminate waste from external activities

- Reduce required paperwork

- Relocate related storage areas to reduce travel and transportation time

- Use a checklist to improve efficiency

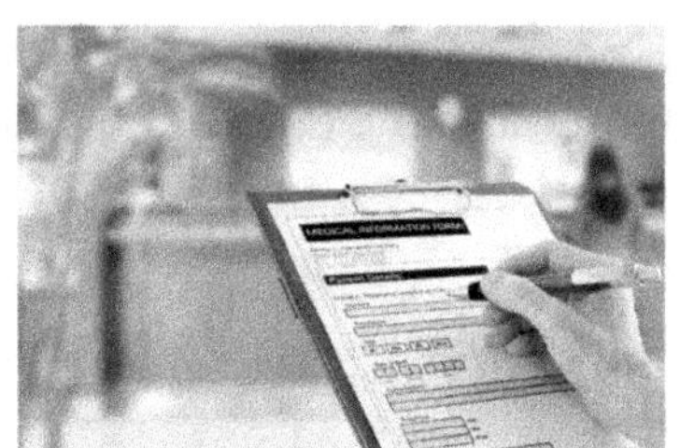

The list should include elements such as:

- Tools, specifications, the number of required workers, etc.

- Correct operating conditions for each process

## 6. Standardize and maintain the new procedure

- Document improved setup procedures.

- Share the new procedures with all involved employees.

- Train everyone involved in the setup.

- Post standardized work instructions in the workplace.

- Establish goals for the setups.

- Measure, publish and keep track of setup times.

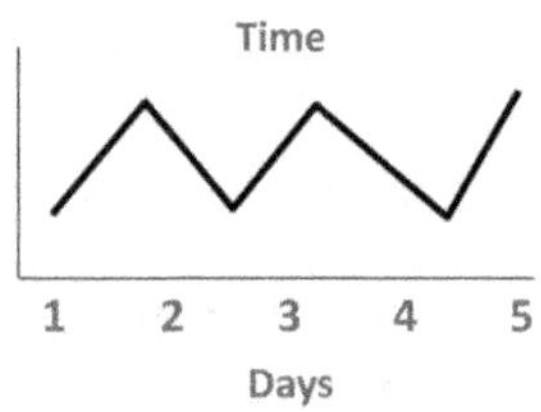

| Before | Now |
|--------|-----|
| 6 hours | 4 hours |

## Rules and considerations for Quick Setups

- For setup initiatives to be successful, it is important that **Total Productive Maintenance** is working correctly.

- Keep in mind that changes are gradual and it will require multiple events to achieve your setup time improvement goals.

- It is required to implement **5s Housekeeping**. Good housekeeping will result in having setup items in their correct places when needed.

## VI. Example

## Reduction in loading time for a bottling company

### WHAT PROMPTED OUR CHANGES?

**Business case:** As a company, our loading times for the logistics, finance, commercial and warehousing areas are not meeting our 30 minute goal. As a result, we are not meeting our customer satisfaction goals and we are losing sales and customers.

Takt Time: 720 min / 45 Loads = 16 min. per loading

Cost per transaction: $ 44.00 per load.

| Entry | Unloading | Loading | Exit | Total |
|---|---|---|---|---|
| 6 | 11 | 42 | 24 | 1:18 |
| 10 | 11 | 29 | 16 | 1:08 |
| 6 | 10 | 25 | 25 | 1:09 |
| 8 | 13 | 9 | 30 | 1:02 |
| 7 | 6 | 42 | 23 | 1:17 |
| | Minutes | | Hours/Minutes | |

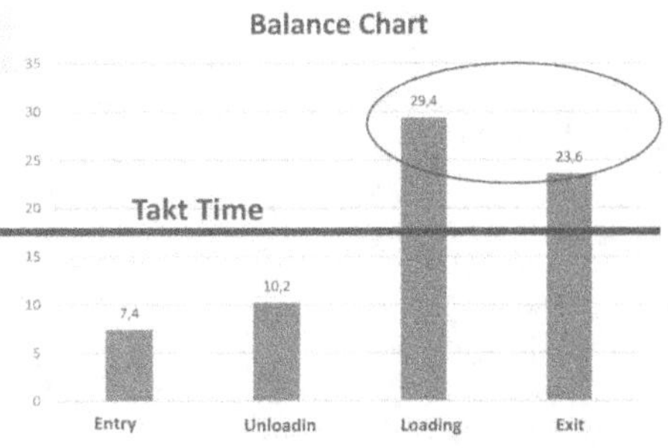

## Transformation phase

### WHAT ACTIONS DID WE TAKE?

**1. Team Training on Quick Setups**

**2. Conducted an analysis to identify process improvement opportunities**

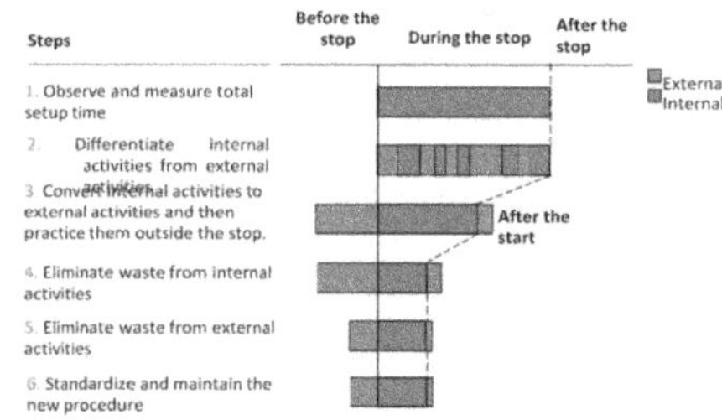


**Entry**: Unscheduled truck loadings

**Unloading**: Lack of coordination by loading personnel. Excess movement of forklift operators.

**Loading**: Loading areas are not defined. In this area, unnecessary movements of people and resources. The area is unsafe, there are unattended vehicles, rework is constantly being performed, paperwork processing is slow, and there is inefficient inventory control.

**Exit**: Long wait times due to slow truck releases.

---

### ¿What we did?

**ENTRY 1 - 2 min.**
- Arrival notice by WhatsApp message
- Pallet arrangement is standardized

**UNLOADING 5 - 8 min.**
- Unload and load area is assigned (bottle unloading in the same area)
- Two forklifts are assigned

**LOADING 7 - 10 min**
- Previous count is performed by finance and logistics
- Checkout receipt is printed in advance
- Product is loaded in both sides of the truck
- Two forklifts are assigned

**EXIT 1 - 2 min**
- Check out information is ready

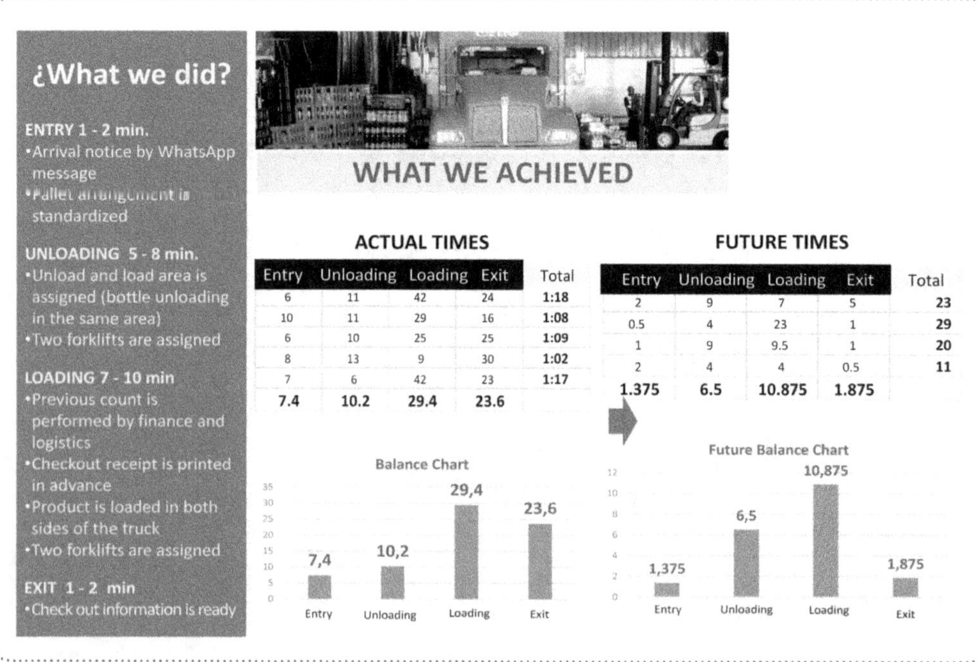

### WHAT WE ACHIEVED

#### ACTUAL TIMES

| Entry | Unloading | Loading | Exit | Total |
|---|---|---|---|---|
| 6 | 11 | 42 | 24 | **1:18** |
| 10 | 11 | 29 | 16 | **1:08** |
| 6 | 10 | 25 | 25 | **1:09** |
| 8 | 13 | 9 | 30 | **1:02** |
| 7 | 6 | 42 | 23 | **1:17** |
| **7.4** | **10.2** | **29.4** | **23.6** | |

#### FUTURE TIMES

| Entry | Unloading | Loading | Exit | Total |
|---|---|---|---|---|
| 2 | 9 | 7 | 5 | **23** |
| 0.5 | 4 | 23 | 1 | **29** |
| 1 | 9 | 9.5 | 1 | **20** |
| 2 | 4 | 4 | 0.5 | **11** |
| **1.375** | **6.5** | **10.875** | **1.875** | |







**LSSI**
LEAN SIX SIGMA INSTITUTE

## Quick Setups help reduce inventory

- Achieving quick setups helps reduce inventory because the company only replenishes items according to customer demand.

- Using forecasts typically results in an excessive accumulation of inventory.

## Example: Hospital ooperating room

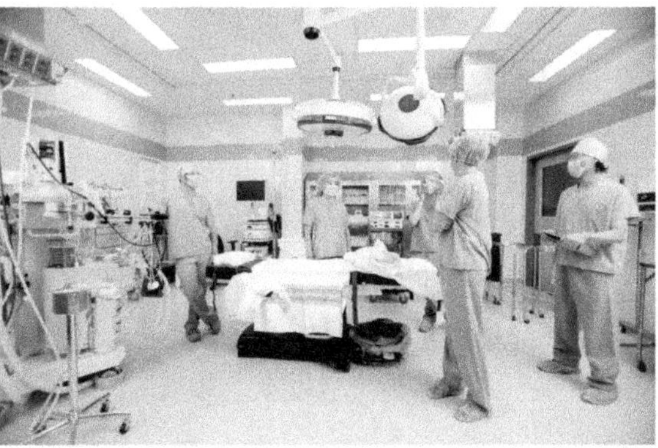

As a result of implementing quick setups, preparation times decreased from 30 minutes to less than 10 minutes.

## SMED applications in different industries

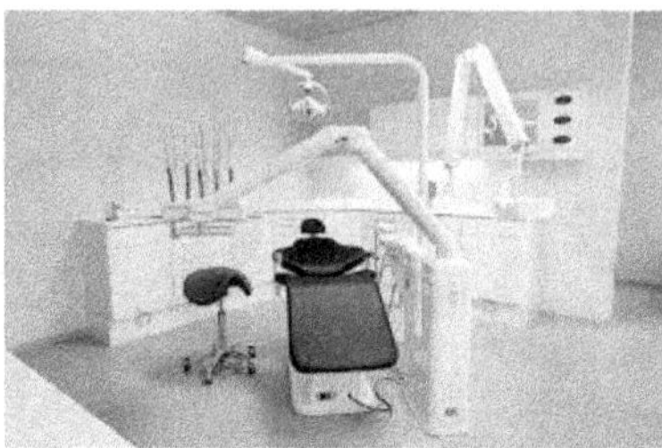

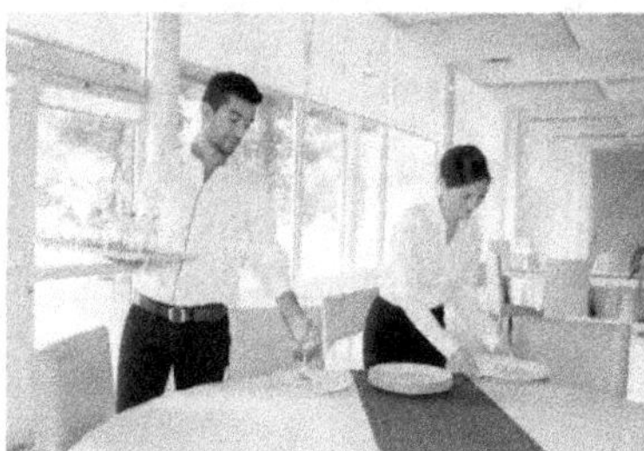

# Kanban

**18**

A "Pull System" consists of optimizing inventory and the product
or service  flow according to the actual demand behavior

## Objectives

1. Understand the *basic concepts* of Kanban.
2. Understand the different *types* of Kanban.
3. Know how to calculate Kanban *sizes.*
4. Know the *procedure* to implement a Kanban system.

## Content

# Kanban



- Japanese executives visited manufacturing plants in the United States to learn about their inventory control systems.

- Taiichi Ohno and his colleagues visited multiple vehicle assembly plants in search of a system that prevents excess inventory. They didn´t find what they were looking for.

- However, after visiting a few supermarkets, they became interested in the way products were restocked after customers took them from the shelves.

- The customers' payments acted as signals to the supplier (store employee) that he/she needed to restock the products that the customer had just purchased (pulled).

## Supermarket

The **Kanban system** was inspired by the way that U.S. supermarkets restocked their shelves. Kanban cards symbolize the dollar bills that served as a signal to the suppliers (employees).

Key features:
- Kanban provides a **visual display** of what is needed in the work area.
- It quickly identifies the **minimum** and **maximum** stock required.
- It **drives the time** for when inventory items must be replenished.
- It ensures a **FIFO** (first-in, first-out) **inventory sequence.**
- It helps **synchronize** the elements of the supply chain.

## II. What is Kanban?

A **Pull System (Kanban)** is a communication system that enables the control of operations, synchronizes manufacturing or service processes with customer demand, and supports production scheduling.

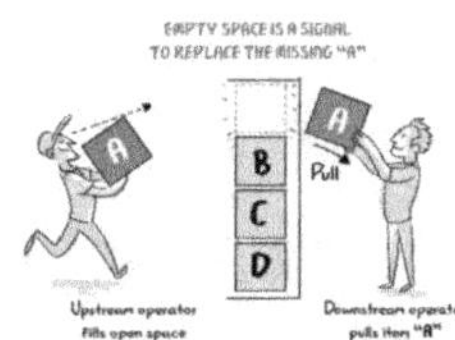


A Kanban is a card that:

- Identifies the items.
- Controls the flow of the items.
- Documents the results.

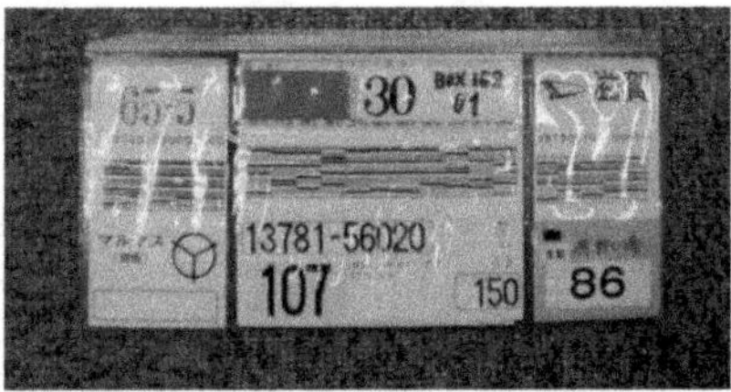

Original Kanban used for
purchasing at Toyota

# Information contained on a Kanban card

- Item number
- Container type and size
- Container capacity
- Location
- Item destination
- Delivery time and place
- Part drawing or picture
- Process where it is used

Information that facilitates **effective material flow**
while eliminating delays and time losses.

## III. Benefits

**Some of the applications and benefits of Kanban are:**

- Ensures that customers will receive their products or services on time.
- Minimizes the need to purchase an excessive amount of supplies.
- Supports the ability to work with low inventory levels.
- Avoids a lack of supplies, which interrupt the flow of services.
- It is a visual system that enable us to compare what is bought and what the service process requires.
- Provides a common system for moving materials through the facility.

## IV. Types of Kanban

### Information Kanban

This information must be available at all times within an assigned area (supermarket) in order to avoid an interruption in the process and maintain a continuous flow.

**Examples:**

- Packing lists to provide an ongoing delivery service to customers.
- Resumes of pre-approved people to be interviewed and potentially hired in a company.

### Kanban of Materials in Service

These are the materials and supplies that must be available at all times in order for the process to mantain a continuous flow.

**Examples:**

- Cure materials in an operating room
- Spare parts for an automotive maintenance service
- Sheets and bedspreads for a hotel room

## V. When is Kanban used?

Kanban is used:

- When it is necessary to provide a structure for the control and administration of inputs (especially when there is a high mix of services).

- After other core Lean Tools such as 5S Housekeeping, Quick Setups, TPM and Continuous Flow have begun to be implemented.

## VI. Procedure

1. Determine items to include in the Kanban.

2. Calculate the number of items in the Kanban.

3. Select the type of signal and container.

4. Calculate the number of containers.

5. Monitor the WIP-to-SWIP indicator  (work in process / standard work in process).

# 1. Determine items to include in the Kanban

- Select items for the Kanban system
  - Parts to produce products
  - Materials to perform a service
  - Finished goods
  - Etc.

- It is important to select items that are already involved in other Lean methods such as Continuous Flow, Quick Changes, TPM, etc.

# 2. Calculate the number of items in the Kanban

- Formula for the number of items: $D \times LT \times L \times (1 + \%VD)$

- **Where:**
  - D = Weekly demand: number of items or information needed to serve customers a week.
  - LT = Internal or external supplier lead time (in weeks), which includes:
    - ✓ **For purchased materials:** Time to generate the order + supplier lead time + transportation time + receiving, inspection, and stocking time
    - ✓ **For information:** Time to generate the order + total processing time + checking time



LSSI
LEAN SIX SIGMA INSTITUTE

## 2. Calculate the number of items

- Formula for calculating the number of items = $D \times LT \times L \times (1 + \%VD)$

- **Where:**
  - **L = Number of locations.** When first implementing Kanban, it is recommended to have 2 full locations, one for the supplier and another for the service area. It is possible that later we will be able to use one single location, but at the beginning with this we ensure continuity in the process.

  - **% VD = Demand variability coefficient**, is the standard deviation of demand for a specific time period, divided by the average demand for that same period.

## Example

**1. Select materials and / or information to be established in Kanban**

Surgery Clothing

**2. Calculate the quantity of items in Kanban**

The demand for surgeries in the last 12 weeks was analyzed. For each surgery, 7 clothing kits (doctors and nurses) are required. Determine the number of kits that we must have in stock to never stop the process

| Week | Demand for surgeries |
|---|---|
| week 1 | 18 |
| week 2 | 22 |
| week 3 | 17 |
| week 4 | 29 |
| week 5 | 20 |
| week 6 | 19 |
| week 7 | 21 |
| week 8 | 16 |
| week 9 | 23 |
| week 10 | 22 |
| week 11 | 21 |
| week 12 | 20 |

## Example

Formula for calculating the number of items = **D x LT x L x (1 + %VD)**

Average weekly demand= 20.7 surgeries per week.

Weekly demand for clothes= (20.7 x 7 kits) = 144.7 kits.

D=144.7 kits

LT= 1 week from the external supplier that delivers it to the hospital warehouse

Locations = 2 (one with the supplier and one with the warehouse).

%VD = Standard deviation/ average demand

%VD = (3.4 / 20.7) = 0.16

**Amount of pieces=** 144.7 x 1 x 2 x 1.16 = 336 kits

## 3. Select the type of signal and container

- In order to apply visual control by part type, it is important that the containers are easy to identify and  handle and are of the same color for a specific Kanban.

- The container can be a box, stand, cart, tray, pallet, etc.

# 4. Calculate the number of containers

$$\text{Number of containers} \quad = \quad \frac{\text{Number of items in the Kanban}}{\text{Container capacity}}$$

If the container's capacity is 7 kits, then the number of containers needed is 48, calculated as follows:

$$\text{Number of containers} \quad = \quad 336 / 7 = 48 \text{ containers}$$

# 5. Monitor the WIP to SWIP indicator

- WIP to SWIP is calculated by dividing the inventory in process (WIP) by the minimum necessary in-process inventory to maintain standard work (SWIP).

$$\text{Formula:} \quad \frac{\text{WIP (Work-In-Process)}}{\text{SWIP (Standard-Work-In-Process)}}$$

- The ideal ratio is **1**, which means that WIP is equal to SWIP.

- If the result is **greater than 1**, there is an excess of inventory in process.

- If the result is **less than 1**, there is insufficient inventory in process and might be at risk of being short in materials or products.

## Kanban rules

- Do not transfer defective items to the next processes.

- A Kanban card is withdrawn when a process withdraws items from the previous process.

- Earlier processes produce items according to the quantity specified by the withdrawn Kanban card (the Kanban makes a production order).

- Nothing is produced, purchased or moved without a Kanban card.

- The Kanban card acts as an attached production order to all items.

- The number of Kanban cards should be decreasing over time.

## VII. Examples

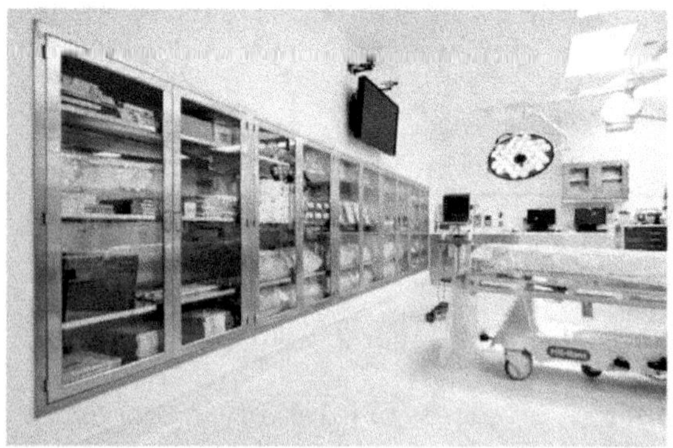

**Kanban supply in an operating room**
The surgery personnel withdraws what they need from the storage area. All of the utilized items are later replenished so they are available for future surgeries.

# Future State Value Stream Map

Whenever there is a product or service for a client, there is a value stream. The challenge is to see it.

## Objectives

1. Identify critical *areas of opportunity* and *bottlenecks* that need Lean improvement actions.
2. Learn *how to develop* a future state map of the value stream, that minimizes cycle times.
3. Know how to develop a *continuous improvement action plan* aimed at transforming the value stream.

## Content

I.    What is a Future VSM?
II.   Benefits
III.  When is it used?
IV.  Procedure

# Future State Value Stream Map

## I. What is a Future VSM?

**Future State Value Stream Map (VSM)**

- A **Future State Value Stream Map** represents the short-term improved solution that we want to incorporate into the production or service system.

- Provides a starting point to develop a new work strategy.

## II. Benefits

- Improved process flow

- Optimized resource utilization

- Improved customer satisfaction

- Improved quality and reduced costs

- Allows us to see things differently than we do initially

- Reduced cycle times

## III. When is it used?

- It is used when the bottleneck has been analyzed, and the following elements have been identified:
    - Root cause of the main problems
    - Any type of waste
    - Variation
    - Overburden

*"We could not build a house without a plan."*

## Value stream mapping process stages

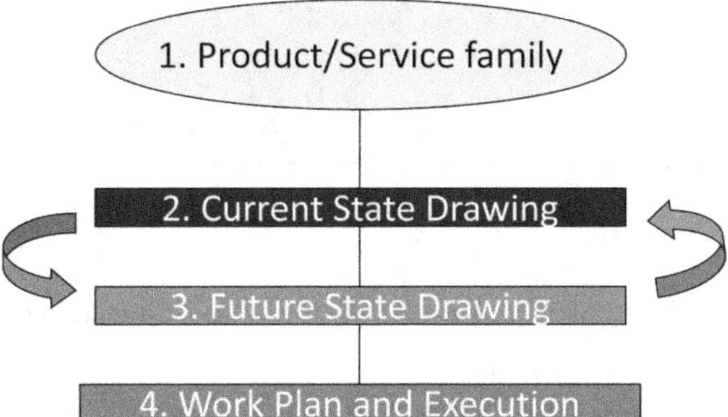


**Develop Value Stream Maps for each of your service families.**

## IV. Procedure

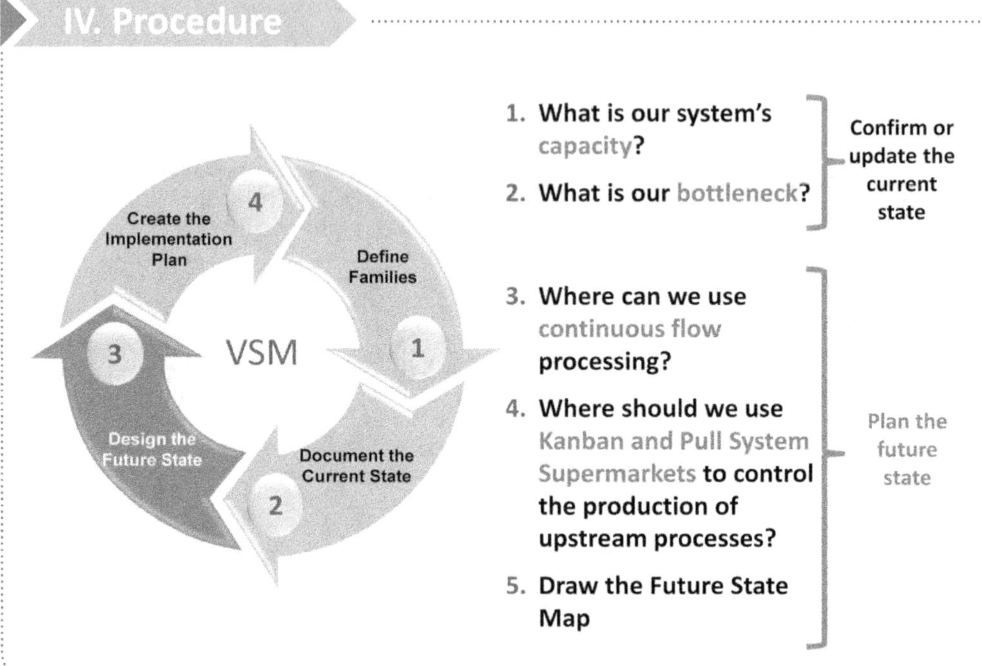



1. **What is our system's** capacity?
2. **What is our** bottleneck?

Confirm or update the current state

3. **Where can we use** continuous flow **processing?**
4. **Where should we use** Kanban and Pull System Supermarkets **to control the production of upstream processes?**
5. **Draw the Future State Map**

Plan the future state

## 1. What is our system's capacity?

Process capacity is calculated as follows:

$$\text{Capacity} = \frac{\textbf{Available Working Time}}{\textbf{Longest Cycle Time}}$$

To work out the capacity, we must graph the Takt time and compare it to the cycle time of each activity.

The Balance Chart summarizes the actual cycle times for each process.

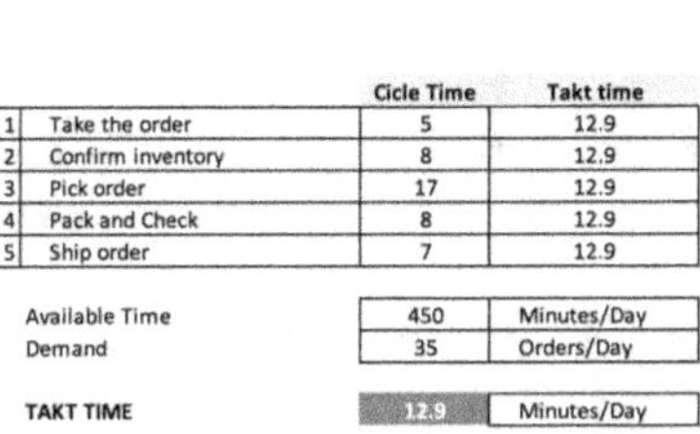

| | | Cicle Time | Takt time |
|---|---|---|---|
| 1 | Take the order | 5 | 12.9 |
| 2 | Confirm inventory | 8 | 12.9 |
| 3 | Pick order | 17 | 12.9 |
| 4 | Pack and Check | 8 | 12.9 |
| 5 | Ship order | 7 | 12.9 |

| | | |
|---|---|---|
| Available Time | 450 | Minutes/Day |
| Demand | 35 | Orders/Day |

| | | |
|---|---|---|
| TAKT TIME | 12.9 | Minutes/Day |

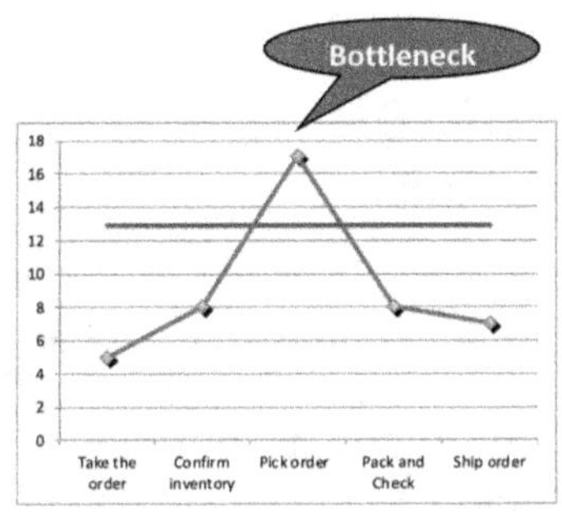



- A system is as fast as the system bottleneck allows.

- The bottleneck is in picking the order.

- Improving any other area at the moment would just be costly and time consuming since we can only make an impact if we focus on the bottleneck

Available time= 450 minutes / day
Longest cycle time = 17 minutes / order

**Capacity** = 450/17 = **26.5** orders / day

# 2. What is our bottleneck?

The bottleneck will determine the system's capacity. It can either be:

- Internal:  If Demand > Capacity

    Or

- External: If Capacity > Demand

For **Wilson Retail**, the bottleneck is in order picking (17 minutes).

The bottleneck is internal because demand is greater than the system's capacity.

Internal: **35 orders > 26.5 orders**

## 3. Where can we use Continuous Flow processing?

- Would there be any reason why we could not integrate all the operations into a single process?

- This should be the first question leading to a continuous flow.

- If it is not possible during the first stage to integrate all the activities that add value into a single flow, they would have to be joined by "pull" systems to achieve a continuous flow.

- In the graph we can see a great imbalance in order picking operation.
- How could we unite the operations in a single process?
- To unite all operations in a single continuous flow, we would have to form a multidisciplinary team that would carry out the entire process from beginning to end and that would require:
  - Staff trained in multiple functions.
  - Continuous communication among all the members of the cell.

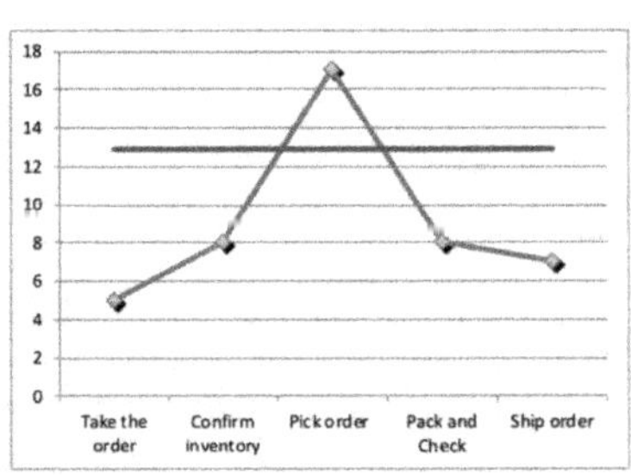




LSSI
LEAN SIX SIGMA INSTITUTE

- When we join several operations into one, we call it a continuous flow cell.

- In this case it is a service cell.

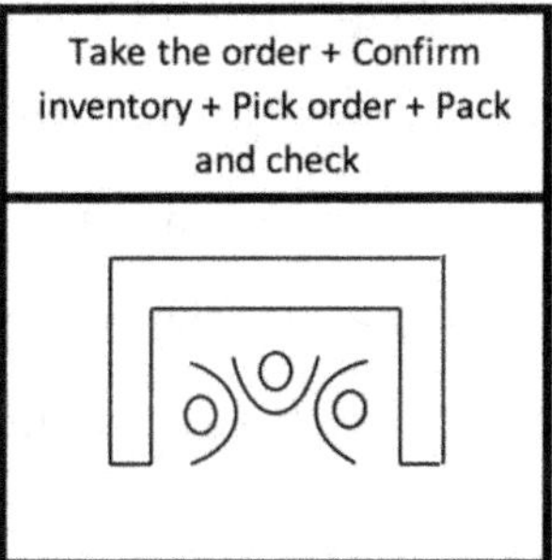


## Order picking

The order picking operation requires us to distribute the load among the other elements of the service cell to enable the **integration** of all of them in the cell.

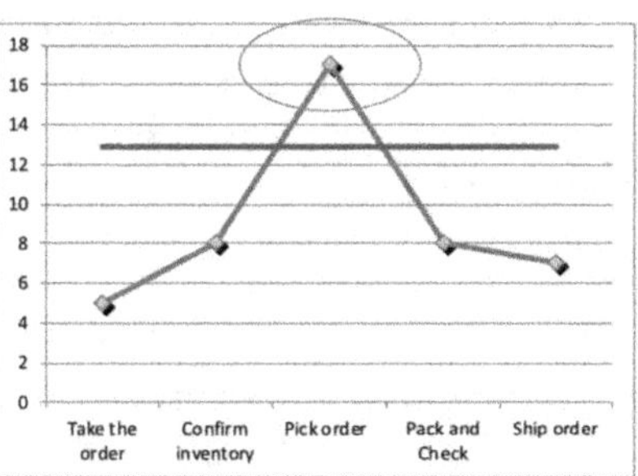

The most important Kaizen must be conducted in order picking operation since it represents the longest time to complete each service and that time is also greater than the customer rate (takt time).

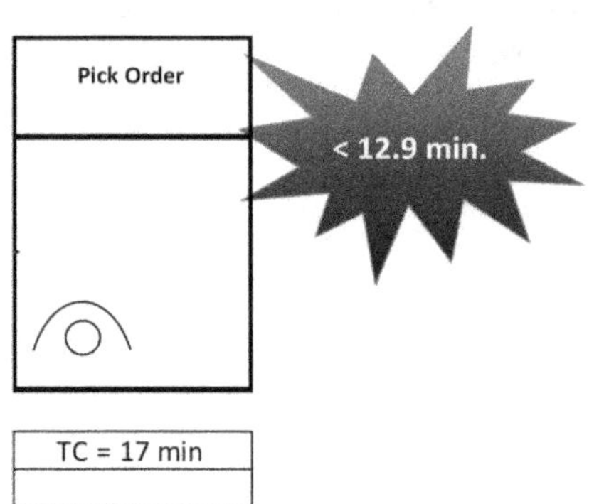


## 4. Where should Wilson use pull system supermarket?

- To connect the cells with the operation of services we could have a supermarket with the product ready to be shipped and thus significantly reduce the time it takes from when the order is received until the order is shipped.

- It is also recommendable to set up a supermarket with the products received from the suppliers to do the order picking. This supermarket shall be replenished using Kanban cards addressed to the Planning Department.

## 5. Draw the Future State Map

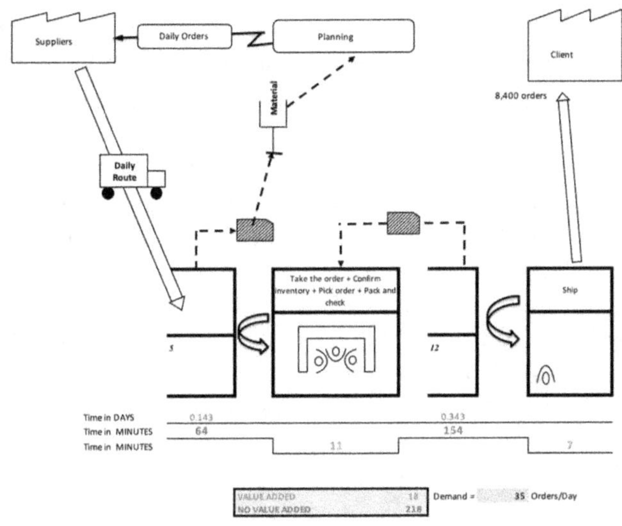


## What have we achieved?

- Reduce delivery time.

- Send customers their order immediately.

- Greater customer satisfaction.

- Greater communication between the members of the process.

## Successful Implementation of the Future States

- To achieve safer implementation, it is advisable to carry out a step-by-step implementation, starting with those tasks that are easiest.

- Once Future State 1 has been implemented, the work team will notice the value that has been created and this will provide initiative and encouragement for the same team to implement Future State 2 and so on upto the Ideal Future State.

- Starting with the Ideal Future State may be acceptable as long as it is being initiated for a completely new process. Otherwise, small steps are essential for successful implementation.

## The Value Plan

It is highly recommended that the current VSM generate an action plan for the selected family of services that establishes the tasks to be performed. This plan must contain the following:

- What the work team plans to achieve, step by step.
- Measurable goals for team members.
- Clear checkpoints with real delivery times and individuals responsible for the tasks to be delivered.
- Explanation of costs and benefits.

## Conclusions

- At this point it is good to share a little secret: one can never reach the ideal state. There will always be waste to remove and added value to generate for the customer.

- However, there is another point that also seems to be a secret for many managers and this is that successive future states that approach the ideal can be achieved and implemented; the secret is in continuous improvement with a view to the ideal state.

- The trick is to take a walk through the entire Value Stream in order to see the big picture and appreciate the value that would be created if the Value Stream were optimized. The challenge is to start, get small success stories that motivate us to generate bigger changes and not look back.

## Quantify future state

| Metrics | Current State | Future State | % Improvement |
|---|---|---|---|
| Value added time | 5.88% | 7.62% | |
| Space | 15,000 sqft. | 9,000 sqft. | |
| Quality | 80% | 99% | |
| Lead Time | 765 minutes | 236 minutes | |
| Conversion cost | $125,000 | $95,000 | |
| Head count | 5 | 4 | |

# Kaizen

**The engine for a Lean Six Sigma transformation.**
**"The wise do not teach with words but with acts."** *Lao-tsé*

## Objectives

1. Understand *how to apply* Kaizen in your *personal life* and in an *organization*.
2. Understand the *role and importance* of Kaizen events in a company's *Lean Six Sigma transformation*.
3. Learn the *procedure* for implementing Kaizen events.

## Content

I. Background
II. What is Kaizen?
III. Types of Kaizen events
IV. What is it used for?
V. Key elements
VI. Procedure

## I. Background

- **Kai** = Change
- **Zen** = Good or improve
- It has its origin in the Buddhist school of India. It is practiced in China, Japan and South Korea by individuals seeking personal improvement.
- The Toyota Motor Company was the first organization to use it as a Lean philosophy and tool.
- Today, many Kaizen concepts and tools come from:
  - The field of Industrial Engineering
  - The teachings of Dr. Edward Deming
  - The book Gemba Kaizen by Masaaki Imai

## Personal Kaizen philosophy

- **Self-control** is the key to mastering life.

- **Success** starts with individuals and then expands to teams.

- **Enlightenment** is achieved through the cultivation of the mind, body and soul.

- The **goal of life** is to find your purpose and carry it out.

## II. What is Kaizen?

The Japanese word "Kaizen" (改 善) means change (kai) to become good (zen).

**Kai**  **Zen**

# 改 善

Change  Good

KAIZEN = **Change for the Better**

---

*"This is not theory ... It's a way of life."*

- For use in organizations, Kaizen means gradual continuous improvement

- Everyone is actively involved

- Kaizen is a powerful tool that many leading international organizations use to improve their people and processes

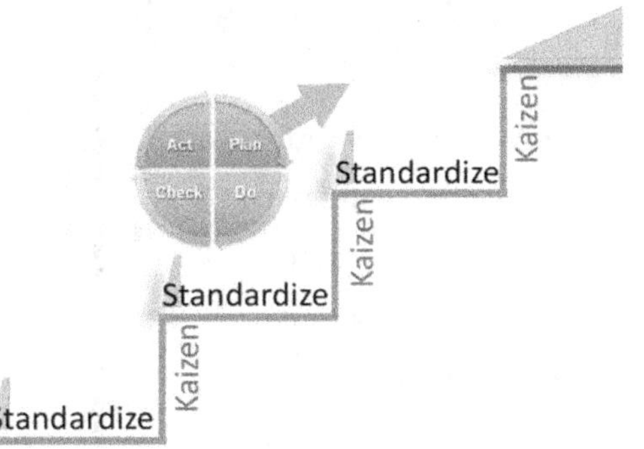

## III. Types of Kaizen events

- **Kaizen Blitz:** To make quick improvements or solve simple problems (3-5 hours)

- **Kaizen Events:** To solve problems and implement Lean tools: TPM, SMED, etc. (3-5 days)

- **Six Sigma Kaizen:** For complex problems and process / product re-design (3-5 weeks)

## VI. What is it used for?



- Improvements with clients
- Sales improvements
- 5 S's implementation
- TPM implementation
- Automation
- Lay-out design
- New product design

- Visual management
- Kanban implementation
- Poka-Yoke
- Continuous flow implementation
- Quick Setup implementation
- Talent Development
- Value engineering implementation (Kaikaku)

## Kaizen benefits

- Provides a way to train employees, enrich their work experience and bring out the best in each person.

- Promotes the personal growth of employees and the company.

- Improves safety, performance, customer service, therefore employee satisfaction.

- Improves leadership.



- A focus on quality

- Human effort

- Total participation

- A will to change

- Communication

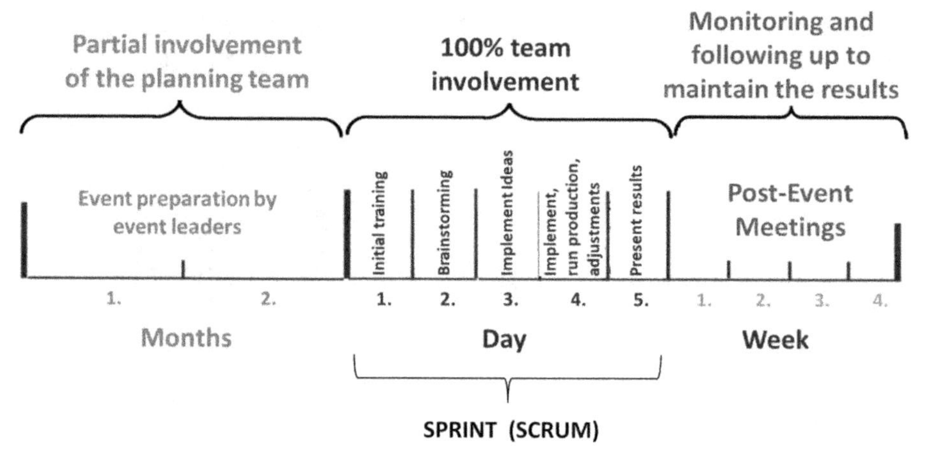


## Relationship between Kaizen and Sprint used in SCRUM

When an agile project is developed based on a future value stream map, each Kaizen event represents a Sprint in which the team is completely focused and dedicated.

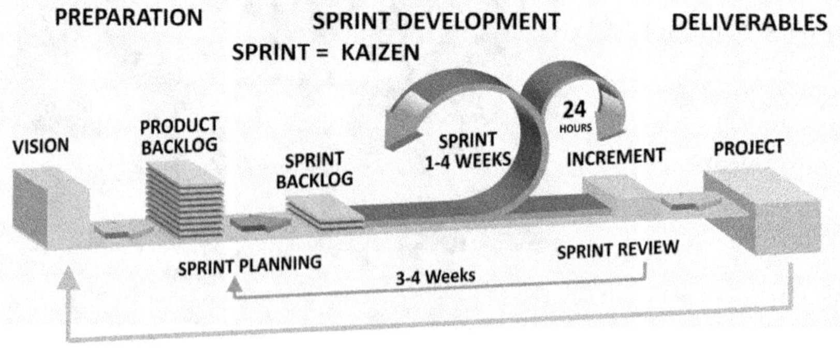

## Opportunity cards used to document ideas during kaizen

- It is important to encourage the team to submit their ideas and when possible, implement them during the event.

- Improvement ideas should be classified as opportunity categories A, B or C.
  - A: These are ideas that can be implemented immediately **(1 to 5 days)**.

  - B: These are ideas that can be implemented during or shortly after the event **(1 to 2 weeks)**.

  - C: These are ideas that require a greater amount of time to implement and may require special authorization, investment, etc. **(up to 2 months)**.

| OPPORTUNITY CARD | |
|---|---|
| Date: | |
| Area: | |
| Opportunity found: (Muda, Muri, Mura) | |
| To do: | Classification |
| Equipment: | |
| Observations | |
| Date: | |
| Area: | |
| Opportunity found:  (Muda, Muri, Mura) | |
| To do: | Classification |
| Equipment: | |

## Improvement principles

- Ignore the traditional or current work methods and consider that there might be a way to do things better
- Think about how the new method will work and not why it won't work
- Don't accept excuses – Refuse the status quo
- Don't strive for perfection
- Fix problems immediately
- Don't spend money on improvements. Instead, use common sense
- Ask "Why?" at least 5 times to find the root cause of any problem
- Use the rule that 10 people's ideas are better than one person's knowledge

# Standardized Work

**Standardization: The Foundation for Improving Any Process**

## Objectives

1. Understand the *essential elements* of standardized work to ensure optimal performance.
2. Know the *procedure* for achieving standardization in any process.
3. Understand the elements that ensure the *proper functioning* of Standard Work.

## Content

I. Background
II. What is Standardized Work?
III. Key Elements
IV. Benefits
V. Procedure
VI. Exercise

# Standardized Work



## Stability

- Stability is the ability to produce consistent results over time.

- Instability is the effect of variability on a process.

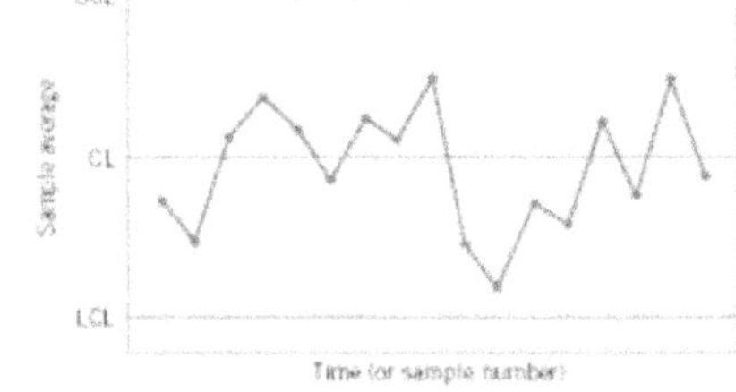

- The first step towards Lean implementation is reaching a maximum level of process stability.

- **What is standardization?**
  The safest, easiest and most effective way to perform any job.

- **What is a standard?**
  A clear picture of a desired condition (something that serves as a basis or a model)

- **Why are standards important in a lean system?**
  Standards allow us to immediately identify anomalies and as a result implement corrective actions

- **Characteristics of an effective standard**
  Simple, clear and visual

## Stability and Standardization

Symptoms of instability and lack of standards:

- High variation in performance indicators

- Inconsistent work methods

- Accumulation of WIP (work-in-process)

- Sequential operations working independently

## II. What is Standardized Work?

- A tool used to guarantee maximum performance and minimal waste.

- Is a set of documents that help us understand how our work meets customer requirements.

## III. Key elements

| White Belt | Yellow Belt |
| --- | --- |

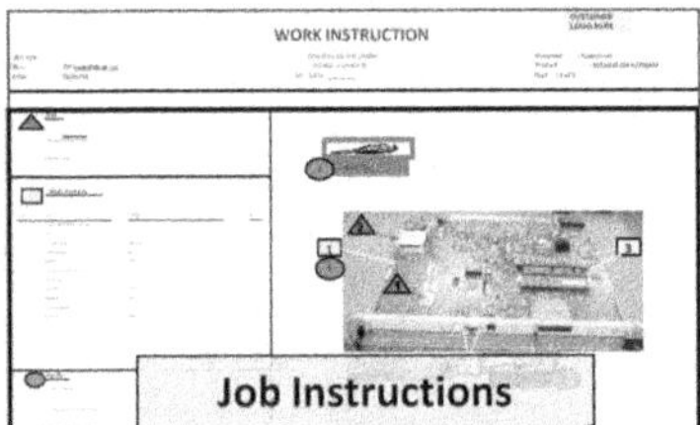


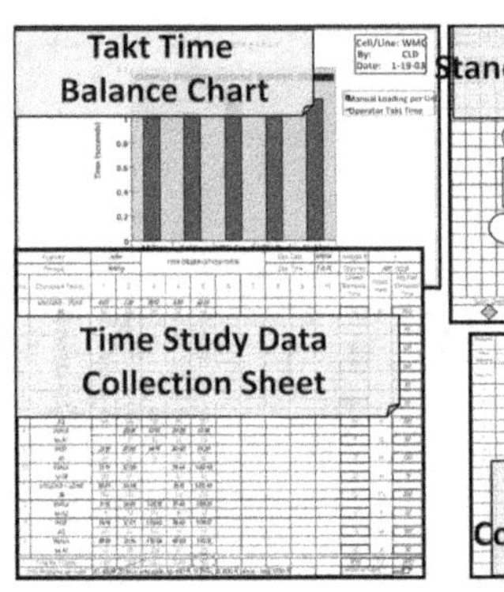


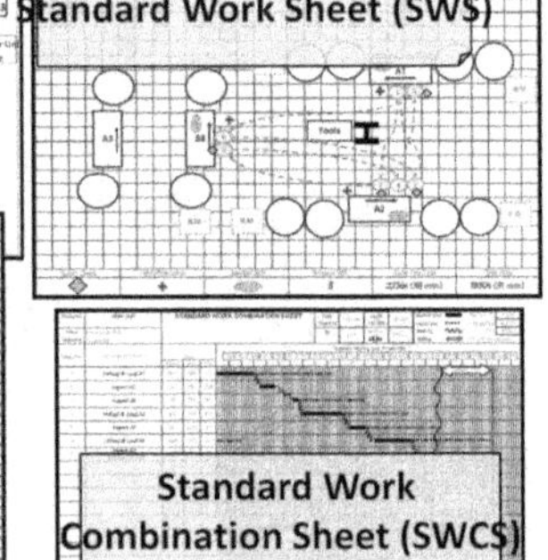


## IV. Benefits

- Achieve process stability

  - Standardization ensures that work is always performed identically to meet quality and speed standards.

- It is a tool that initiates improvement actions

- Establishes a baseline to evaluate and manage processes and assess their performance

- Ensures safer and more effective operations

- Extraordinary source of information.

1. Select a specific process or operation within a process

2. Conduct a time study and record data on the "Time study data collection sheet"

3. Calculate process or operation capacity and fill out capacity form

4. If necessary, balance the operation

5. Design or document the capacity's optimal sequence on the "Standard Work Combination Sheet" (SWCS)

6. Draw the process in the "Standard Work Sheet"

7. Document work instructions

## How to implement standarized work?

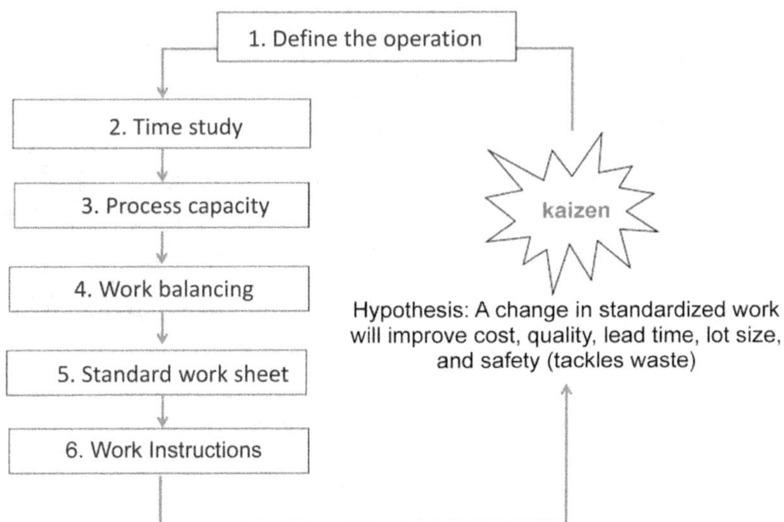

## 1. Define the operation

- It is recommended to begin by selecting the operation bottleneck found in the Value Stream Map or some critical operation.

## 2. Conduct a time study

The Time Study Data Collection Sheet includes work element start and end times. Each work element is measured and standard times are established for each operation in the process.

| Process | **LSSI** LEAN SIX SIGMA INSTITUTE | TME STUDY DATA COLLECTION SHEET | | Date | | Process # | |
|---|---|---|---|---|---|---|---|
| | | | | Time | | Observer | |
| # | Work elements | Measure point | 1 | 2 | 3 | 4 | 5 | 6 | 7 | 8 | 9 | 10 | 11 | 12 | 13 | 14 | 15 | Lowest repeated time |

# 3. Process capacity analysis

The capacity of any process is determined by the slowest step.

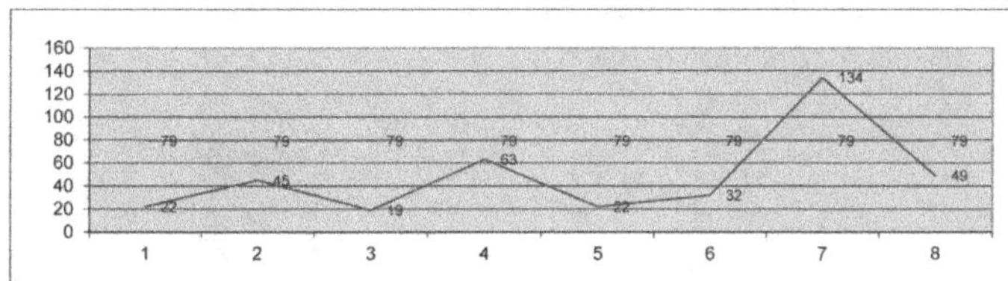

**Capacity** = Available time / Longest time

**Capacity** = 27,000 secs / 134 secs

= 201 units/shift

**Note:** Document in the Current Standard Work Combination Sheet and Standard Work Sheet

# 4. Work balancing

The standard work combination sheet allows us to graphically see the sequence of the process in order to evaluate it and optimize the capacity. It is also useful for balancing operation workload in relation to takt time.

| Project & Model | Chocolate Cake | STANDARD WORK COMBINATION SHEET | Date Prepared | | Units per shift | | Man | |
|---|---|---|---|---|---|---|---|---|
| | | | Prepared by | | Takt time | 55 | Auto / Walk | |
| Area | Bakery | | Operation time (seconds) | | | | | |
| | | Time | 1  5  10  15  20  25  30  35  40  45  50  55  60  65  70 | | | | | |
| Step | Operation | Manual | Auto | Walk | | | | |
| 1 | First bread | 3 | | | | | | |
| 2 | First chocolate layer | 2 | | | | | | |
| 3 | Second bread | 2 | | | | | | |
| 4 | Second chocolate layer | 3 | | | | | | |
| 5 | Third bread | 3 | | | | | | |
| 6 | Put chocolate on top | 4 | | | | | | |
| 7 | Spread chocolate on top | 10 | | | | | | |
| 8 | Spread chocolate on side | 12 | | | | | | |
| 9 | Take off excess chocolate | 13 | | | | | | |
| 10 | Place cake on tray | 3 | | | | | | |
| 11 | Clean plate | 5 | | | | | | |
| 12 | Place cake on plastic box | 3 | | | | | | |
| | Totals | | | | | | | |

## 5. Standard work sheet

- The Standard Work Sheet includes a design of the process (layout) including the operator or service provider and material flow to determine the most efficient movements.

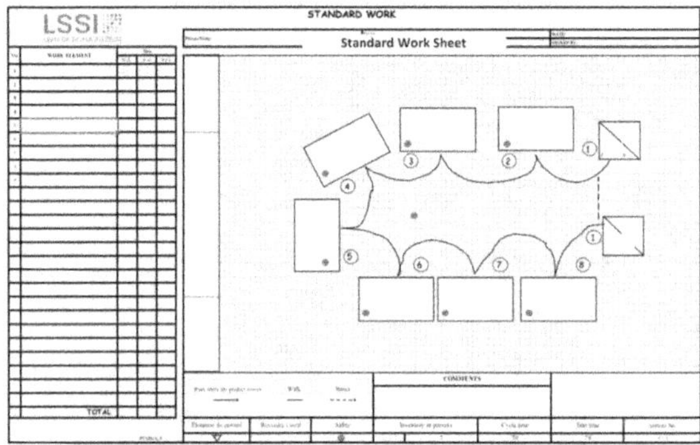

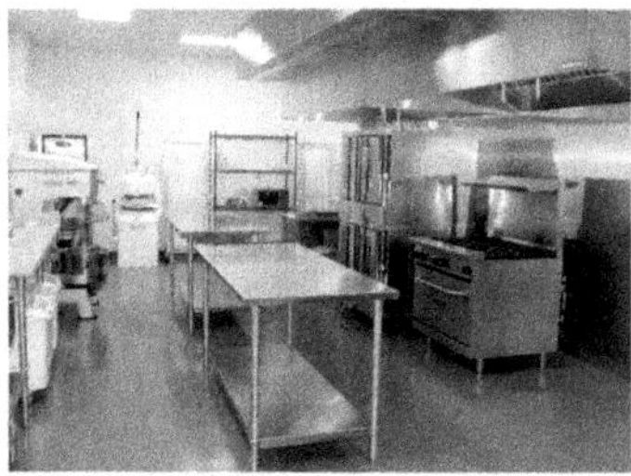

- The operations are analyzed as a group to give a clear view of the sequence and flow.

## 6. Document the work instructions

| | WORK INSTRUCTION | | | | | |
|---|---|---|---|---|---|---|
| Department: | | Area: | Operation: | Type of product: | Made by: | Pg. 1 of 1 |
| NO. | SEQUENCE OF OPERATIONS | | KEY POINTS | | ILLUSTRATIONS | |
| 1 | | | | | | |
| 2 | | | | | | |
| 3 | | | | | | |
| 4 | | | | | | |
| 5 | | | | | | |
| | | | | | | |

| CHANGES | | | | | SAFETY CONSIDERATIONS | SIGNATURES | | | |
|---|---|---|---|---|---|---|---|---|---|
| Date | Rev | Description of Change | Elim. | Approved | | Date | Shift | Supervisor | Operator |
| | | | | | | | | | |
| | | | | | | | | | |
| | | | | | | | | | |

It is recommended that operators, service providers, engineers, quality personnel and HR staff all participate in the creation of work instructions to ensure all aspects are included.

### VI. Exercise

- Form teams

- Analyze combined work (takt time = 55 seconds)

- Recommend improvements and share your diagrams with the group

# Poka Yoke

**First Time Quality**

## Objectives

1. Understand the *importance* of implementing Error-Proofing (Poka-Yoke) mechanisms.
2. Learn the *basic principles* for implementing Poka-Yoke mechanisms.
3. Understand the *classification* of Poka-Yoke mechanisms.

## Content

I.   Background
II.  What is Poka Yoke?
III. Benefits
IV.  Classification
V.   Procedure

### I. Background

- In the 1960's, quality control was only about inspection activities.

- However, no matter how rigorous the inspections were, Shigeo Shingo, an industrial engineer and consultant for many companies, realized that the goal of having zero defects could not be met.

- After concluding that most defects are due to human error, he realized that the best way to ensure quality was to integrate simple mechanisms to detect errors before they became defects.

- Shingo called them "Poka-Yoke mechanisms" (mistake proofing).

## The error

- Many things can go wrong in a work environment.

- Every day, there are opportunities to make mistakes which can result in defective products or services.

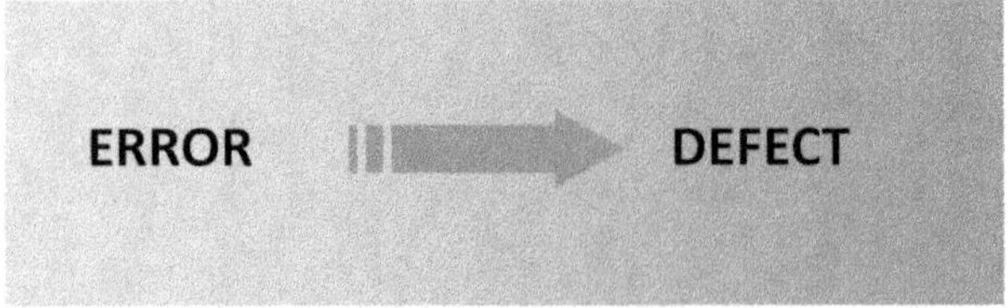


The key to success is eliminating the error.

# There are two essential attitudes towards human error

**Traditional thinking**

Errors are inevitable! We are humans!

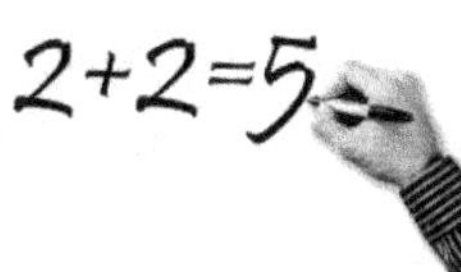

**Lean thinking**

Errors can be avoided!

If we develop a way to eliminate the cause

# Source of defects

| Materials | Manual | Methods | Machines | Measurements | Environment |
|---|---|---|---|---|---|
| ▪ Damaged<br>▪ Incorrect<br>▪ Out-of-specifications | ▪ Improper training<br>▪ Inadvertent errors<br>▪ Mistakes<br>▪ Negligence<br>▪ Incorrect operation of equipment | ▪ Incomplete<br>▪ Lack of documentation<br>▪ Obsolete<br>▪ Incomprehensible or complex | ▪ Improper maintenance<br>▪ Incorrect adjustments<br>▪ Inadequate changeovers<br>▪ Dirt and contaminants affecting products<br>▪ Inadequate installations | ▪ Improper calibration<br>▪ Incorrect Sampling | ▪ Humidity<br>▪ Excessive heat<br>▪ Cold |

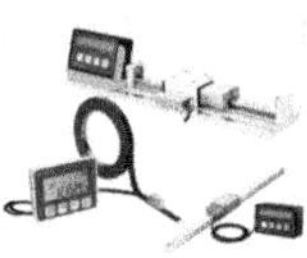

## II. What is Poka Yoke?

"Poka-Yoke" is a mechanism that anticipates, prevents and detects the error before it becomes a defect.

The term "Poka-Yoke" comes from Japanese:

"Poka" = inadvertent mistake          "Yokeru" = prevent

## Basic principles

- Errors and defects can be avoided.

- We need to detect the error before it turns into a defect.

- The best tool to prevent a defect is the one that most  effectively isolates the source of the problem.

## III. Benefits

**Some of the applications and benefits of implementing Poka-Yoke are that it:**

- Eliminates or reduces the possibility of errors

- Prevents accidents caused by human distraction

- Eliminates actions that depend on memory and inspection

- Ensures quality at every workstation

- Is inexpensive to implement and simple to use

## Example: Poka-Yoke and Andon

**Poka-Yoke** was born from simplicity and can be either really inexpensive and simple or very expensive and complex.

**Poka-yoke combined with Andon to prevent train accidents**

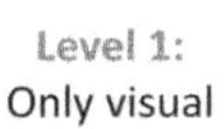

| Level 1: | Level 1: | Level 2: | Level 3: |
|---|---|---|---|
| Only visual | Visual and audible | Visual, audible and restrictive | Mistake Proof |

## Poka-Yoke effectiveness

1. Detects the defect after it has already occurred.

2. Detects the error as soon as it occurs and before it turns into a defect.

3. Eliminates or prevents human error before it occurs.

## IV. Classification

Richard Chase and Douglas Stewart have defined 4 basic types of Poka-Yoke:

1. Physical

2. Sequential

3. Counting and Grouping

4. Information

# 1. Physical Poka-Yoke

## 1.1 Guide

**Type of Error:** Orientation or positioning

The shape of the device prevents it from being inserted incorrectly.

**Type of Error: Space**

## 1.2 Template

**Type of Error:** Presence or absence of data

# Marking Required Fields in Forms

* **Name**   *Required*

* **Email Address**   *Required*

## 1.3 Conditions indicator

**Type of error:** temperature, time, pressure, etc.

## 1.4 Dispenser

**Type of Error:** Quantity and / or positioning

## 2. Sequential Poka-Yoke

- When order or sequence is important, any change or omission in the order can result in errors.

- Therefore, ways to restrict incorrect sequencing have been developed so that only a predetermined order is followed.

**Sequence is frequently a key factor for packaging, preparation, assembly and inspection.**

**Type of Error:** Incorrect sequence

1. Open
2. Keep near by
3. Close

## Healthcare

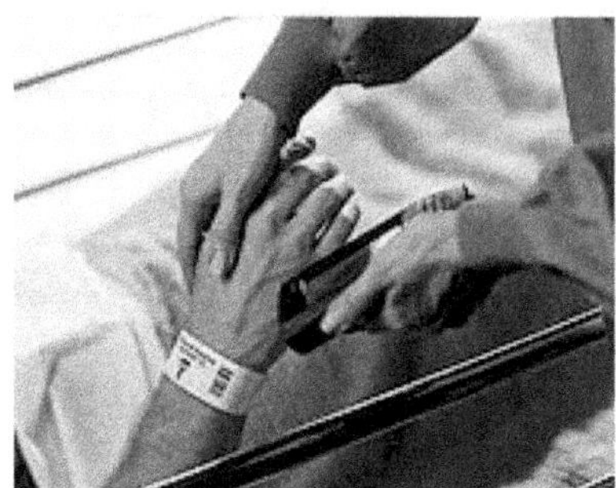 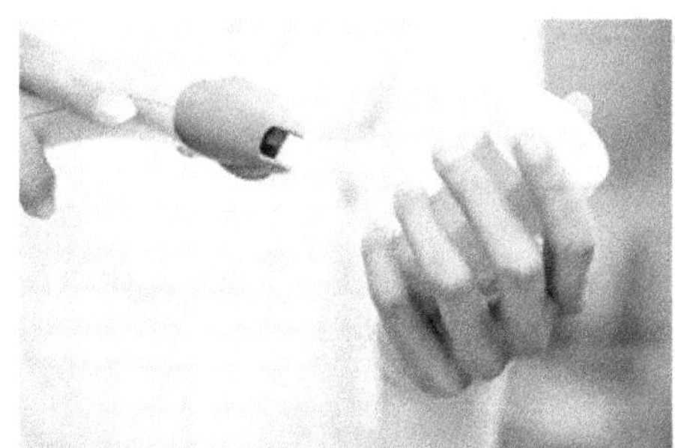

1. The bracelet is scanned to ensure the correct patient.
2. The medicine is scanned to ensure that it belongs to the right patient and it is given at the right time.

## 3. Counting and Grouping Poka-Yoke

**3.1** Counting Poka-Yoke

A counter keeps track of parts, cycles, exits, etc., for a particular machine or operation. A counter can be mechanical or electrical and can be combined with machines or equipment such as sensors.

### 3.2 Grouping – kits

**Type of error :** Missing items

- Use of kits

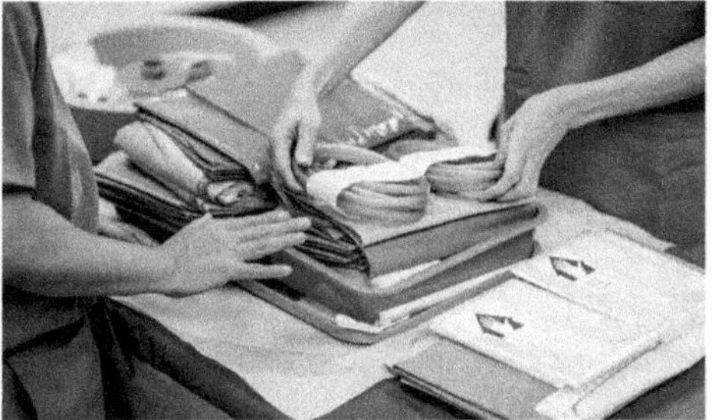

Surgery kit example

Nothing should be left behind when the fire officer leaves the station.

# 4. Information Poka-Yoke

**Alert method:**

Usually the device is a visible or audible alarm, or a combination of both, which notifies the person in charge that an error has occurred and there is a need to resolve the issue.

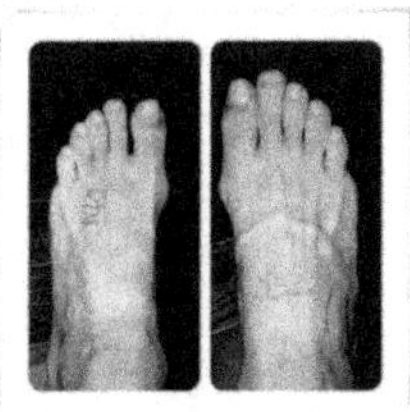

A simple mark is used to identify which foot should be operated on.

## V. Procedure

1. **Identify the stages of the process:**

   The step-by-step stages of each process are identified to know the sequence of operations.

2. **Identify the type of Poka-Yoke that can be used:**

   When we establish controls or mechanisms to test errors in the critical inputs of the processes, we are applying **preventive mechanisms.** When we establish controls for the outputs, we are applying **reactive mechanisms.**

3. **Characterize the inputs and outputs:** the objective is to identify the inputs and outputs of each operation that could become failures or errors.

**Note:** When defining the process for which the Poka-Yoke will be used, be sure to identify places where the risk of failure is high due to the severity of the process, level of occurrence and degree of detection by the system. Use FMEA (Failure Mode and Effect Analysis) if possible.

# Kata

**The art of leadership at the place where value is added**

## Objectives

1. Understand the concepts of a powerful methodology to *develop leaders.*
2. How to use Toyota Kata to *solve problems* and *improve* specific situations in the work place.

## Content

I. Background
II. What is Kata?
III. What is Kata for?
IV. Key elements
V. Who participates?
VI. When is it used?
VII. Procedure
VIII. How long does it take?
IX. Example

## I. Background

**Imagine a management system that:**

- Generates initiative among employees to adapt to changing business conditions
- Keeps the organization moving (improving)
- Is easy for everyone to understand, even though Kata is different

**This is the goal of Toyota Kata**

Organizations typically have a sense of frustration due to the difference between expected and actual results

## Recurring problems

- Most companies are led and operated by hardworking people who want their colleagues and organization to succeed

**Conclusion: The problem is not the people!**

*It is the Management System*

## Definition of Management

> The systematic search of target conditions by using human capabilities in the most effective way

Because we cannot predict the future,

an effective management system will make the organization able to adjust to:

- Unpredictable events
- Dynamic business conditions
- Changes in customer requirements

## Toyota makes mistakes too

**But no other company seems to adapt and improve every day as Toyota does**

Implementing Lean Company

does not mean  there will be no problems, but  that we will be able to solve them more quickly and effectively

**Kata is the way Toyota manages continuous improvement and adaptability to changing business conditions**

## Research on Toyota Kata

2004 – 2009
*Mike Rother*

How to apply the management system in companies different from Toyota:

1. What are the invisible thinking and management routines behind Toyota's success in   relation to its improvement and constant adaptation system?

2. How can other companies develop similar routines and thinking processes?

**"If we study Toyota's management system long enough, a common thinking and acting pattern will emerge and become evident in every level within the company."**
*Mike Rother*

*Visible*

| Methods | Tools | Principles |

| Management thinking and routines |

*Invisible*

## Improvement based on waste reduction

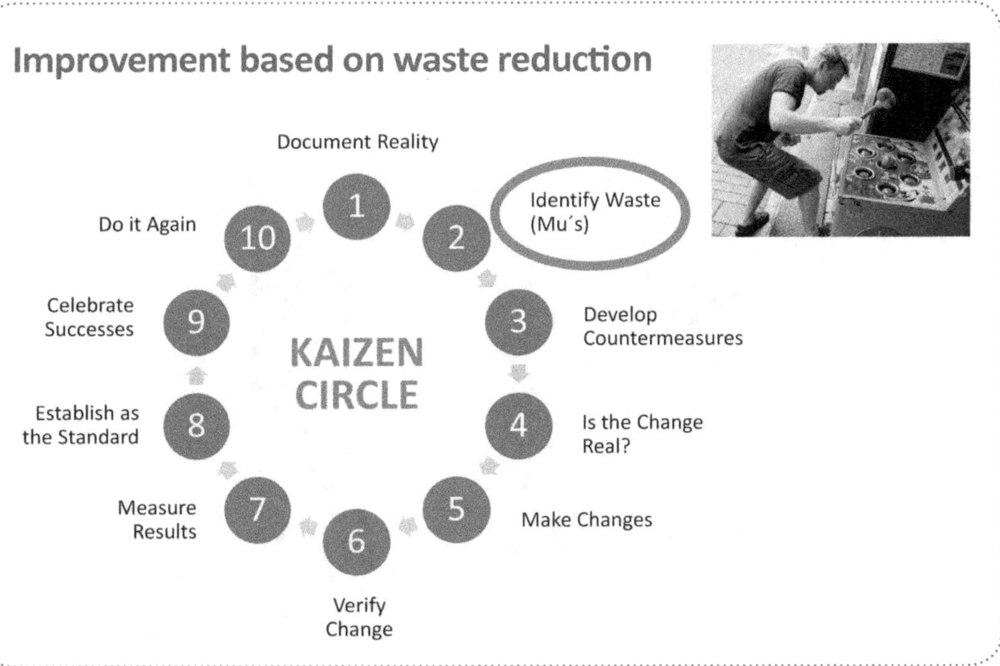

**Katas are routine practices that help us adopt new ways of acting and thinking**

KATA

## What is improvement Kata?

It is a pattern of scientific thought that is combined with practical routines which help us adopt new ways of thinking and acting.

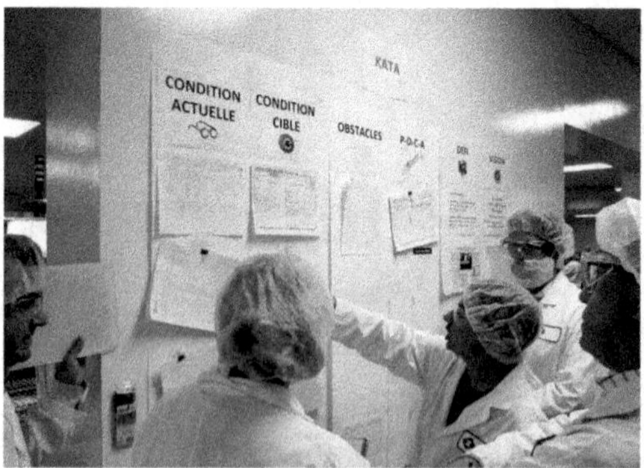

## III. What is it for?

It helps us achieve the goal we seek in a process, without generating unfocused ideas, but with a focused model of improvements based on well-founded hypotheses, experiments and frequent monitoring.

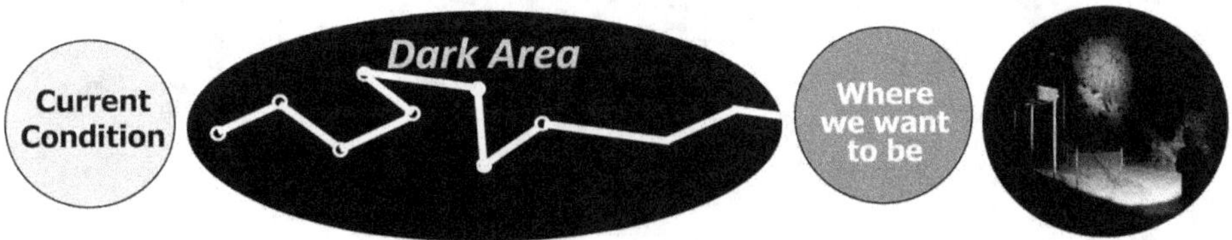


## Principles

To develop new habits, you must practice new routines and experience the sense of progress once you have mastered them.

**The following ingredients will help us re-wire our brains to acquire new skills and a new mentality.**

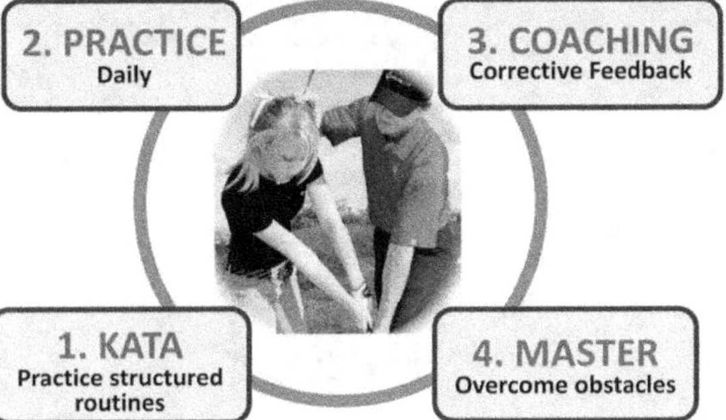

## 1. Kata: structured routines

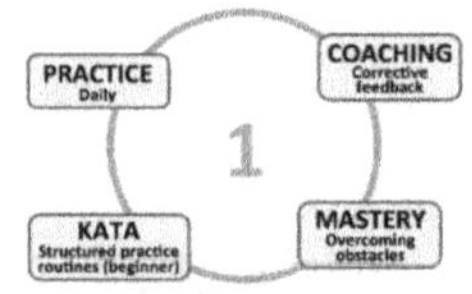

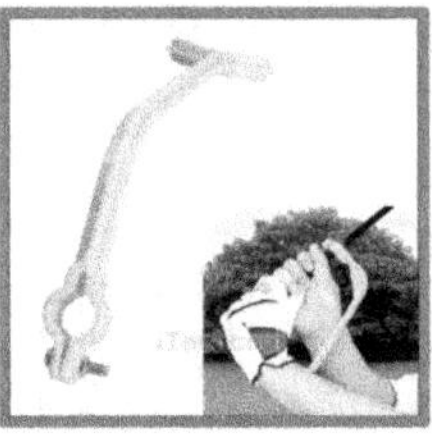 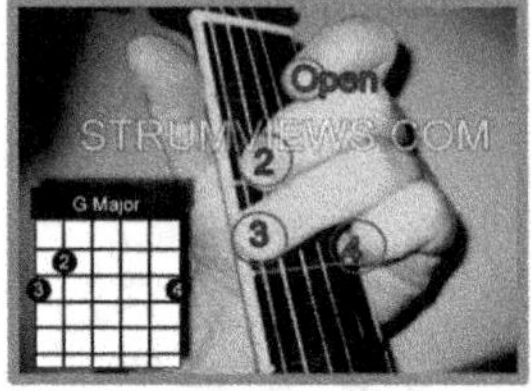 

**KATA: Structured Routines**

- The foundation to build a learning process

- A way to transfer and develop skills and share a thinking method among the organization

## 2. Daily practice

If we occasionally practice improvement events (Kaizen) –and the rest of the time it is "business as usual"– then, according to neuroscience, what we are really teaching is "the usual."

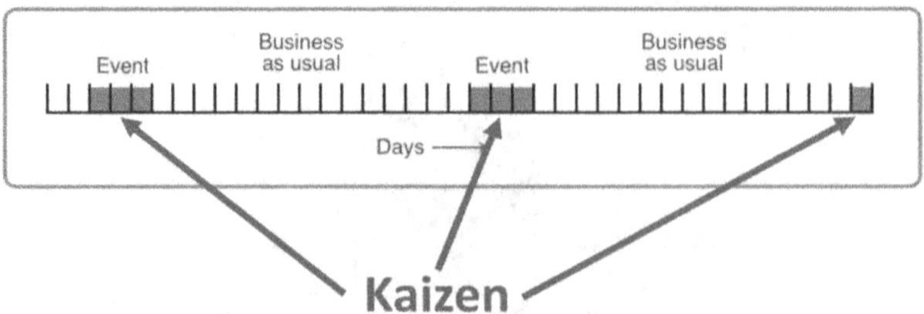

# 3. Coaching: corrective feedback

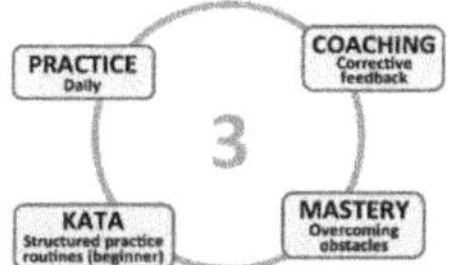

If we leave our trainees alone, they will practice existing habits.

The coach (manager) provides **corrective methods** to ensure the student practices the new routine in the right way.

The coach´s job is not to provide solutions, but to develop and improve their students' skills.

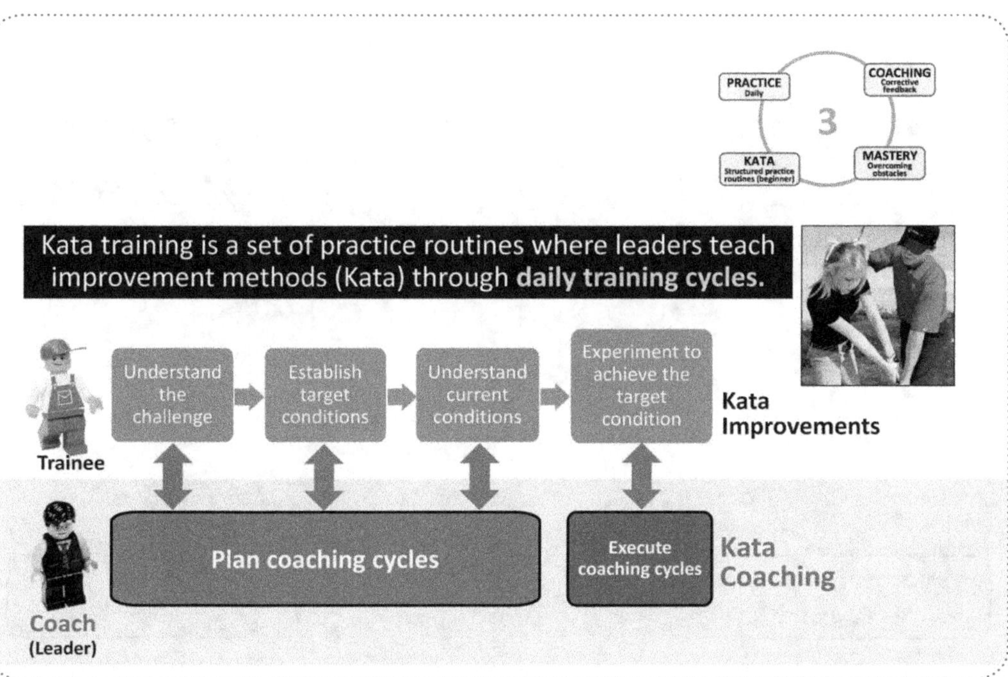

## 4. Master: overcome obstacles

To learn new skills and a new mentality, the student must practice in a learning zone beyond their comfort zone to feel they are making progress.

This is a responsibility of the coach.

## IV. Key elements

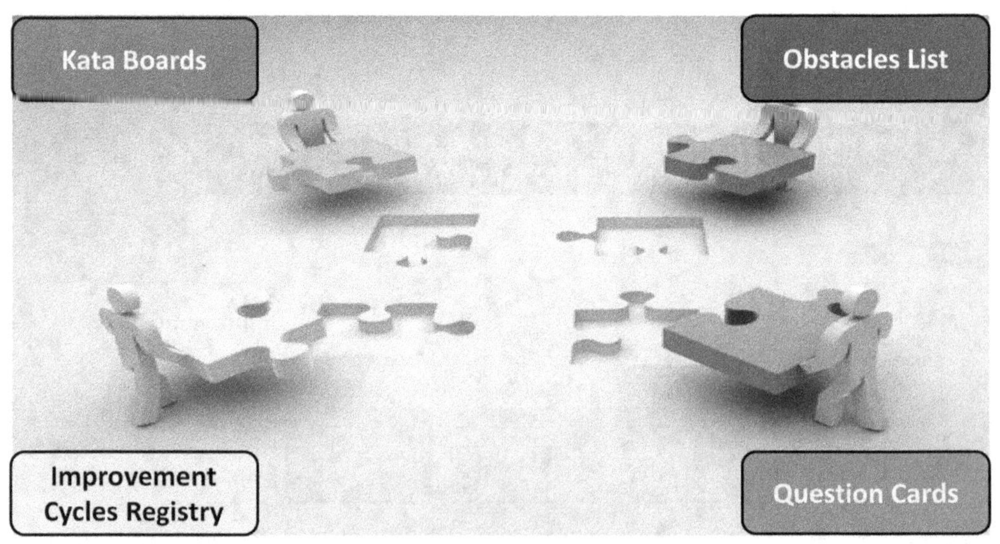

# Kata Board (Storyboard)

The Kata Board should be located in the work place

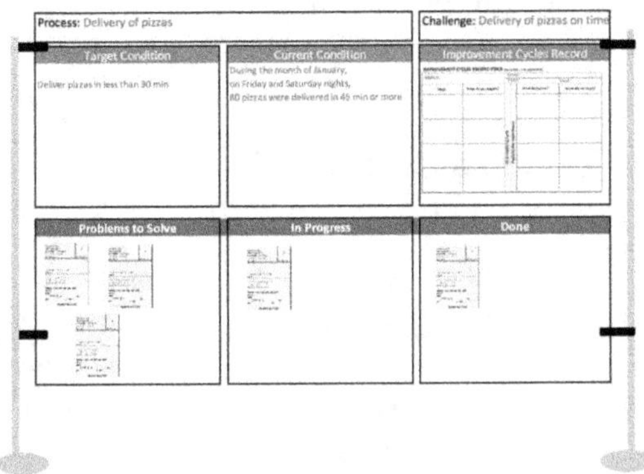

# Question cards

- Kata is made by a sequence of questions and answers.

- Question cards contain the questions to be asked by the leader or coach.

- Usually the coach has authority over the learner.

- Cards can be carried along with a company name tag.

| | The Five Questions |
|---|---|
| Coaching Kata | **1.** What is the **Target Condition**? |
| | **2.** What is the **Actual Condition** now? |
| | **3.** What **Obstacles** are preventing you from reaching the taget condition?<br><br>Which *one* are you addressing now? |
| | **4.** What is your **Next Step** (next experiment)? What do you expect? |
| | **5.** When can we see what we **Have Learned** from taking that step? |
| | *You'll often work on the same obstacle for several PDCA cycles |

# List of obstacles

All the problems, opportunities or obstacles that prevent reaching the target condition are listed, or at least the most important ones, using the opportunity cards seen in the White Belt training.

- Each problem (opportunity) is recorded on a card to make it visible and is shared with the team.

- Opportunity cards are placed on the Kata boards.

**Classification**

A = 3 – 5 hrs.
B = 3 – 5 days
C = 1 – 2 months

| OPPORTUNITY CARD | | |
|---|---|---|
| **Date:** January-10-18 | **Number:** 001 | |
| **Area:** Delivery | | |
| **Opportunity detected: (Muda,Muri, Mura)** During the month of January, on Friday and Saturday nights, 80 pizzas have been delivered late | | |
| **CAUSE** Lack of standard to capture data | | |
| **SOLUTION** Develop a standard form to document the customer's address including the apartment number | | **Classification** A |

# Record of improvement cycles

Used by the student to document experiments (steps), expectations, results and what was learned

**IMPROVEMENT CYCLES RECORD PDCA** (Every line = one experiment)

| Obstacle: | | | Process: Trainee: | | Coach: |
|---|---|---|---|---|---|
| **Step** | **What do you expect?** | Do a coaching cycle / Perform the experiment | | **What happened?** | **What did we learn?** |
| | | | | | |
| | | | | | |
| | | | | | |

# Card and improvement record

The 5 questions card and the improvement record are used together in every Kata.

| | The Five Questions |
|---|---|
| | **1.** What is the **Target Condition**? |
| | **2.** What is the **Actual Condition** now? |
| Coaching Kata | **3.** What **Obstacles** are preventing you from reaching the taget condition? Which *one* are you addressing now? |
| | **4.** What is your **Next Step** (next experiment)? What do you expect? |
| | **5.** When can we see what we **Have Learned** from taking that step? |
| | *You'll often work on the same obstacle for several PDCA cycles |

### Coach

**IMPROVEMENT CYCLES RECORD PDCA** (Every line = one experiment)

| Obstacle: | | | Process:<br>Trainee: | | Coach: |
|---|---|---|---|---|---|
| **Step** | **What do you expect?** | | **What happened?** | **What did we learn?** |
| | | Do a coaching cycle / Perform the experiment | | |
| | | | | |
| | | | | |
| | | | | |

### Student



All leaders at all levels perform **Katas** with their collaborators

## VI. When is it used?

Every time we need to achieve an objective in terms of:

- Quality
- Sales
- Safety
- Delivery
- Inventory
- Cost
- Etc.

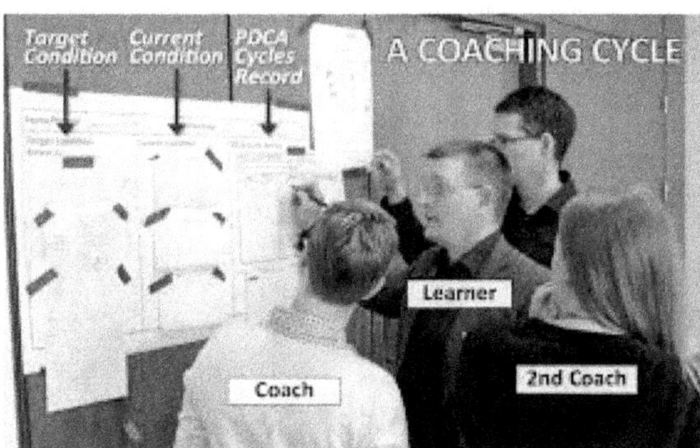


## VII. Procedure

Improvement Kata

**Practice the scientific method to achieve improvements**

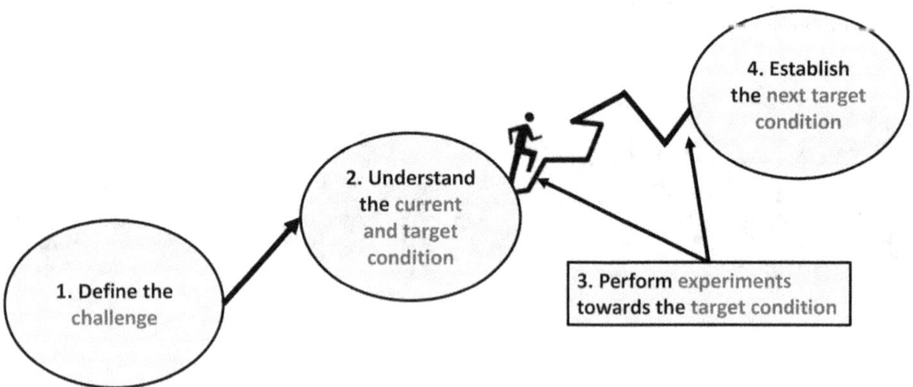

## VIII. How long does it take?

- Average Kata = 10 - 15 minutes.

- It is a simple process, but the fact of doing it continuously solves big problems, in small amounts of time.

## IX. Example

| COACH | TRAINEE |
|---|---|
| - Good morning, Peter! Nice to see you. How are you?<br>- I'm very interested in the **challenge** that you and your team have in the electrical components production process | - Good morning, John.. I'm doing well.<br>- The challenge we face in our value stream is to increase our production capacity |

# Kata coaching example

**1** — What is the target condition?
- Increase our production capacity per shift to 600 pieces with the current staff

**2** — What is the current condition?
- Our current production capacity per shift is 500 pieces

What is the current condition?

When do you plan on reaching it?
- By the end of year, which means 4 months from today

**3** — What obstacles are preventing you from reaching the target condition?

We have identified 4 main obstacles:
- Material deliveries come in lots
- Production stops due to a lack of materials (purchasing or incoming inspection)
- Occasional high defect rates
- No cross training

Which obstacle are you addressing now?
- Production stops due to a lack of materials (purchasing or incoming inspection)

**4** — What is your next step? (Experiment) and
- To assign people dedicated to receiving materials only

What do you expect?
- To find out in what we need to focus on in order to improve

**5** — What happened?
- They don't have a sampling plan
- They don't know how to do sampling

What did you learn?
- We learned that receiving inspectors need additional information and training

**4** — What is your next step? (Experiment) and
- Learn about sampling

What do you expect?
- Develop an optimal sampling plan

**Process:** Electronic Components

**Challenge:** Increase Capacity

### Target Condition

600 pieces per shift with the current staff by the end of year (4 months)

### Current Condition

500 pieces per shift with the current staff

### Improvement Cycles Record

### Problems to Solve

### In Progress

### Done

## PDCA CYCLES RECORD

| Obstacle: | | Process: | | | |
| --- | --- | --- | --- | --- | --- |
| | | Learner: | | Coach: | |
| **Step** | **What do you expect?** | | | **What happened** | **What we learned** |
| Assign people solely dedicated to receiving materials | To find out what we need to focus on to improve | | Do a coaching cycle / Conduct the experiment | They don't have a sampling plan and they don't know how to interpret sampling levels | Receiving inspectors need additional information and training |
| Study the information and develop a sampling plan | Learn about sampling needs and develop an optimal sampling plan | | | | |
| | | | | | |
| | | | | | |

## Conclusions

**Leaders are** teachers (by default)

With everyday words and actions, leaders teach their staff about the proper mentality and focus,
which has a significant effect on creating problem solving capacity and culture.

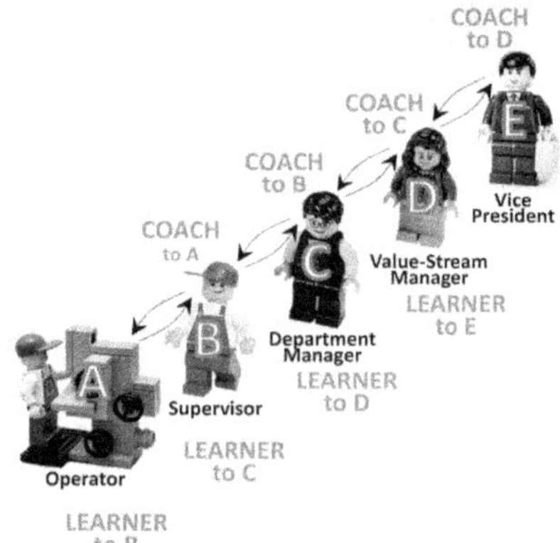

# Tools for the Management of Organizations

**Sales and operations planning.
S&OP in 14 steps**
*Cristina Peña Andrés*

**Manual de estrategia
de operaciones**
*Ángel Caja Corral*

**Cómo participar
en ferias comerciales**
*Cristina Peña Andrés*

**La Industria 4.0
en la sociedad digital**
*Antoni Garrell Guiu,
Llorenç Guilera Agüera*

**Cerebro, inteligencias
y mapas mentales**
*Zoraida G. de Montes,
Laura Montes G.*

**Manual del comercio
electrónico**
*Eva María Hernández Ramos,
Luis Carlos Hernández
Barrueco*

# Lean Six Sigma Management System

**Lean Six Sigma.
Management system
for leaders**
*Luis Socconini, Carlo Reato*

**Lean Company.
Más allá de la
manufactura**
*Luis Socconini*

**Lean Energy 4.0.
Guía de
Implementación**
*Luis Socconini,
Juan Pablo Martín*

**Lean Manufacturing.
Paso a paso**
*Luis Socconini*

**Lean Six Sigma Yellow
Belt. Manual de
certificación**
*Luis Socconini*

**Certificación Lean
Six Sigma Green Belt
para la excelencia
en los negocios**
*Luis Socconini*